The Growth of Islam among the Yoruba, 1841-1908

Ibadan History Series

Christian Missions in Nigeria 1841–1891
by J. F. A. Ajayi

The Zulu Aftermath
by J. D. Omer-Cooper

The Missionary Impact on Modern Nigeria 1842–1914
by E. A. Ayandele

The Sokoto Caliphate
by Murray Last

Benin and the Europeans 1485–1897
by A. F. C. Ryder

Niger Delta Rivalry
by Obaro Ikime

The International Boundaries of Nigeria
by J. C. Anene

Revolution and Power Politics in Yorubaland 1840–1883
by S. A. Akintoye

Power and Diplomacy in Northern Nigeria 1804–1906
by R. A. Adeleye

The Segu Tukulor Empire
by B. O. Oloruntimehin

The Warrant Chiefs
by A. E. Afigbo

The New Oyo Empire
by J. A. Atanda

The Evolution of the Nigerian State
by T. N. Tamuno

The Malagasy and the Europeans
by P. M. Mutibwa

Western Yorubaland under European Rule 1889–1945
by A. I. Asiwaju

The Judicial System in Southern Nigeria 1854–1954
by Omoniyi Adewoye
Press and Politics in Nigeria 1880–1937
by F. I. A. Omu

In preparation

Benin under British Administration
by P. A. Igbafe

Ibadan History Series

General Editor J. F. A. Ajayi, PhD

The Growth of Islam among the Yoruba, 1841-1908

T. G. O. Gbadamosi

Humanities Press

First published
in the United States of America 1978
by Humanities Press
171 First Avenue,
Atlantic Highlands,
NJ 07716

Library of Congress Cataloging in Publication Data
Gbadamosi, T   G   O
    The growth of Islam among the Yoruba, 1841–1908.
        (Ibadan history series)
        Revision of the author's thesis, Ibadan University.
        Bibliography: p.
        1. Yoruba – History.   2. Muslims in Nigeria –
    History.   3. Yorubas – Religion.   I. Title.
    II. Series.
    DT513.G33   1978   966.9'1   77–28068
    ISBN 0–391–00834–X

Printed in Great Britain

Contents

v

0743218   106424

List of Maps

Abbreviations

ADS	Ansar Ud-Deen Society
B	Brockelmann
BSOAS	*Bulletin of the School of Oriental and African Studies*
CAD	Centre of Arabic Documentation, University of Ibadan
CMI	*Church Missionary Intelligencer*
CMS	Church Missionary Society
EI	*Encyclopaedia of Islam*
IFAN	L'Institut Fondamental d'Afrique Noire
JAS	*Journal of African Society*
JHSN	*Journal of the Historical Society of Nigeria*
NAI	National Archives, Ibadan
NAK	National Archives, Kaduna
NUD	Nuwair Ud-Deen Society
PP	Parliamentary Papers (British)
UIL	University of Ibadan Library

Glossary

A'jamī	Non-Arabic language written in Arabic
Baba Adini	Patron of the Religion (Islam)
Balogun	Commander of the veteran warriors
Baḷẹ	Head of certain towns
Egungun	Masquerade
Giwa	Secretary
Gọmbọ	A type of Yoruba facial marking
Ifa	A form (god) of divination
Ile-kewu	An elementary Muslim School
Jamā'a	A group, community (Muslim)
Khuṭba	The Friday or 'Īd religious sermon
Ladani	Muezzin
Lemọmu	al-Imām, the leader of the Muslim community
Lemọmu Ratibi	Imām of a part or quarter of the town
Mallam	*Mu'allim*, a learned Muslim
Mukadamu	*Muqaddam*, leader of a Muslim brotherhood
Ogboni	A Yoruba secret politico-religious body
Onitafusiru	Qur'ān commentator (*Mufassir*)
Oṣugbo	An Oro-cult; a politico-religious body
Ọya	A Yoruba goddess, wife of Ṣango
Pele	A type of Yoruba facial marking
Sarumi	Commander of the cavalry
Seriki	Commander of the young warriors
Ṣango	A deified Alafin of Ọyọ
Yidi	'Īd, a Muslim festival

Foreword

This book is a revised version of my thesis – a work I undertook when the University of Ibadan awarded me a University scholarship to undertake post-graduate work; and Ondo Boys' High School kindly released me from their service, thereby making it easy for me not only to accept the scholarship award but also to continue my academic career. I wish, therefore, to express my appreciation and gratitude to the two institutions, and to Professor J. C. Anene, who was at that time the Head of History Department, University of Ibadan, and J. A. Iluyọmade, the Principal of O.B.H.S.

My supervisor for the thesis was Professor J. F. Ade Ajayi, who has done much more than merely draw my attention to a research topic which I have since found useful and satisfying. I here recall with thanks his guidance, encouragement and help in various ways.

In the course of my research, I received assistance from many people, some of whom are mentioned in the notes. Here, I wish to record my gratitude to B. G. Martin and J. O. Hunwick for guiding me further in the study of Arabic; the staff of the National Archives at Ibadan and Kaduna, and the staff of the Africana Section of the University of Ibadan Library for their patient help. Above all, I acknowledge my indebtedness to all Muslims in Yorubaland for their incalculable co-operation and support in the course of my field work.

I must record my thanks to Professor A. B. Aderibigbe, for his invaluable help and moral support, especially in the compilation of this thesis, and to Professor Abdullahi Smith for the inspiration and stimulating analyses that he often gave. All my drafts were read by Professor O. Ikime and Dr H. O. Idowu; and parts of it were read by Professors F. H. El-Masri, I. A. B. Balogun, T. N. Tamuno, B. O. Olọruntimẹhin, R. J. Gavin, Oyin Ogunba and Biodun Adetugbo. To them all I am grateful for their valuable comments and suggestions.

It would be difficult to estimate how much the successful completion of this work is due to the moral support and help of my friends, in particular Lare Akinyoyenu, Rẹmi Adelẹyẹ, Ladi Ọbakin, Kọla Fọlayan and Lateef Adegbite. And I must mention my sister Mulikat Aduke and my wife Tayibat Jumoke as outstanding symbols of a helpful family.

Last but not least, I thank Mr J. O. M. Pẹluọla who prepared the original maps, and all my typists, especially Kaṣimawo, E. Kẹhinde and C. O. Akinbọade for their labour and toil over my scripts.

T. G. O. Gbadamosi

Introduction

This work attempts to shed light on the Muslim history of the Yoruba – a subject that has hitherto not been seriously studied, and has suffered considerably from speculation and guesswork. The Yoruba are one of the most enterprising peoples in West Africa and since the majority of them are now Muslims, constituting a very conscious and dynamic body with far-reaching connections, it is obviously essential to try to understand their past experience, development, ideas, hopes and aspirations.

My viewpoint in this work has been largely socio-political, and little attention has been given to the literary, spiritual and economic activities of Muslims. Other scholars, I hope, will embark on studying these aspects and enrich our present knowledge. In collecting material for the present history I have consulted Muslim, Christian and government sources, as the bibliography indicates. It is hoped that the conclusions drawn from these sources will serve as bases for new questions that should provoke further enquiry.

It must be emphasised here that this work deals mainly with the Muslim history of the largest concentration of the Yoruba, inhabiting the present Lagos and Western States. A full-length history of nearby Yoruba Muslim communities, especially of the Yoruba Muslims in Dahomey and Ilorin, has not been undertaken here largely because ever since they came under new political masters, the course and pattern of their history have followed channels strikingly different from those of the Yoruba Muslims in the Lagos and Western States. For example, with the success of the *Jihad* led by ibn Salih, Ilorin, alone in Yorubaland, became an emirate of the Sokoto Caliphate and thereby belonged to a juridical and political system unparalleled in the rest of Yorubaland. More important, the pattern of the development of Islam there was no longer typical of the course of Islam in Yoruba society at large. Consequently, it has been found more useful in this study to deal with the main body of Yoruba Muslims who, on the whole, have had a distinctive pattern of Muslim history and development. Reference has been made to the history of Yoruba Muslims in Ilọrin or Dahomey only where this has been considered relevant to an understanding of the historical development in the core area of Yorubaland.

As a Muslim history of a Nigerian people, this study, in a way, complements certain scholarly works dealing with the activities and influence of the Christian missions in Nigeria. The most notable among such works are those by J. F. Ade Ajayi, *The Christian Missions in Nigeria*; E. A. Ayandele, *The Missionary Impact of Modern Nigeria*; and J. B. Webster, *The African Churches among the Yoruba*. I believe that an evaluation of the Nigerian past will benefit greatly from a more balanced appreciation of the influences which both the Cross and the Crescent have exerted on the Nigerian peoples.

More important, however, this study hopes to further our understanding of the growth and influence of Islam especially in the West African periphery of the Muslim world. This work is restricted in both scope and time to a homogeneous group, and it thus contrasts with the wide-scale exercise undertaken by J. S. Trimingham (*A History of Islam in West Africa*) with the pitfalls common to such general works. It falls more in line with the work of J. F. Hopewell (*Muslim Penetration into French Guinea, Sierra Leone and Liberia before 1850*), N. Levtzion (*Muslims and Chiefs in West Africa*), and the studies of the history of Islam among the Wolofs, Asante, and Mossi undertaken by V. Monteil, Ivor Wilks and E. P. Skinner respectively. Evidently, there is a strong case for this type of close historical study of the different Muslim groups to enable us to understand better the role and effects of Islam in West African areas frequently regarded as peripheral to the Muslim world.

Thus the focus of this work is the outstanding development and activities of the Muslim community among the Yoruba in the second half of the nineteenth century. Before this period, Islam had been established in certain parts of Yorubaland and had developed certain features. The Jihad of 1804, and the political disintegration of Old Ọyọ Empire, considerably affected the Muslim community, and tended to prejudice Yoruba society against Islam. However, in spite of the generally inauspicious circumstances immediately created, the Muslim community succeeded in regrouping itself, and before the turn of the century it had grown very remarkably in size, status and strength. It even essayed to introduce Islamic law and establish an Islamic state *de facto*. An effort is made in this work to analyse not only the peculiar salient factors responsible for this phenomenal development, but also the nature and pattern of this Muslim growth.

As the history of the growth of Islam among the Yoruba is studied in the socio-political context of the period, the nature and development of the relationship between the Muslims and the rising forces of Christianity and colonial rule are discussed; and the overall significance of the community to the society is described. Drawing upon traditional social values, and adjusting itself to the new forces of Westernism, the Yoruba Muslim community constituted one of the major dynamic forces shaping the nature and course of Yoruba life and history.

A word about Yoruba orthography. Yoruba orthography is being modernised, I am informed; and, on expert advice, the new form has been used much in this work. But in certain cases, especially place and personal names, I have found it more convenient to spell these as they occurred in the contemporary records.

Bibliographical details of works listed in the bibliography are not repeated in full in the notes.

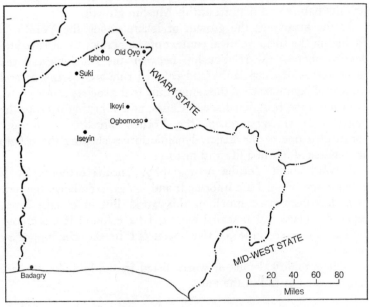

Major centres of Islamic distribution in Yorubaland before 1830

1 Islam in Yorubaland in the period before 1840

In the period under study the Yoruba mostly lived in the area which constitutes the present Western and Lagos States.[1] The Yoruba could be divided into a number of sub-ethnic groups – the Ọyọ, the Ẹgba, the Ẹgbado, the Ijẹbu, the Ekiti, the Ondo, the Akoko, the Ikalẹ and so on. These groups can, for easy reference, be classified into three rough geographical zones. Along the coastal rain forests to the south were the Ijẹbu and the Mahin; in the deciduous forests of the hilly interior were the Ijẹsa, the Ondo, the Ekiti and the Akoko; in the open derived savannah to the north-west and west were the Ọyọ, the Ẹgba and the Ẹgbado. By far the largest unit, and the most populous, was the open derived savannah group which at the beginning of the nineteenth century contained a substantial number of the largest Yoruba towns, especially Ọyọ, the metropolis of the Ọyọ Empire.

Each sub-ethnic group developed its own dialect, local culture and traditions; but in spite of these local developments and variations, there was unity in Yoruba culture and we can identify five main characteristics relevant to this study.

First, there was the role of Ife as the cradle of the Yoruba.[2] In popular belief the Yoruba were 'Ọmọ Oduduwa', descendants of Oduduwa of Ifẹ; and practically every important Yoruba traditional ruler jealously traced and preserved his link with this town. This belief gave some homogeneity to the group and marked it off from groups of a different ancestry.

In addition to common descent, the Yoruba had another bond in their common language. There are dialects within the language and, on the basis of linguistic and some ethno-historical criteria, they have been classified into three major groups: North-west Yoruba, South-east Yoruba and Central Yoruba.[3] But these dialects are mutually intelligible and are variants of the standard form. This form gained an orthography in the last century, thanks to the efforts of the Christian missionaries.[4] This orthography, it has been pointed out,[5] initially represented to a large extent the phonemes of the Abẹokuta dialect, and the morpho-syntax the Ọyọ Ibadan dialects; but later standardisation has tended to lean more on the Ọyọ dialect. This has remained essentially the standard form of the written language.

More relevant to our present study are the other three marks of Yoruba unity. The Yoruba culture was basically urban.[6] The people lived mostly in cities and large agglomerations, and this fact manifested itself in various aspects of their life, particularly in the quality, polish and sophistication of their politics, economic attitudes, dress, language and behaviour. A significant aspect of this pattern of settlement was the close relationship between the town and the outlying rural area; the townsmen owned farms outside the towns, and the dwellers in the countryside regularly came to the towns for various social, political and economic activities.[7]

The frequency of social interaction not only between towns but also between the urban centres and outlying areas helped to maintain a considerable degree of homogeneity of culture, and facilitated the diffusion of new ideas and styles. This city-village life style later proved important for the spread and growth of Islam in Yorubaland.

Within its own geographical area, each sub-ethnic group evolved its own political organisation with its system of unwritten laws and sanctions. The Ọyọ Empire, which was the largest political unit that evolved, lay in the open derived savannah region and did not include all the Yoruba, although it embraced non-Yoruba elements such as the Igun and the Fọn. There were local variations in the political systems that evolved in the various areas. The Ikale, for example, did not have the Ogboni, so prominent a feature of the political life of the Ẹgba, among whom the Ogboni has been rightly described as a Senate.[8] Similarly, in the Ọyọ-speaking areas of the Yoruba country there was the Parakoyi, an organisation which was in charge of markets and traders, especially long-distance traders; but this institution remained unknown to, or became defunct among, the Ondo, for example.[9] Nevertheless there were a recognisable political system and a substantial body of political practices and concepts which were common to all of them. The political structure[10] was hier-

archical, with the Ọba or Balẹ at its apex; and among the institutions within that structure there was a balance of power and
authority. Most important for our study was the integration into
the political and judicial system of various religious and semi-
religious beliefs, systems and institutions such as Ifa, *orịṣa*, the
Ogboni, the Oṣugbo[11] and the Oro.[12]

Indeed, the integrating role of the body of Yoruba traditional
beliefs and worship[13] constituted the single most important factor
of Yoruba culture. Again, there were some local beliefs in certain
'gods' and traditional 'pagan' practices. For example, peculiar to
the Ọyọ was the belief in Ṣango, a deified Alafin, and in Ọya and
Ọṣun.[14] There were some variations in certain traditional features
such as the *Egungun*.[15] Moreover, some of the beliefs and practices were not indigenous, but were introduced to the Yoruba
country; a good example here was Ifa, which probably came from
Nupe.[16] These local beliefs and practices, as well as the imported
ones, eventually spread among the Yoruba; and they could be
distinguished from the core of the Yoruba traditional pantheon.
Essentially, this consisted of belief in Olọrun (Olodumare)[17] and
in a panoply of 'gods' (orịṣa) such as Esu, Ogun, Orịṣala and the
like.[18] The belief in Olodumare, orịṣa and ancestors, together with
the practice of magic and medicine, may rightly be said to be the
chief element of Yoruba traditional religion.[19]

This body of Yoruba beliefs permeated the whole fabric of
Yoruba life and culture. Ifa and other diviners were consulted
everywhere by all Yoruba who had to formulate policies or make
important decisions. The social taboos were essentially what the
'gods' hate; and festivals were mainly celebrations in honour of
these 'gods'. Security and protection both in public and private
life were expected from the 'gods', whose favour was solicited
through the amulets and sacrifices made by their priests. Even
artistic works, such as carving, were inspired by concepts of these
gods, and were largely oriented towards their service.[20] Thus,
perhaps, the single most important factor in Yoruba life, important
because of its pervasive and determinant quality, was the body of
Yoruba traditional beliefs and worship.[21]

In the course of its development in Yorubaland, Islam[22] had to
reckon with these very characteristics. Some of these factors, such
as common language, city-village life style and political hierarchy,
were to assist the spread and growth of the religion. Others, such
as the complexity of Yoruba religious beliefs and practices, were,

in some regards, obstacles to the progress of Islam. Moreover, new factors such as Christianity, Western European values and British rule entered the situation later. It will be seen how Islam spread and grew amidst these challenging and changing circumstances.

Beyond Yorubaland there were areas that had in varying degrees become 'Islamised'. Bornu had welcomed some Ummayyad Muslim refugees in about the eleventh century and had since become progressively Muslim.[23] In the Songhai Empire, Islam was introduced early in the eleventh century and had become a powerful force by about the fifteenth century.[24] From such Islamised empires as Bornu, Songhai and Mali, Kano and other parts of Hausaland had received Islam in about the fourteenth century, thanks to the Mandinka traders and missionaries.[25] Nearer, Nupe evidently had a Muslim ruler by the close of the eighteenth century, and may have accepted Islam much earlier than that.[26]

Yorubaland had some contact with these Islamised areas both in war and in peacetime through the activities of soldiers, settlers and above all traders. This varied contact meant some intermingling of peoples and ideas, an intermingling which facilitated the infiltration of Islam into Yorubaland. From the Islamised areas, especially those to the north-west of Yorubaland, had come the first Muslims in Yorubaland.

The date of entry of Islam to Yorubaland cannot be fixed with precision. It was unannounced and unplanned; and, for the most part, the first Yoruba Muslims had to worship privately and secretly. What is fairly certain is that in the seventeenth century, mention was made of Muslims in Yorubaland.[27] Towards the close of the eighteenth century the position of Islam was already such that the Yoruba were propagating Islam as far afield as Porto Novo and Dahomey.[28] The evidence shows that by 1840 there was considerable degree of Islamisation in Yorubaland.

In many of the large towns there were at least some sprinklings of Muslims. Owu, before its destruction in 1825, contained many Muslims.[29] Badagry evidently had some Muslim community whose colourful celebration of the '*Íd al-Fiṭr* was watched by Lander on 27 March 1830.[30] At Ardra, Captain John Adams saw at some time in the last two decades of the eighteenth century a group of local Muslims at worship and he noted that the adherents of Islam were many.[31] These were, according to him, generally 'dressed after the Moorish fashion with large loose trowsers [*sic*], short shirt, and sash'.[32] At about the same time, al-Ṣāliḥ (about whom more will be said) passed through the northern parts of Yorubaland; and he met some thriving Muslim communities, for example, at Ikoyi and Ogbomoṣo.[33] At Ketu, Islam was long established,[34] and by the close of the eighteenth century Muslims constituted a noticeable force in Ketu's army.[35] In Lagos mention was made of the presence of Islam first at the court of Adele I (1775–80, 1832–4).[36] He permitted the practice of this religion, at the expense of his throne in 1780.[37] When he came back to Lagos in 1832, Islam was again firmly planted in his court in Lagos, and Muslims in and outside the court enjoyed his patronage. In these towns Islam was established though in varying degrees.

Larger and firmer communities existed in a few towns. This was so, for example, at Igboho, a town to the north-east of Yorubaland. A town of some considerable size,[38] Igboho had a fairly extensive section, called Moḷaba, completely settled by Muslims[39] (also known as *Mọlaba* or *Mọlawa*), who were in considerable numbers[40] and had their quarter and central mosques in their own area.

Similarly in Iseyin, there was an established Muslim community. Most of the Muslims were settled at Oke Baba Dudu and at Ijemba,[41] where they practised their faith. The early Muslims reportedly came from Songhai or Mali area, and were regarded as having introduced the faith which they and succeeding generations had helped to sustain since then. Prominent among them were Kanuri and Dendi Muslims. It is from among some of these families that the first few Imams, and many of the later ones, have been selected.[42]

Above all, in the capital of the Oyo Empire, Islam was fairly well established. It had been introduced by Afaa Yigi,[43] of Arab descent,[44] probably some time during the reign of Alafin Ajagbo.[45] This Arab had stayed in the palace, it is said, at the request of the Alafin; and it was around him that the nucleus of converts gathered. The size of the Muslim community was probably small, but it throve and was considerably reinforced by the ingress of other occasional Arabs and the Hausa slaves and men who were brought to Oyo.

Evidently then, Islam was established before 1840 in Ardra Badagry, Igboho, Ijana, Ikoyi, Iseyin, Ketu, Lagos and Oyo.[46] Two remarkable points emerge from this. First, these were market towns or ports, providing a congenial environment where Islam could easily thrive. The second and more interesting point is that almost all the important centres of Islam in the period before 1840 were based in the Ọyọ Empire. Largely as a result of this, early Yoruba Islam was very much permeated by Ọyọ custom.[47]

One of the customs in the early days, it was said, was to give 'Pele' and 'Gombọ' facial marks to the Muslim converts.[48] It may well have been that some families or sub-ethnic groups with these facial marks became so Islamised that the marks were identified with adherence to Islam. Also, the Muslims may have wanted to distinguish themselves by adopting this type of facial mark. This custom of facial marking of Muslims was not widely observed long after the rebellion of the eighteenth century, since this event, as will be seen later, stigmatised the Muslims.[49]

These early Muslim communities were composed of Yoruba and non-Yoruba, such as Dindi, Mọlawa, Mọlaba, Hausa, Bornu and Nupe Muslims. In this diverse group many of the Hausa were in fact slaves,[50] obtained through war and trade,[51] and served in various capacities depending on their skills and circumstances. Some were barbers, rope-makers and cow-herds;[52] others were expected to carry out domestic chores but particularly to take care of the horses.[53] Others were free-born, though there is no evidence that their social position was high. Those who were knowledgeable in Islam and Arabic were, however, held in high esteem in the society for their learning, piety and ability to make powerful charms. Lander observed, with a touch of merry exaggeration, that the Muslim learned man 'never toils or spins but is bountifully fed and pampered in luxury by his lay countrymen'.[54] It was this indefinite number of learned men who conducted teaching, led the prayers and helped to nurture the religious life of the community.

In spite of their low, or at best middling, social position, some of the well-informed mallams felt strong enough to challenge openly erring political heads. Johnson records[55] how in the reign of Alafin Ajiboyede, the last Alafin at Igboho, a certain Muslim *mu'allim* from Nupe appeared and launched a protest against him for his cruelty in murdering his allegedly hypocritical nobles and chiefs. 'This is a sin against God who took away the life of your son', he reportedly rebuked the Alafin.[56]

The communities organised themselves generally under their Imam. In some of these areas, particularly Igboho and Ọyọ, some active role seems to have been played by the Parakoyi in the organisation of the early Muslim community. For some time in Igboho the Parakoyi was known to be the head of the Muslim community;[57] and no less prominent seems to have been his role in Ọyọ, Ogbomọṣọ and Oṣogbo. In Oṣogbo, indeed, he was also virtually the leader,[58] and his leadership was superseded only later by that of the Imām.[59] This active role of the Parakoyi in the leadership of the early Muslim community may have been due to his position as the 'toll collector'[60] which exposed him to, and invested him with some authority over, strangers and long-distance traders.

The existence of these Muslim communities was bound to create some tension in society.[61] This was easily the case when Muslims became ardent in the cause of their faith, or were caught in any political tussle. For example, in Lagos certain dynastic trouble broke out around 1832 between two royal groups, led by Adele and Eshilogun respectively.[62] The Muslims became involved in this because they had been close to royal personages, and when their side lost, they together with their Imām, Idris Salu Gana, were expelled to Ibi.[63] This dynastic trouble was confined to Lagos; but the Muslim misfortune was only part of the general fate which overtook Islam during the early years of the nineteenth century.

In the Ọyọ Empire more momentous events were already taking place. Early in the nineteenth century this area witnessed the stirrings of two important forces that later rocked the whole of Yorubaland. First, there was the political or constitutional crisis in Ọyọ, which can be dated as far back as 1793 when Alafin Aole attacked Apomu, an Ife town, and consequently broke his coronation oath.[64]

Less well known but equally important was the second force: the movement for Islamic reform which was going on at the time in Yorubaland. The northern section of this empire and, indeed, the capital itself witnessed an intensive amount of Muslim evangelisation and reformist preaching. In Ọyọ there were 'no less than five holy men, two or three of whom were Arab Emirs . . . spread[ing] the dogmas of their faith amongst the inhabitants, publicly teaching their children to read the Quran'.[65] Two of these active Muslim preachers were particularly notable. The first was an Arab, Muhammad Ben Haja Gumso[66], who stayed in the palace of the Alafin. The second mallam had a more crucial significance. By name al-Ṣālih,[67] he was popularly known as

Alimi.[68] He had travelled extensively in the area, particularly to Ọyọ, Iseyin, Ogbomọṣọ and Kuwo,[69] over a period of some years,[70] and had devoted himself to the cause of Islamic reform. He moved and taught within the Muslim communities and became very much revered for his piety and learning. For his religious activities and popularity he was, according to some tradition, driven out of Ọyọ by the Alafin,[71] but he continued his travels and reformist preaching in the northern part of the empire.

This intensive Islamic activity caused considerable concern and aggravated the latent tension between the Muslims and the traditional authorities in this part of the Ọyọ Empire. Lander was informed everywhere in 1825–6 that so intensive and successful was this Muslim activity that the pagan votaries were more than alarmed. Consequently they went all 'in a body to their monarch . . . threatening him with the loss of his Empire if he persisted in tolerating the religious principles broached by the mallams'.[72]

The upshot of this Islamic ferment in the Ọyọ areas was violent. Toleration was replaced by persecution. The Alafin massacred such of the Muslims as could be gathered into the palace;[73] only Ben Gumso escaped, naked, to Sokoto, where Clapperton found him to be 'an influential and trusted official'.[74] This massacre terrified the Muslims, and made them bitter against the entire traditional system. They were now clearly in danger of their lives, and whether they could survive the policy of persecution and extermination must have seemed doubtful. But widespread and reasonably established as the Muslims were, the issue was not likely to be resolved swiftly. Indeed, this apparent religious problem only further complicated the political problems of the empire.

The politico-constitutional crisis within the empire soon reached a head with the revolt of Afọnja. The events of the Afọnja Revolt are too well known to require more than a brief narration here for the elucidation of the history of Islam in Yorubaland.[75] While the Ọyọ Empire was in the throes of political troubles Afọnja, the Arẹ-Ọna Kakanfo, revolted against the authority of the Alafin about 1797.[76] He refused to pay tribute to Ọyọ, and assumed independence.[77] He was with his yet tiny forces at Ilọrin, his home town within the Empire, which he strove to make the base of his rebellious operations.

An important development of this revolt was the way Afọnja cast about for support. He needed a force that could match that of his former lord in the event of a confrontation. More pressing, however, was the advancing force of Ojo Agunbambaru, a son of Basorun Gaha,[78] who was moving in from Bariba with 'an immense' army, and had set off for Ilọrin.[79] Afọnja needed all his resources; and his idea was to forge an alliance with the Muslims and Hausas in the Ọyọ Empire. In this connection, he secured the help of al-Sālih (Alimi) who, widely-travelled in the area and known and respected among this group of people as a Muslim reformer, had his own complaints and grievances against the current pagan system and practices.[80]

This alliance of Afọnja and al-Sālih was a diplomatic master-stroke of considerable significance. In the meantime, Afọnja successfully withstood the forces under Ojo Agunbambaru.[81] More important, the alliance underlined a change in the original character of the Afọnja Revolt: the political revolt continued but it was now conjoined with religion. The politico-constitutional crisis became mixed up with the Islamic ferment and agitation of the time.

As religion became an issue in the conflict, local (Yoruba) Muslims (for political reasons as well) threw in their lot with Afọnja and al-Sālih against the Alafin. They trooped into Ilọrin from the nearby towns, and settled at Oke Suna[82] in Ilọrin, constituting a considerable Muslim force for Afọnja. It was effectively under the leadership of Ṣọlagbẹru, a rich Muslim friend of Afọnja; but it formed part of the entire *Jamā'a* of al-Sālih. In the course of time al-Sālih invited down to Ilọrin his two sons, 'Abd al-Salām and Shitta. He did this on the insistence of Afọnja, his grateful and beleaguered host.[83] Later, when the opposition against Ilọrin appeared formidable, Ilọrin solicited and won the military support of the Sokoto Jihadists.[84] It was largely through this double Muslim support, local and external, that Afọnja was able to carry through his revolt, making himself and his followers at Ilọrin independent.

Afọnja's success, however, was short-lived. He had had hopes of establishing his own political authority in Ilọrin and probably beyond; but no less ambitious were the victory-flushed jamā'a of al-Sālih. Between them there ensued a struggle for political supremacy, a struggle which strained the erstwhile union of the political gamblers and the religious zealots. In a desperate but belated attempt to rid himself of his chokingly powerful and

9

ambitious supporters, Afọnja himself was slain in a pitched battle fought out by the two groups.[85]

The fall of Afọnja did not immediately ensure the supremacy of the Sokoto forces under al-Ṣālih and his two sons. The local Muslim forces which, under the leadership of Ṣọlagbẹru, had championed Afọnja's cause were still considerable, and could draw on reinforcements more readily than the Jihadists from Sokoto. What was more, these local forces, after the fall of Afọnja, soon began to resent the growing power and raids of the Sokoto forces. No less bitter were the religious purists among the followers of al-Ṣālih, who scorned the Muslim followers of Ṣọlagbẹru for the *bada'* present in their practice of Islam.[86] Internal religio-political tension soon broke out and the two sides appealed to the arbitration of the sword. In the subsequent battle, the Sokoto Jihadists proved stronger and victorious; they killed Ṣọlagbẹru and firmly established their political dominance in Ilọrin. Thus Ilọrin came under the control of new masters, Muslim and non-Yoruba. From here was launched a series of wars not only against the Ọyọ Empire but also into the surrounding areas.[87] The militancy of the Ilọrin Jihad reached its apogee in Yorubaland when Alafin Oluewu was made to come to Ilọrin 'to tap the Qur'ān,'[88] some time between 1827 and 1830.[89] But it was signally checked in 1840 when Ibadan defeated Ilọrin at the battle of Oṣogbo.

The pertinent issue here is the effect on Islam in Yorubaland of this chain of events which began with the Afọnja Revolt and resulted in the launching of a jihad.

The first obvious effect of this revolt-turned-jihad was the establishment of Ilọrin as a Muslim stronghold. Initially a small village, Ilọrin in the course of the revolt attracted a large number of Muslims from inside and outside the Ọyọ Empire, and this Muslim group became the dominant power in Ilọrin. Henceforth Ilọrin remained to Yorubaland a sort of Islamic lighthouse, a local Mecca to which the Yoruba Muslim turned for study and guidance. But this very success also had certain negative and damaging implications on the fortunes of Islam in Yorubaland.

The building up of Ilọrin had meant the evacuation of Muslim leaders from the rest of Yorubaland. For, the introduction of a religious issue into the Imperial conflict encouraged a sizable number of ardent Muslims to flee and join at Ilọrin the standards of Ṣọlagbẹru and al-Ṣālih in their joint assault upon the Alafin and his authority. These Muslims from Yorubaland included Hausa and Fulani, some of whom were in a servile position.[90] Most of the Muslims had fled Kuwọ, Kobẹ, Ikoyi – the big towns in the northern sector of the Ọyọ Empire, through which, incidentally, that revered religious man al-Sālih had passed. This reduction in Muslim ranks meant more than a numerical loss: it involved also loss of talent, for the fleeing and persecuted Muslims necessarily included many of the more ardent and knowledgeable ones.[91] The loss was felt for many decades, especially since the fleeing Muslims settled in their new abode which, as has been noted, passed into the hands of new masters.

The immediate depletion of the Yoruba Muslim ranks was carried further by the reaction shown by some towns and people in Yorubaland. As the revolt became a jihad, the ardent Muslims and the Jihadists constituted inevitably an extremely serious and fundamental challenge to the political authority of Ọyọ. In addition, the success of the revolt encouraged the Muslims to use their new stronghold Ilọrin as the base from where they launched incessant wars and raids against various towns within the Ọyọ Empire. The more such successful raids there were, the more the Muslims and the Hausa slaves were encouraged to rise in revolt and flee to Ilọrin. All this could not but provoke the Yoruba traditionalists into a determined reaction against the Muslims. They opposed and fell upon the Muslims, local and alien, in their midst. Clapperton observed in 1826 that:

> the Yoruba confirmed Kaffers, on the invasion of the Fellatahs ... put all the Mahometans [*sic*] to death whether natives or in caravans trafficking; quite denying the plea that God had given to the faithful their land and houses, and their wives and children to be slaves.[92]

This reaction against Islam might not always have been as fateful and bloody as Clapperton noted; but it was widespread and protracted, and in some cities Muslims were 'roughly handled by the people'.[93] This Yoruba reaction against Islam was due largely to the fear of Ilọrin, a fear which lingered down to the late 1820s and beyond.[94] The flight of the Muslims in Yorubaland to Ilọrin as well as their persecution at the hands of irate traditionalists were concurrent, two developments that crippled Islam in both size and stature in these areas of Yorubaland.

Some Muslims, of course, remained behind and survived such persecution as there was in their areas. In 1825–6 Clapperton and Lander still encountered some Muslims and Hausa mallams in places such as Ilaro, Jannah and Ọyọ.[95] But these Muslims had to contend with a problem greater than those arising from the numerical and intellectual depletion of their ranks; hemmed into their localities, and deprived of some of their leaders, they failed to evince the necessary courage to sustain their faith. Moreover, a thick cloud of suspicion was cast over the Muslims by the non-Muslim Yoruba especially in and around the capital city.[96] They were suspected as secret collaborators with Ilọrin or as being simply subversive of the established order.[97] They were also held responsible for the raids and devastation in Yorubaland. Thus, they were under 'irksome restraint',[98] and the preaching and teaching of Islam to children of the inhabitants were suffered only on the pain of death.[99] Indeed the tendency was to curtail the activities of the Muslims within Yorubaland.

Another effect of the revolt-turned-jihad was that Muslim establishments fell along with the towns that were sacked, deserted or destroyed.[100] As such towns as Igboho, Ikoyi, Kuwọ and Ọyọ fell or were deserted,[101] the Muslims were scattered, and their organisation and spirit were broken. For the history of Islam among the Yoruba, this collapse of Muslim communities was of double significance: it meant that the remaining Muslims were further thrown into considerable disarray. Faced with security problems, they (together with non-Muslims) fled to such nearby areas as could afford protection. Where the circumstances proved favourable, they founded new settlements.

By 1840 then, the picture of Islam among the Yoruba was largely a dismal one, depicting considerable depletion and disarray. And in a very real sense, Islam in Yorubaland in the period after the rebellion virtually had to re-establish itself, outlive strong local prejudice, recover and reorganise itself, and rebuild its stature and strength.

In its efforts to re-establish itself it could draw support from three main sources. First, there was the basic Yoruba attitude of religious toleration which finds its finest expression in the belief that the Yoruba Ọba was to be 'the father of all' irrespective of religion. This basic principle of religious toleration might be shattered in times of crisis and religious ardour such as that ushered in by the period of rebellion; but the balance was soon restored 'when tempers cooled'. This began in 1840 with the victory of Ibadan over Ilọrin. Secondly, the depletion which Yoruba Islam suffered was, as already indicated, a tremendous gain to Ilọrin, one from which Yoruba Islam was later to derive immense support once Ilọrin itself became settled and well established. The same Ilọrin that had been so richly reinforced from both the Yoruba and Hausa Muslim sources became, in spite of its change of political masters, a particularly nourishing source for the regeneration of Islam in Yorubaland. Thirdly, the very disarray into which the Yoruba Muslims were perforce thrown was later to prove advantageous since, as will be shown below,[102] the fleeing Muslim refugees from the sacked Yoruba towns became, as it were, agents of Islamic propagation in their new centres of abode.

The era of the rebellion thus marked in effect a watershed in the history of Islam in Yorubaland. A second phase began from about 1840 when Islam started to be re-established in Yorubaland.

Notes

1 Many Yoruba are to be found outside this area in Ilọrin, as well as in Ketu, Porto Novo and other parts of Dahomey. Ilọrin, however, came under Fulani rule early in the nineteenth century, and politically cannot be strictly regarded as part of Yorubaland. Similarly, Ketu, Ardra (Porto Novo) fell away from Yoruba (Ọyọ) control and came under the rule of Dahomey in the nineteenth century. After this political change of masters, these areas developed in a way different from that of the other Yoruba settlements. The latter remained closely inter-related in war and peace, and manifested a remarkable degree of uniformity in their historical development. It is these settlements which constituted the core of Yorubaland, and this study is concerned mainly with the Yoruba resident in this area.

2 S. Johnson, *The History of the Yoruba*, p. 15. There is the more recent work by S. O. Biobaku, 'The origin of the Yorubas', in *Lugard Lectures*, in which he tries to trace the Yoruba ancestry. He pursues a suggestion by S. Johnson (pp. 3–5) that the Yoruba came from the East, particularly Mecca. This does not, however, invalidate either the Yoruba belief of common ancestry or their belief that Ife was their 'distribution centre' in Yorubaland.

3 Abiodun Adetugbo, *The Yoruba language in Western Nigeria: its major dialect areas.*

4 See J. F. Ade Ajayi, 'How Yoruba was reduced to writing', *Odu.*

5 A. Adetugbo, *op. cit.*, p. 245.

6 Some scholars have studied this urban nature of Yoruba settlements; e.g. W. R. Bascom, 'Urbanisation among the Yoruba', *American Journal of Sociology.* See also B. Awe, *The Rise of Ibadan as a Yoruba power in the nineteenth century.* She tries to show that the urban character of Yoruba settlements antedated European advance and influence. See also A. L. Mabogunje, *Yoruba Towns*, and Eva Krapf-Askari, *Yoruba Towns and Cities*, Oxford, 1969.

7 As regards the economic relations between town compound and farm hamlet, Goddard tries to show that in spite of the rootedness of the Yoruba town in the surrounding farms, there is considerable economic discontinuity; see S. Goddard, 'Town–farm Relationships in Yorubaland: a Case Study from Ọyọ', *Africa*, xxxv, 1, Jan. 1965.

8 S. O. Biobaku, 'Ogboni, the Ẹgba Senate', *Proceedings of the C.I.A.O.*, pp. 257–64; 'An historical sketch of Ẹgba traditional authorities', *Africa.* See also J. H. Blair, *Intelligence Report, Abeokuta*, 1938.

9 N. A. Fadipe, *The Sociology of the Yoruba*, I.U.P., 1970, p. 225. The question raised by Biobaku as to whether the Parakoyi was a guild of traders or not remains unsolved; see S. O. Biobaku, *The Ẹgba and their Neighbours*, p. 6. See also articles by P. C. Lloyd, particularly 'The Yoruba Town Today', *Sociological Review.*

10 For more about this see N. A. Fadipe, *op. cit.*, pp. 198–242; and articles by P. C. Lloyd, especially 'The traditional political system of the Yoruba', *South Western Journal of Anthropology.*

11 Various Intelligence Reports on Ijẹbu deal with this. See in particular A. F. Abell, *Intelligence Report on the Ijebus*, 1933; T. B. Bovill-Jones, *Intelligence Report on Ijẹbu Ode Town and Villages*, May 1941; Captain J. A. Mackenzie, *Intelligence Report on Ijẹbu-Igbo*, 22 April 1940; and A. F. B. Bridges, *Intelligence Report on the Waterside Areas, Ijẹbu*, July 1940. Evidence shows that the Oṣugbo exercised administrative and judicial powers.

12 Peter Morton-Williams, 'The Atinga Cult among the South-Western Yoruba', *WAISER*, 1952.

13 Much has been written on this. The notable and scholarly works include A. B. Ellis, *The Yoruba-speaking Peoples of the Slave Coast of West Africa*; S. S. Farrow, *Faith, Fancies and Fetish*; P. A. Talbot, *The Peoples of Southern Nigeria*, vol. 1; J. O. Lucas, *The Religion of the Yorubas*; and E. B. Idowu, *Olodumare: God in Yoruba Belief*, S. Johnson, *op. cit.*, pp. 34-6. Ṣango was the fourth Alafin. E. B. Idowu (*op. cit.*, p. 70) feels that Ṣango was one of 'the earliest' gods and, therefore, a 'principal' divinity.

15 Adamuoriṣa, for example, is unknown in some parts of Yorubaland, notably in Ijẹbu and Ondo. Mr J. Adedeji, who has done a Ph.D. thesis on Yoruba drama, communicates that the Egungun is mainly an Ọyọ affair. For further information see P. Morton-Williams, 'The Egungun Society in South-Western Yoruba Kingdoms',

Proceedings of the Third Annual Conference of the West African Institute of Social and Economic Research.

16 S. Johnson, *op. cit.*, pp. 32–3.

17 The novel suggestion has been made recently that the 'vital power', 'supreme being' in Yoruba religious concept, might be 'Ase' and not Olǫrun, the Owner of the Sky – a word which is associated with death. See Pierre Verger, 'The Yoruba High God', *Odu*. A modern exposition of the old and popular idea can be found in P. Morton-Williams, 'An Outline of the Cosmology and Cult Organisation of the Ọyọ Yoruba', *Africa*.

18 The definite number of these oriṣa is difficult to fix. According to oral evidence, it has ranged from 201 to 1,440 (E. B. Idowu, *op. cit.*, pp. 67–8). He has even put the number at 1,700 in his more recent work *African Traditional Religion*, pp. 159ff. It is difficult not to agree that, as he said in his earlier work, 'to quote any of the figures is now "only a manner of speaking"'. Besides, no work has yet been able to list *all* these 'gods'.

19 E. B. Idowu, *African Traditional Religion*, pp. 139–202.

20 J. W. Cordwell, *Some Aesthetic Aspects of Yoruba and Benin Cultures*. He shows how figurines and other artistic works are inspired and oriented towards religion.

21 For gods in Yorubaland see also I. O. Delano, *The Soul of Nigeria*, pp. 175–86.

22 Very many scholarly works are available on this subject. These include A. Ali, *The Spirit of Islam*, London, 1965; A. Jeffrey (ed.), *A Reader on Islam*, pp. 457–521; H. A. R. Gibb, *Mohammedanism*, Oxford, 1965, pp. 35–107; and W. M. Watt, *Islamic Philosophy and Theology*.

23 The Mahram of Umme Jilmi (translated and published by H. R. Palmer), *Bornu, Sahara and the Sudan*, pp. 14–15. See also Palmer's *Sudanese Memoirs*, III, pp. 3–5; quoted by T. Hodgkin, *Nigerian Perspectives*, pp. 68–9.

24 J. S. Trimingham, *A History of Islam in West Africa*, pp. 86–7. He here quotes the well-known Arab historians of the Western Sudan: 'Abd al-Rahmān b. 'Abdullāh al-Sa'd, *Ta'rikh al-Sūdān* (published and translated by O. Houdas, Paris, 1898), pp. 3–5; Mahmūd Ka'ti b. al-Hājj Ka'ti, *Ta'rikh al-Fattāsh* (published and translated by O. Houdas, M. Delafosse, Paris, 1913), pp. 332–3. See also E. W. Bovill, *The Golden Trade of the Moors*, pp. 133–8.

25 *The Kano Chronicle*, translated and published by H. R. Palmer in *Sudanese Memoirs*, III, pp. 104–6. See also J. S. Trimingham, *op. cit.*, pp. 130–1.

26 S. F. Nadel, *A Black Byzantium*, p. 76.

27 'Abdullah Muhammad b. Massanih, *Shifā' Rubā fi tahrir fucahā Yurubā*. The author and this work were mentioned by Muhammad Bello in *Infāq al-Maisūr*, p. 8. See also A. D. H. Bivar and M. Hiskett, 'The Arabic Literature of Nigeria to 1804: A Provisional Account', *BSOAS*, xxv, 1962; H. F. C. Smith, 'Arabic Manuscript Material Relating to the History of the Western Sudan', *Supplement to Bulletin of News*, Historical Society of Nigeria.

This negates the statement made by S. Johnson (*op. cit.*, p. 26) that Islam was introduced into Yorubaland only at the close of the eighteenth century.

There is a Yoruba saying: 'Ile la ba Ifa, ile la ba, Imale osangangan ni ti Igbagbo' ('we met Ifa at home, we met Islam at home, but it is in the afternoon that we had Christianity'). By this the Yoruba stress that Ifa and Islam had been with them long before Christianity.

28 A. Akindele and C. Aguessy, *Contribution à l'étude de l'histoire de l'ancien royaume de Porto-Novo*, p. 131. See also their *Dahomey*, pp. 48–9. These Porto-Novo historians show that the Yorubas introduced Islam to Porto Novo in the reign of Ayikpe, 1775–83.

S.O. also E. G. Parrinder, *The Story of Ketu*, p. 33, where he says that Islam was introduced to Ketu in the latter half of the eighteenth century.

29 See Biobaku, *The Egba and their Neighbours*, p. 26. From Owu fled the people who later formed a whole quarter preponderantly Muslim in Abeokuta. See Ch. 2, p. 24. See also P. Curtin, 'Narrative of Joseph Wright' in P. Curtin (ed.), *Africa Remembered*, p. 318, fn. 3.

30 Richard and John Lander, *Journal of an Expedition to explore the Course and Termination of the Niger*, pp. 24–7.

31 Captain J. Adams, *Remarks on the Country extending from Cape Palmas to the River Congo*, pp. 78, 220–1.

32 *Ibid.*

33 Ahmad b. Abī Bakr Kokoro, *Ta'līf Akhbār al-qurūn min umarā' bilād Ilūrin*. I am grateful to El-Masri and B. G. Martin for allowing me to see the original of this document. Interviews with the Imam Abegunde of Ogbomọṣọ (May 1965) and with the leading Imams in Ilọrin (April–May 1965), confirm this point that al-Sālih met Muslim communities in these places and at Isẹyin 'O ba 'male nibi yi ni' ('He met Islam in these places'). See Bibliography: Oral Evidence.

34 E. G. Parrinder, *op. cit.*, pp. 33–4. Parrinder's assertion that the introduction of Islam to Ketu 'dates from the latter half of the eighteenth century' is not supported by any evidence.

35 *Ibid.*, see also pp. 52–3.

36 J. B. O. Losi, *The History of Lagos*, pp. 21–3. See also A. I. Animasaun, *The History of the Muslim Community of Lagos* (Lagos, n.d.), pp. 2–3 *et passim*. Moloney's statement that Islam was 'introduced into Lagos about 1816' has to be taken with a grain of salt; see A. Moloney, 'Notes on Yoruba and the Colony and the Protectorate of Lagos, West Africa, *Journal of the Royal Geographical Society*. Islam was in Lagos by 1816, but its introduction antedated 1816. Compare J. A. O. Payne, *Table of Principal Events* . . . p. 21, who affirmed that Islam was introduced to Lagos in the reign of Idewu Ojulari, the Ọba after Oshilokun.

37 J. B. O. Losi, *op. cit.*, pp. 21–3. One of the reasons for his expulsion from the Lagos throne was the latitude he gave to Muslims, and the consequent neglect of traditional worship.

38 Crowther in 1841 mentioned Igboho as one of the 'principal towns in the country of Yoruba'; see J. F. Schön and S. Crowther: *Journals*

of Rev. J. F. Schon and Mr. S. Crowther of an Expedition on the Niger, 1841, London, 1842. Bowen estimated around 1850 that the population of Igboho was 20,000: see T. J. Bowen, *Adventures and Missionary Labours in the Interior of Africa, 1849–1856*, p. 218.

39 Interview with Salami Jaiyeola, Chief Imam, and members of the Muslim community, Igboho, April 1965.

40 *Ibid.* There were seventy homesteads at Mọlaba, it is believed. If there were an average of five people for a homestead, the Muslims would have numbered at least three hundred and fifty.

41 Interviews at Iseyin with the Muslim community and Ijemba Muslims in particular, April 1965. Notable informants were al-hajj Yaya of Ijemba Quarter, al-hajj Abudu Wahabi of Agbaji Quarter. See Bibliography: Oral Evidence.

42 See Appendix I.

43 See S. Johnson, *op. cit.*, p. 164. Johnson mentions a certain 'Baba Yigi' as coming from Tapa country to castigate Alafin Ajiboyede for the murder of his chiefs. See Note 45 below. This Afaa Yigi was 'a white man' (Yoruba: *enia funfun, Larubawa ni*). *Afaa* is the Yoruba term for a Muslim scholar or cleric. Compare the use of *alufa* for his Christian counterpart.

44 *Ibid.* His appellation was 'Afaa Yigi to ko 'Male wo Ọyọ' ('Afaa Yigi who brought Islam to Ọyọ'). The Parakoyi also claims that his family has this praise-name; but this is doubtful in view of the well-corroborated migration of a few Muslim Arabs to Ọyọ. See pp. 6–7 below for discussion about the Parakoyi.

45 Interview with the Chief Imam, Ọyọ, March 1965. This Alafin was the sixteenth, according to Johnson; while Ajiboyede was the thirteenth. It is doubtful if both sources refer to the same person. Johnson's 'Baba Yigi' was Tapa, and he went back; whereas this other source maintained that 'Afa Yigi' was 'a white Arab' who settled and became an Imam.

46 Compare the view of some scholars who feel that Islam in Yorubaland was a very recent phenomenon. See particularly R. C. Abraham, *A Dictionary of Modern Yoruba*, p. 307; C. H. Elgee, *The Evolution of Ibadan*, p. 30; J. S. Trimingham, *op. cit.*, p. 230; J. Mendelsohn, *God, Allah and Juju*, pp. 109–10.

47 The full significance of this will be seen later when Muslim refugees from the Ọyọ-speaking areas came to reinforce Islam in other parts of Yorubaland. See Chapter 2.

48 Various sources, notably H. Higgins's Report contained in *PP, Correspondence Respecting the War between Native Tribes in the Interior*, C.4957, February 1887, and *PP, Further Correspondence Respecting the War between Native Tribes in the Interior* (in continuation of C.4957) C.5144 February 1887. Interview with the Chief Imam, Ọyọ. See also S. Johnson, *op. cit.*, p. 107. The evidence of Higgins is the same as that of the Ọyọ Chief Imam.

Johnson, however, assigns only the Pele to the Muslims, and asserts that the Gọmbọ are Ọyọ marks. The second half of this statement goes, however, to confirm the statement of Ọyọ preponderance among early Yoruba Muslims. The Pele and Gọmbo as given by Higgins are / / / and ≡ respectively. Johnson's Gọmbo is more elaborate and his Abaja (Ọyọ) marks are similar to Higgins's Gọmbo ≡. The Ọyọ Chief Imam makes slanting marks: / / / or \ \ \.

49 See pp. 11–12. Higgins, however, still heard echoes of the practice in 1893.

50 See S. Johnson, *op. cit.*, pp. 193–4. Particularly see R. and J. Lander, *op. cit.*; J. Adams, *op. cit.*, pp. 21–2.

51 E. J. Arnett, *The Rise of the Sokoto Fulani*, p. 16. See also J. Adams, *op. cit.*, p. 80 'Slaves of the Hausa nation are brought to Ardrah by the Eyeo trader and then sold . . .'

52 S. Johnson, *op. cit.*, p. 193.

53 J. F. Ade Ajayi, 'Narrative of Samuel Ajayi Crowther', in P. Curtin (ed.), *Africa Remembered*, p. 299 f. 20. He stresses the military importance of their role as stablemen.

54 R. Lander, *Records of Captain Clapperton's Last Expedition to Africa*, vol. I, p. 275.

55 S. Johnson, *op. cit.*, p. 164.

56 *Ibid.*

57 Interview with the Muslim community, Igboho, April 1965. See Bibliography: Oral Evidence.

58 Interview with the Chief Imam, Oṣogbo, and with the descendants of the first Parakoyi. See Bibliography: Oral Evidence.

59 See Chapters 2 and 3.

60 In some Yoruba towns, this was the chief function of the Parakoyi; see J. H. Blair, *Intelligence Report, Abeokuta*, 1938. For a different interpretation see B. A. Agiri, *Development of Local Government in Ogbomoso 1850–1950*, pp. 92–3. He believes it meant the officer running errands (Yoruba: *para*, go often) to Ikoyi.

61 This tension was quite understandable in view of the desire of Islam to reform society in a particular way (see Chapter 7. For a treatment of this tension in the Western Sudan of the nineteenth century, and for its role in the Jihād, see H. F. C. Smith, 'The Islamic Revolutions of the Nineteenth Century', *JHSN*.

62 For further details about this dynastic tussle, see J. F. Ade Ajayi, 'Political Organisation in West African Towns in the Nineteenth Century: the Lagos Example', in *Urbanisation in African Social Change*.

63 A. Moloney, *op. cit.*, gives the name of the Imam as 'Iaris Daha'; but he probably meant Idris Sule Gana, who was in fact the Chief Imam at this time. See Chapter 2.

64 S. Johnson, *op. cit.*, pp. 188–9. Johnson gives the background to the attack on Apomu. See also I. A. Akinjogbin, 'The Prelude to the Yoruba Civil Wars', *Odu*.

65 R. Lander, *op. cit.*, I, p. 279.

66 *Ibid.* See also H. Clapperton, *Journal of a Second Expedition into the Interior of Africa*, p. 230. He describes Ben Gumso whom he met in Sokoto as 'an influential and trusted official'. M. Last, *The Sokoto Caliphate*, Longman, 1968, makes no mention of him.

67 Ahmad b. Abī Bakr, *op. cit.*

68 He may well have been so called because of his reputation for learning and piety. Schacht supposes that the name is derived from al-Azim; see J. Schacht, 'Islam in Northern Nigeria', *Studia Islamica*. But he gives no other basis for this supposition than that in northern Nigeria the letter Z is pronounced as an emphatic L.

69 *Ibid.* This document only mentions his having been to Ogbomoṣọ, Ikoyi and Kuwo.

70 Ahmad b. Abī Bakr, *op. cit.* He spent 3 months in Ogbomoṣọ, 1 year at Ikoyi and 3 years at Kuwo. Altogether, he was probably in this area for four years.

71 Interview with al-hajj Salmon in Ọyọ, March–April 1965. The reason for his expulsion was not known. Al-hajj Salmon here states what was a fairly general belief. It has not been easy to determine which Alafin this was. It may have been either Abiodun or Aole, since this expulsion took place before the 1797 rebellion of Agonja against Aole (1789–96); see I. A. Akinjogbin, 'A Chronology of Yoruba History', *Odu.*

72 R. Lander, *op. cit.*, pp. 277–9.

73 *Ibid.*

74 H. Clapperton, *op. cit.* pp. 195–6. Lander also met him in Sokoto, and he informed Lander that he owed his life to one of the wives of the Alafin, who planned his escape. R. Lander, *op. cit.*, pp. 277–9.

75 See J. A. Atanda, 'The Fall of the Old Oyo Empire: A Reconsideration of Its Cause', *JHSN*, v, 4, June 1971, pp. 477–90. He has recently reviewed the traditional explanations about the fall of the Empire. One important point that he drew attention to was that Apomu was not attacked at all, contrary to Akinjogbin's view which predicated a constitutional crisis on the sacrilegious attack on Apomu.

76 This was within the 'first phase of Afọnja's revolt', to use Akinjogbin's phrase; see I. A. Akinjogbin, *op. cit.*

77 S. Johnson, *op. cit.*, p. 193. He was not alone here: Opele, the Balẹ of Gbogun also refused.

78 S. Johnson, *op. cit.*, p. 194.

79 *Ibid.* Johnson infers that Ojo opposed Afọnja because the latter's father was 'one of those who swelled Oyabi's army for the overthrow of his father the Basorun Gaha'. Ojo may, however, not have been more than one of the many military adventurers in that age, of whom Afonja himself was one.

80 In view of the activities and standing of Alimi prior to the Afonja revolt, it is unsatisfactory and simplistic to say that 'Alimi's role was to be that of the priest who would ensure Afọnja's success through supernatural means'. J. A. Atanda, *op. cit.*

81 *Ibid.*

82 This is the name which the Yoruba give to an area inhabited mostly by Muslims.

83 Oral tradition stresses this. See also Bibliography: Oral Evidence.

84 R. Lander, op. cit., pp. 96–7. For example, Ọyọ sought the help of a 'Monjia'; see S. Johnson, op. cit., p. 201. Tradition varies as to who obtained this Sokoto support; Alimi or 'Abd al-Salām. Possibly, they both did at various times; but it is certain that 'Abd al-Salām was the first Emir, a fact which indicates that he obtained help and authority from Sokoto. Last writes that 'Abd al-Salām communicated Sokoto as to the legality of castration, and received a fatwa on this in 1829; see M. Last, op. cit., p. 92 f. 11.

85 S. Johnson, op. cit. See also Ahmad b. Abī Bakr, op. cit. It is extremely difficult to agree with H. A. R. Johnston in assuming that Afọnja became a Muslim convert. Yoruba and Ilọrin sources – written and oral – prove otherwise. Afọnja died a pagan. See H. A. S. Johnston, The Fulani Empire of Sokoto, p. 140.

86 Interview with Imam Fulani, Ilọrin, April to May 1965. Whispers of this can be heard in Ilọrin today. Bada' is an innovation, alteration of established Muslim practice and therefore unacceptable. It means syncretism here. See EI, article on 'Badā'.

87 H. A. R. Johnston, op. cit., deals with Ilọrin's role in the early 1830s. In many ways, this account raises an eyebrow. For example, he affirms (p. 144) that after the decisive battle of Ọyọ in 1837 (a doubtful date) the Fulani in Ilọrin 'were content to consolidate their power in Ilọrin . . . and did not attempt to exploit their victory by further conquests.'

88 S. Johnson, op. cit., pp. 258–9. This means conversion to Islam.

89 This event took place a little before the Eleduwe war in 1830, and the Sack of Ọyọ in 1835. At the time of the Landers' visit, this had not happened.

90 There were many Hausa slaves in Ọyọ and Yorubaland generally – such as to call forth a protest from Muhammad Bello in his Infāq al-Maisūr. These are better presumed, with some justification and correctness, to be Muslims. Johnson, op. cit. pp. 193–4 and Lander, op. cit. pp. 143ff, suggest that the opportunity for looting and of earning their freedom might have induced the Hausa domestics to rise against their masters and rally round the Muslims in Ilọrin. Plausible as this argument may sound, it seems to have underplayed the Muslim religious fervour which dominated that first decade of the nineteenth century. This was the fervour which spurred the intense Muslim activity and made Yoruba free-born Muslims rally round the same standards as did the so-called Hausa freebooters.

91 Oral tradition collected at Ilọrin particularly from Imam Oke Male, Afa Salawu and others, April to May 1965. See Bibliography: Oral Evidence.

92 H. Clapperton, op. cit., p. 204.

93 R. Lander, op. cit., I, pp. 277–9.

94 Ibid. The Alafin in 1826 entreated Lander to free him from his over-powerful Muslim subjects. The nature of this fear may have been religious: fear of forced conversion to a different faith (here Islam). It may also have been political: fear of subjection to the Fulani and Hausa (some of whom were only slaves until that time).

95 Evidence of this abounds. Note particularly that Lander and Clapperton met a couple of Muslims here and there in their trip inland from
Badagry in 1825–6. Lander, *op. cit.*, p. 277, notes: 'mallams from
Houssa [*sic*] reside in almost every town of consequence which we
passed . . .' In Ọyọ itself, Clapperton noted that he was given an
account of the religion by 'a native of Bornu, a Muhammedan, and a
slave of the caboceer of Jannah'. H. Clapperton, *op. cit.*, p. 51.
96 R. Lander, *op. cit.*, I, pp. 279–80. Lander affirmed that the mallams
were 'looked upon with the greatest suspicion'.
97 R. and J. Lander, *op. cit.*, I, p. 68, note that 'a very prevalent notion'
was that 'the fellatahs are . . . spies from Sokoto'. Compare also the
view of Biobaku, *op. cit.*, p. 13, that in the early years of Abeokuta
the Muslims were 'fifth columnists'.
98 R. and J. Lander, *op. cit.*, I, p. 138.
99 *Ibid.* In Badagry the mallams were not allowed to show themselves
to Lander. This might have been due to a slight suspicion of Lander
himself! After all, on coming back to Badagry he was allowed to see
them only after *he* had taken the fetich water as a test of his fidelity
bona-fide; *ibid.*, p. 280.
100 Lander and Clapperton record the tales of woe and devastation
caused by this complex Revolt-Jihad movement; Lander, *op. cit.*,
pp. 96–7; Clapperton, *op. cit.*, p. 204.
101 The fall of these towns (and others) is dealt with in unsurpassed
detail by S. Johnson, *op. cit.*, Chapters 7 to 14.
102 See Chapter 2.

2 The resurgence of Islam, 1840-1860

The first two decades of the nineteenth century saw the disarray and depletion of the ranks of Yoruba Muslims, generally and the prospects of recovery seemed bleak. The greater part of the country was in considerable confusion because of the series of wars that ravaged towns and villages. The belief lingered that the Muslims were the chief cause of these troubles, and they were suspected as collaborators of Ilọrin. But in spite of these handicaps, the position of Islam improved. The southward advance of Ilọrin into Yorubaland was halted in 1840 when Ibadan routed its forces at Oṣogbo.[1] Henceforth, Ibadan steadily forced Ilọrin back, and kept it at bay. Although Ilọrin soon directed its military efforts eastwards to Ekiti and Ijẹsa areas, yet it was to meet Ibadan there also.[2] The containment of the menace of Ilọrin meant that Islam was ceasing to be a threat to a greater part of Yorubaland in this period. Islam could settle; and a major and interesting feature of the period 1840 to 1860 was how Islam revived, and succeeded in rebuilding itself out of the debris of the previous decades.

The regeneration of Islam in this period was naturally preceded by the settlement of the mass of people cast adrift by the incessant wars and raids of the previous decade. The general resettlement involved two major processes. First, it involved the integration of the refugees into towns where they had found shelter and protection. This was the case in such places as Ifẹ, Oṣogbo, Iwo, Ogbomoṣọ and Ẹdẹ. Secondly, it involved the foundation of new towns such as Ibadan (c. 1829) and Abẹokuta (c. 1830), and the resettlement of Ọyọ (c. 1837). For almost a decade, the problems of resettlement – both internal and external – were to perplex these new towns, especially those newly founded. But as this process got under way, Islam re-established itself, and even began to play a part in the solution of these problems of general resettlement.

Lying south of Ọyọ were the areas of Ẹgbado and the Ẹgba, once districts of the old Ọyọ Empire. These semi-savannah areas offered easy progress for the fleeing Ọyọ people, just as some well-defended places in the area afforded the refugees the necessary physical protection and security. The population[3] of towns such as Ilaro, Oke-Ọdan, Ajilete was swollen by refugees from Ketu and the northern section of the Ọyọ Empire. There is considerable evidence that among these Ọyọ refugees in Ẹgbado there was a good number of Muslims who became agents for the propagation and re-establishment of their professed faith. Thus in Ilaro there was the outstanding example of the members of the Adẹyẹmi family, a scion of the Ọyọ royal family, who, as fleeing Muslims, took refuge in the town[4] and were largely responsible for the regeneration of Islam there and in its immediate environs.[5] They gathered together the few Muslims in the town, and organised them into a community. The leadership of this new community was given to one Adẹyẹmi, partly by virtue of his royal descent and partly by virtue of his comparatively superior Islamic know-ledge.[6] It is particularly instructive to observe that it is this family that has since supplied the leadership of the Muslim community.

In Shaki, a comparable situation developed. Among its diverse refugee population were some Muslims who later joined the very few Muslims who had been left in the town to organise the Muslim community. This Muslim community was built up at the time of Alafin Oluewu;[7] it comprised local Muslims such as Afa Asumo Ismaila[8] and his father, together with immigrant Muslims from other places in the neighbourhood. From Old Ọyọ came people like Mọmọ (later the Balogun Imale)[9] and his retinue, while Afa Yesufu came from Kishi;[10] Afa Mumini of Okaka and his family came from Gbanga whence they had been driven by the Dahomey wars, and a few others such as Afa Suta, a Dindi, were refugees from Dahomey area. Though these Muslims were few in number and of diverse origin, they constituted a Muslim community in Shaki. This young community held its open communal prayers in a small fenced sandy area[11] (Yoruba: *girigiri*) with the permission of the Ọba and the support of the Balogun, and was reinforced as more individual refugees arrived.

The cases of Ilaro and Shaki adequately illustrate how immigrant Yoruba Muslims helped in some Yoruba towns to organise and establish the Muslim community. This is also true of such other 'old' towns as Ogbomọṣọ, Oṣogbo and Ẹdẹ which, in this period, provided a haven for many refugees, some of whom were Muslims. In these towns they had the status of settlers, and some time elapsed before they became fairly well integrated into their new environment. Some of these refugee or 'settler' Muslims were clearly more distinguished than their hosts either by birth or in Islamic knowledge. Consequently, it was usual for them to play an active part in the organisation of the nascent Muslim community. In Ilaro, the Adeyemi family was active; in Ede, there was the 'Imale Compound'[12] and in Ogbomoso, families such as the Muse family at Oke Masifa, and Gbadamosi at Adurin formed the cream of Muslim leaders.[13]

There were also cases where the Muslim immigrants were absorbed into an established Muslim community. The case of Iseyin amply illustrates this. It will be recalled that in Iseyin, Islam had been early established, and that Shaikh al-Sālih, on coming to this town, before even reaching Ilorin, had met there a community of Muslims. In the general confusion and holocaust which engulfed the northern section of the old empire at the time of the rebellion, Iseyin had stayed firm and unscathed. By virtue of its strong natural and man-made defences,[14] it proved a welcome harbour of refuge for the people fleeing from the fear and destruction of the wars.

Among the notable Muslims who took refuge here were the Ijemba people, who in fact had long been Muslims in their former homestead[15] (Jemba-Ile);[16] they set up an Ijemba quarter at Iseyin and considerably strengthened the Muslim community in that town. New mosques such as the Mosalasi Alalikimba[17] were built in the quarters to cope with the demands of the enlarged Muslim population. The community, however, remained one. It repaired and widened the oldest mosque and used it as the central mosque.[18] A product of communal effort, this central mosque was the seat of the Chief Imam, the head of the community. Thus in such towns where Islam was fairly well established the Muslim refugees naturally joined the community and were prepared to accept the existing leadership.

What was the position of Islam in the towns created by the shifting population of refugees? In Abeokuta there was a considerable number of Muslims who came from the surrounding areas that were being deserted or devastated. Most of the fleeing Muslims were from Owu, and they formed in Abeokuta a preponderantly Muslim quarter.[19] Others, Yisa and Sunmonu

Adelokun for example, came from elsewhere and settled in other parts of Abẹokuta.[20] As the settlement of this composite town went on apace, the Muslims tried to settle down. Sunmọnu Adelokun reconstituted the Muslim community[21] together with other notable Muslims such as Sunmọnu Oyegebi, Sofo of Igbore, Buraimọ of Itoku, Aliyu Sopeyin of Iporo, Disu Oligbaje Ogun of Ilawo (Imam of Oke-Ọna) and Akeyan Balogun of Ikija. Sunmọnu Ọnasokun was chosen as the leader of the community; but this position was later taken over, with the consent of the Muslim community, by one Imoru, son of Salu Balẹ Itoku of Oke Aleji. This Imoru, sometimes referred to as Baba Badaru, was the first formally acknowledged Chief Imam of Abẹokuta. The Muslim community continued to expand and grow. In Owu quarter alone there were at least two mosques by 1848.[22] A few learned men (*mu'allimun*) such as Afa Fulani established Quranic Schools for the community.[23] This activity of the Muslims alarmed the various separate authorities in Ẹgba, who knew too well from their past experience what a cataclysmic force Islam could be. Thus the 'pagan priests' and the local authorities fell upon the Muslims. They 'troubled the Muslims sorely'; and in 1849 they tried 'on several occasions, to pull down their mosques'.[24] In spite of this persecution, however, the community stood firm and strong.

At Ibadan and Ọyọ the situation was not much dissimilar. Amid the great concourse[25] of people who founded the town of Ibadan about 1829 were a few individual Muslims. For some time, because of the prevailing suspicion and unfavourable circumstances of war,[26] many worshipped privately and secretly. They once endeavoured to build their mosque at Ọja-Ọba but this first attempt to hold an open public service came to grief. Basorun Oluyọle ordered the mosque to be razed to the ground;[27] and earnest Muslims had to content themselves with private and secret worship for some years yet. Meanwhile the Muslims succeeded in winning the favour of some prominent people in the town. One such was Opeagbe, who became a notable patron of the Muslims in Ibadan;[28] he was a valiant soldier and a wealthy immigrant from Ogbomọsọ.[29] In Ibadan, a town of immigrants and open competition, Opeagbe soon proved his mettle. He rose from the minor rank of a Sarumi under Oluyọle to become, in the late 1840s, an Osi Balogun, the third leading war chief. In about 1850 he became the Balẹ of Ibadan.[30] Under his patronage, the Ọja-Ọba mosque was rebuilt[31] and open joint worship was begun again. The

Muslim community was thus resurrected, and Abudulahi Gun-nugun[32] of Ayeye area was appointed Imam to conduct the congregational prayers and direct the community. After him, a certain Shaikh Uthman[33] became the Imam. Thus, the Muslims settled down, and their community began to develop roots.

The unique case of Ẹpẹ should also be mentioned here. Before 1851, Ẹpẹ was a small settlement of Ijẹbu farmers and fishermen. In that year, however, Ẹpẹ received its own peculiar refugees. For, when the British Government exiled Kosọkọ and his party of about 1,500[34] from Lagos, it was at Ẹpẹ that they came to settle.[35] These new settlers, or Eko Ẹpẹ, as they were better known subsequently, were mostly Muslims, and they included such gallant war chiefs as Balogun Ajeniya, Oṣodi Tapa and Posu.[36] They outnumbered the non-Muslim settlers, and consequently they virtually turned Ẹpẹ into a Muslim settlement. They built mosques, and formed a community under the leadership of Mallam Idris Salu Gana who had been their leading mallam in Lagos.[37]

Islam in Yorubaland was also reinforced by a considerable migration from across the seas. In this period, there was the return to West Africa of liberated slaves. Most of them were, indeed, Christians, about whom the sponsors of their liberation and return entertained great hopes for the successful establishment of Christianity and the radiation of European civilisation in West Africa. Attempts were thus made to facilitate their return not just to Liberia and Freetown but also from the latter place to other parts of the West African coast. This deliberate promotion of the return of the freed slaves was facilitated by the thriving oceanic trade that linked the West African coastal towns – a coastal trade that grew as these immigrant colonies expanded. Partly as a result of the promotion of this return movement and partly as a result of this flourishing coastal trade, the liberated Africans returned to Yoruba country.

Some of the Akus[38] in Sierra Leone were Muslims,[39] including those who had been Muslims even before their capture and export as slaves. Some Aku Muslims clearly remembered their particular homesteads – Oyọ, Ọtta and the like.[40] Others, probably the greater number, hardly knew their Yoruba towns, and were converted to Islam only in their foreign environment. While they were still in Sierra Leone, these Aku Muslims were anxious to join in the return movement to Yorubaland. Crowther noted that 'when it was known that we had chartered a vessel to take us to Badagry we received applications from every direction from Mohammedans and pagans . . . offering themselves to be employed as labourers and servants.'[41] The offer of free passage and the hope of employment and protection in Badagry might have encouraged the Aku Muslims to seize the opportunity to return home, but their eagerness to do so must have arisen partly out of nostalgic feelings and love for their homeland in that era when the cry was 'back to the mother country'. To some of the Aku Muslims, there was hardly any conceivable reason why they should not remember and go back to their town 'when everybody was returning to his own'.[42] But it would appear also to have arisen out of their desire to be free of the difficulties, political and otherwise, which they faced in Sierra Leone. They did not live happily enough with the others[43] in Sierra Leone; and they must have felt almost ostracised not only by the well-meaning and ardent Christian evangelists but also by the high-handed administrators. These two classes of people were less concerned about the Aku Muslims than about the nucleus that was to propagate Christianity and civilisation.[44] In the circumstances, the Aku Muslims kept closely to themselves at their two main centres: Fourah Bay and Foulah Town.[45] When the return movement to Yorubaland set in among them, they were quite understandably anxious to avail themselves of any proffered opportunity.

Among the Christian sponsors of the exodus of native Christians from Sierra Leone there was some hesitation about the idea of encouraging alongside their own scheme the return of the Aku Muslims and pagans. The missionaries 'were to make the country good first';[46] consequently, they tried to pour cold water on the Muslim schemes as much as possible. They exaggerated tales of hardship which people such as the Duke of Wellington brought back about the batch of Sierra Leonean emigrants in Badagry. But understandable as Christian hesitation was in these circumstances, it was no doubt directed particularly at the 'pagans'.[47] In any case, the Aku Muslims did not have to rely on Christian support. Quite a number of them paid their passage back home; and the prominent ones among them, such as Shitta and Savage, organised their own groups for the return. Muhammad Savage, who was the Muslim Aku headman at Fourah Bay, bought his own ships, and at least fifty of his own people sailed back home in a group.[48]

As a result of these individual and group efforts, Aku Muslims found their way back to Yorubaland during the period under study. In Badagry there were a number of these Muslims, some of them, according to Crowther's testimony,[49] possessing copies of the Arabic Bible given to them in Sierra Leone.[50] Perhaps the most notable group of the Muslim emigrants who came to Badagry was that headed by Salu Shitta.[51] This Shitta had gathered his family together with their one-year-old son and left Waterloo in 1831 for Fourah Bay in Sierra Leone.[52] Here, the older Shitta became the Imam of the Muslim community of the town – a post he held for some years. In 1844 he decided to leave Sierra Leone and join the Aku Muslims farther down the coast. At the head of a group of about fifty of his followers with their wives and children, he came down with his own family to Badagry in 1844.[53] Here the family stayed for a considerable period, mixing freely with other Muslims in the town.

Lagos, much more than Badagry, was the destination of the returning Muslim emigrants. Here grew up two distinct groups: the Sierra Leonian and the Brazilian. The first group was (and still is) commonly known as the group of Fourah Bay or Saro Muslims.[54] They settled at Olowogbowo and Isalẹ Eko area and were more numerous than the Brazilian group. Among them were some members of such well-known families as Abdallah Cole, Amodu Carew, Muhammad Savage, Umar and Williams.[55] Their number, common experience and outlook as well as the contiguity of their residence made them erect their own first big mosque at Olowogbowo in 1861.[56] Initially called the *Jami'u al-Mubariq* (the Blessed Mosque), it later became more popularly known as the Horobay Mosque.[57]

The Brazilian group,[58] better known as Aguda,[59] came to Lagos a little later than the Sierra Leonians. The first group of repatriates was reported to have arrived about 1840.[60] Their number rose steadily from 1,237 to 1,800, especially from 1847 onwards after the guarantee of safety and encouragement received from Chief Tapa Oṣodi.[61] Many as they were,[62] the number of Aguda Muslims never equalled that of the Sierra Leonian group. Muslims were to be found among notable families in this Aguda group: Pedro, Martin, da Silva, Tiamiyu Gomez, Yahya Tokunbo, Salvador and Agusto.[63] They settled mainly at Bamgbose Street in Lagos, where they erected their own mosques such as the Olosun Mosque, Alagbayun Mosque, Tairu Eko Mosque and the Salvador Mosque.[64]

Some of the Muslim repatriates after they had settled in their initial areas of disembarkation (Lagos and Badagry), soon remembered their former towns and homes farther inland and, after some earnest enquiries, succeeded in moving over to them.[65] Thus they were to be found in small numbers about the Yoruba country in Ibadan,[66] Ilẹsa and so on. One reunion of such repatriates is expressed vividly in the story of Buraimọ Aina. A native of Ọtta, he had been taken as a slave but was liberated in Sierra Leone where he redeemed himself, marrying and settling down till 1838 'when everybody began to go back to his own country'.[67] Consequently, Buraimọ Aina remembered his own people, got himself ready, and collected all his family into a ship *en route* for Lagos. When he arrived in Lagos in 1842, he bought a piece of land on which he built his house at a place now called Akanni Street. But Buraimọ remembered his people at Ọtta, and used to ask those from Ọtta who came to Lagos about his people at home. His perseverance was soon rewarded. Through the help of some Ọtta people, he came down to Ọtta itself in 1847. The vivid and dramatic language of the narration justify quoting the story in the author's own words:

> Nigbati o de awọn enia rẹ ko tun mọ mọ, nitoripe wọn ti mu ọkan kuro lara rẹ bi ẹniti o ti ku ti pẹ, ti a si ti ṣe ọfọ rẹ.

> Ṣugbọn nigbati o ri awọn enia rẹ o mọ wọn o si ṣe apejuwe ara rẹ fun wọn ki nwọn to ṣẹsẹ wa mọ; ṣugbon nigbati nwọn mọ gbogbo wọn bẹrẹ si sunkun bi oku ti o ṣẹsẹ ku.

> Ṣugbọn lẹhin eyi wọn tun bẹrẹsi yọ ayọ nla wọn si bere pe nibo li o gbe de si, o si sọ fun wọn pe ni ita Akanni ni Eko . . . [68]

His was a reunion as memorable as it was deeply touching. It was nevertheless only one of the fairly numerous cases of Yoruba Muslim repatriates who returned home from Lagos.

It is true, however, that many more of these Muslim repatriates did not rejoin their people farther inland, but simply remained in Lagos. Some could not remember their original homes; some were born abroad and knew little of the interior; some held back because of dismaying tales of hardship, theft and the like which were told about the interior; and some simply preferred to remain in Lagos where they settled and carried on with their trade and religion. But even in the case of these people who remained in Lagos, there exists some evidence that they maintained beneficial contact with the Islamic communities inland. For example, the Shitta Bey family soon moved, around 1852, from Badagry to Lagos, settling down at Martin Street.[69] Muhammad, his younger son, soon took to trade in the interior, where he served as the agent of the Pinnock B. Co. until he could stand on his own. Together with his brother, he later established at Egga a flourishing trade of his own.[70] As he became well-off, he was very munificent in the cause of Islam not merely in Lagos but throughout the Colony,[71] and as far away as Sierra Leone.[72]

A pertinent question that arises here is the historical significance for the Muslim community of these immigrant Muslims from overseas. First, their return meant some accession in numbers to the Muslim community of the respective areas. This numerical increase immediately necessitated the expansion of the places of prayer such as '*Id al-Fiṭr* grounds or, more often, the construction of new mosques in the town in order to cope with increased membership. Thus more mosques sprang up: in Lagos, for example, there were the Alagbayun Mosque at Taiwo Street, the Brazilian Salvador Mosque at Bamgbose Street and the Horobay Mosque.[73]

In spite of the existence of the two easily identifiable groups of Aguda and Saro Muslims, there is no evidence of any jealousy between them. Indeed, there was a remarkable amount of co-operation, facilitated by their different experiences and skill. Whenever there was any division among the entire Muslim community, it was, more often than not, on religious and political issues and did not necessarily follow communal lines.

More important was the value of the overseas Muslims to their religious group. This was significantly out of proportion to their number.[74] Among them there were many tailors, carpenters, masons, master bakers and other skilled men.[75] Their practical skill and talent enhanced their position in the society and benefited the Muslim community considerably. For example, the building of the large central mosque in Lagos was at one time abandoned by the local architects;[76] the work was, however, taken up and completed by Sanusi Alaka, a talented Muslim trainee of Señor Joas da Costa, the leading master-mason in Lagos.[77] On completion, the mosque was generally regarded as one of the most stately buildings in Lagos.[78]

Their contributions to the growth of the Muslim community were more than technical, however, for these overseas Muslims considerably boosted the confidence of the nascent Yoruba

Muslim community. This development was very apparent in Lagos.

Islam, it will be recalled, had percolated into Lagos long before 1840. The Muslims were, however, few and had twice suffered expulsion from Lagos. They had gained favour with another prince, Kosoko;[79] but on their return to this town in 1840, they still occupied an uncertain position. Many of them were 'foreigners' of lowly state – Gambaris;[80] and they could practise their religion only in the secrecy of their homes.[81] Their position, however, soon began to improve, with the arrival of the overseas Muslims. These did not just increase the number of Muslims; as respected men of talent and overseas experience,[82] they injected a strong dose of confidence and courage into the Muslim group. Soon enough, open worship of Islam was permitted[83] around 1841 when the first Friday congregational prayer was held publicly on a spot later known as Animasaun Lane.[84] No doubt with the patronage of Kosoko, a community was formed praying under the leadership of Salu, a Hausa mallam in Kosoko's retinue.[85] In August 1845 Kosoko assumed power in Lagos,[86] a factor which further helped the community to develop roots in the society. As the overseas Muslims built their own mosques, the religion waxed stronger still. But misfortune struck when, in 1850, Kosoko was exiled from Lagos, and many Muslims, including the Chief Imam Salu and other eminent leaders, followed him.[87] The position of Islam had become so strong, however, that this defection did not obliterate Islam from Lagos. Another capable mallam was appointed to lead the prayers and act as Imam for the community, Mallam Nafiu Gana,[88] and the community continued to worship as before. When Burton visited Lagos around 1860 and met the Muslim community, he estimated its number to be between 700 and 800 at the least.[89] Evidently, the survival of the Lagos Muslim community in the period 1840 to 1862 owed much to the influence of these Muslim immigrants.

The influence of the overseas Muslims was no doubt felt more quickly in their immediate environment, Lagos and the like. But later their influence was more widespread, and the most lasting aspect of this was their promotion of 'Western culture' among the Muslims; for the overseas group were also purveyors of such 'Western' ideas and practices as they had perforce imbibed in their sojourn abroad. Consequently they stood in the vanguard of the reformation and modernisation movement which later swept

Islam in Yorubaland. Particularly, these overseas Muslims played an important role in transforming the attitude of Muslims towards Western education.[90] Yoruba Muslims were initially averse to Western education because of its Christian monopoly and tinge,[91] but the Muslims from overseas were conspicuous among those who, in later years, were instrumental in making the Muslims adopt and support Western education. They constituted one factor which set Islam in Yorubaland along paths of 'modernity'.[92]

It can be perceived easily how, in the period under study, Islam in Yorubaland was reinforced by two streams from different directions. From the coast there was the stream of overseas Muslims: they were more literate in English or Portuguese than in Arabic, and they were traders and artisans rather than Muslim evangelists. From the hinterland, particularly from the northern Ọyọ-speaking areas, there was the larger stream of Muslim refugees, among them evangelists, professional *afas* and scholars. The two groups put their respective talents and previous experience at the service of their co-religionists among whom they moved. As these two streams flowed in, Islam in Yorubaland was rehabilitated. Muslim communities were set up in the hinterland, especially in Ọyọ, Iwo, Ogbomọṣọ, Ẹdẹ, Ibadan, Shaki and Abẹokuta as well as along the coast, notably in Badagry, Lagos and Ẹpẹ.

It will be noticed that east of this area, that is in Ekiti, Ilẹṣa, Ondo, Okitipupa and southwards in Ijẹbu area, there was as yet little or no trace of Islamic activity. This can be attributed to the relatively little contact which areas in the south-eastern parts of Yorubaland had, both in peace and in wartime, with the Muslim centres to the west and the north. In the case of the Ijẹbu, in particular, the capital, Ijẹbu-Ode, was still closed to non-Ijẹbu[93] (Muslims and non-Muslims alike), thereby shutting the door, though not completely,[94] against the penetration of new disruptive ideas and religions.[95]

Certain factors help to explain why the people in these eastern parts of Yorubaland had such little contact with the Muslim centres nearby. They were essentially self-contained agricultural communities; and they did not have much external trade with the partially Islamised western parts of Yorubaland. A few of their products, such as the Ijẹbu cloth or northern Ekiti kola, might travel far outside the area of production,[96] but the people themselves were less dispersed; and their areas had few or no migrants or settlers from the Islamised centres. They lived in the thick deciduous forests, mostly as small-scale farmers having little need for Hausa slaves, horses and Hausa stablemen.[97]

The north-eastern parts of Yorubaland – the Ekiti, Akoko, Ijẹṣa and so on – could find some justification for not accepting Islam at a time when they were sorely molested by foraging warriors from the nearby centres of Islam, Ilọrin and Bida. Ever since 1840 when they were checked in their expansion southwards, Ilọrin had been the more persistent and serious invader of the Ekiti. As the Ekiti had to resist not only the Ilọrin but also the Ibadan 'invaders' who had come in the guise of Ekiti helpers,[98] Ekiti became an important theatre of Yoruba wars.[99] Peace was to be secured not by Ekiti acceptance of Islam, but by a mixture of effective military check and diplomacy of later decades.[100] For the time being, opposition to Ilọrin in the self-contained communities of Ekiti meant the rejection of subjugation to the Hausa/Fulani authorities of Ilọrin and to the religion they professed.

The rehabilitation of Islam in the western parts of Yorubaland was one dominant feature of this first half of the nineteenth century. In view of the continuous wars of the period, and more significantly in view of the former disorganisation and unpopularity of Islam, this re-establishment was a remarkable achievement. It was a measure of this achievement that the Muslims and their community as a whole were being recognised by the society. Where they were qualified because of their personal merits or other considerations, Muslims were allowed to hold office. Two examples may be cited: in Abẹokuta, Yisa of Itoku was the Balogun, the war chief; and Sunmọnu Adelokun, the head of the Parakoyi.[101] Even in Ọyọ, which owed some of its troubles to Islam and Ilọrin, Yesufu, the Alafin's uncle, was the Parakoyi,[102] and Atiba, the Alafin, was even favourably disposed towards Islam.[103] Furthermore, the rulers often summoned the leaders of the Muslim community on matters affecting the community, or the town generally. On special occasions such as time of war, plague or famine, these leaders held prayers or rendered such help as were necessary or required by the society.[104]

In view of the successful reconstitution of Islam in this period it would, perhaps, be useful to pause here and highlight some of the factors which made this possible and, indeed, which made it take the pattern it did. Pertinent here were some local factors, especially the help rendered to some communities by the Muslim chiefs,[105] and by a few rulers like Opeagbe and Kosọkọ who, as has been pointed out above, were sympathetic to Islam.[106] There were, of course, more general and basic factors. First, there was the tolerant attitude of the Yoruba society.[107] Although this society had been disturbed earlier on by Islam, it soon settled down to its basic liberal attitude on religious matters. Persecution of Muslims became infrequent and less violent. The establishment of Islam, however, was obviously the work of Muslims; and significant in this regard was their role in the society. Evidence shows that, in this period, they began to adjust to local circumstances. They settled down peaceably enough, and when there was a war, they participated. This adjustment had a double effect: it helped to disarm the suspicious; and it gave to the Muslims the opportunity to establish their community.

Among the Muslims themselves, very remarkable were the efforts of the itinerant mallams in establishing Islam in this period. Travelling at their own expense from one town to another, these migrant Muslim savants preached and taught about Islam.[108] A few of them were from outside Nigeria, such as the 'white Arabs' and the Shaikh 'Ali b. Muhammad al-Mekkawi, a Moroccan al-hajj whom Burton met in Lagos in 1860,[109] but greater in number was the 'Hausa' group of mallams, many of whom were to be found in Badagry, Ijaye, Abẹokuta, Isẹyin and other big Yoruba towns.[110] The largest and most prominent group of these itinerant Muslim savants was that of the Yoruba-speaking mallams from Ilọrin or from the neighbouring centres of Islam, who were to be found all over the big Yoruba towns. The position of Abẹokuta illustrates this. Situated about eight days' journey from Ilọrin, three from Isẹyin, four from Badagry, and two from Lagos, Abẹokuta was well placed for the influx of the itinerant scholars. In December 1847 Gollmer met 'a Popo Mohammedan'.[111] In November 1852 Bowen met many Muslims from Ilọrin just as Burton did around 1860.[112] In 1860, Burton met and spoke with 'a handsome young *alufa*[113] or Moslem who told him that he was an Arab born at Bornu: he certainly spoke the purest Semitic'.[114]

The contribution of these itinerant teachers at this stage should not be exaggerated. Almost all the Arabs were passers-by, not staying long. Many of the local, and possibly all of the foreign, itinerant mallams themselves were traders first, whom the necessities of trade and profit in cloth, kola nuts, trona, onions and the like compelled to travel from one big market town in Yorubaland to another. Even then, some of them tarried too little in a (market) town to make any deep impact. Some of the teachers and preachers themselves also stayed only for a while, which largely accounts for the scanty facts and dim recollection about many of them.[115] But there were cases where mallams of repute remained and lived with the people, preaching and teaching about their faith until they died. There were in Ibadan[116] Afa Ahmad Qifu and Abu Bakr b. al-Qasim, to mention only two; and in Abẹokuta[117] a certain Afa Fulani. In Ẹpẹ a 'white Arab' stayed until he died around 1860.[118] In most cases, these were relatively distinguished scholars, often persuaded to remain if not permanently then, at least, for a long while. They were essentially the group of itinerant mallams whose contribution to the establishment of Islam in this period was considerable. By teaching and preaching, they nurtured the Muslim communities and served as a vital stimulant to them. As widely-travelled men or, to borrow Skinner's phrase, 'travel-wise counsellors', they also gained for Islam the respect and awe of the rulers of the society.[119] It is principally the leavening contributions of these resident itinerant *mua'llimim* which were supplemented by those of the occasional Arab visitor and the mallam who was perpetually on the move.

In the process of successful re-establishment, Islam showed certain notable features. First, Yoruba Islam was orthodox (Sunna). The Muslims observed the five fundamental pillars of the religion – the five daily prayers; the *Zakāt*; the *Ramaḍān*; the belief in Allah, His Messenger, the Angels and the Resurrection. There were few pilgrims yet in Yorubaland and the general lack of *al-hajj* in this period can be attributed to a number of factors including the insecurity and high cost of long distance travel in the period ushered in by the turbulent years of the rebellion, and, above all, the overriding problem of settlement. Remarkably enough, in the 1860s Burton, on his visit to Lagos, met and mixed a little with the Muslim community among whom he found 'several who had pilgrimaged to Meccah'. Many of these had also travelled overland to Tripoli *en route* to Mecca.[120]

Islamic knowledge at this time would appear to have been found mainly among the group of itinerant mallams and such teachers as performed the commentary of the Qur'ān or established their own piazza schools. The depth, coverage or quality of their knowledge can hardly be determined now partly because of the paucity of their own literary productions. These schools were to be found mostly in the large growing towns such as Isẹyin, Iwo and Lagos where there were mallams who drew to themselves pupils from even outside their own towns. At Iṣẹyin, as was reported in 1858, there were many Muslims who could 'read Arabic, and there were schools where it was taught'.[121] Some of the teachers in Iṣẹyin were from Bornu.[122] Burton realised around 1860 that in Lagos 'there were books amongst those Moslems, a Qur'ān of Bombay lithography and sundry risalat [treatises] of the Maliki school to which they all belong'.[123] By the reports of their pupils, the teachers appear to have been quite familiar with the whole Qur'ān, with Arabic Grammar as taught by Ibn Malik the Qur'ān commentary of Jalāl al-Dīn; the *Risālat*; and to have had considerable acquaintance with the Zabūr of Dāwūd.[124]

The dissemination of knowledge was primarily through study at the feet of these informed mallams. They had elementary schools (*ile-kewu*) where the Qur'ān, which was divided into sixty parts, was memorised in well-drawn-out stages, some of these stages being enlivened by gay festivities when any pupil reached them. The ile-kewu has been so much vilified that it has to be stressed that it was not simply a school for memory work in Arabic. It was in the school that the young or old pupils were taught about the simple tenets of their religion, some history of the Prophet and of Islam. Here also they were oriented towards an Islamic way of life. In the hands of the teachers, the school was therefore an important seminal institution for sustaining the life of the Muslim community that was becoming established.

Knowledge was provided to a much smaller class of students who, after going through the elementary 'school', desired to deepen their knowledge by studying some particular books on certain aspects of Islamic knowledge. In an effort to do this, they often had to seek out their own teachers, a search which took them out to mallams of repute in the larger centres of Islam. This search was endless, taking them from one teacher to another, and from one town to the other. It is not to be assumed that it was only to nearby Islamic centres in Yorubaland that students went even in this period. Evidence exists that quite a number went to Ketu, Ilọrin and possibly a little farther to the north to study. The importance of this class of itinerant student was to be seen in future years when they came back to their home towns, with their accumulated experience and knowledge.

But, perhaps, the most popular means of disseminating knowledge was open-air preaching.[125] This was often organised by any mallam, who might sometimes be an official (*Onitafusiru*[126]) of the Muslim community. Such open-air teaching was particularly widespread at the time of Ramadan, the month of Muslim fasting. It was through this mass medium that the Jamā'a (as well as the animist population) was enlightened further about the religion, its beliefs and tenets. An important and abiding feature of this preaching and admonition was the use of short ditties incorporating a religious issue for the easy recollection of the audience. A recollection of ditties before 1861 is extremely difficult although a few that stress the vital points of the religion have survived.

In so far as Ialamic knowledge is concerned, it is striking that, at least in the late 1850s, the Yoruba scholars were making efforts to write the Yoruba language in Arabic characters.[127] These efforts were single-handed and scattered, unlike the Christian attempt at about the same time.[128] The result of the Muslim effort was the production of writings little understood[129] by other Yoruba mallams, who invariably had their dialects to transliterate into Arabic. Their efforts, therefore, proved largely futile. This was a sad example of the effect of over-localised and unorganised independent struggle and development of Islam in Yorubaland.

As the Muslims settled down, practising and teaching their orthodox faith, they began to occupy strategic positions in society. It has been noted how some held office in the state. Many more served the civil and military leaders as advisers, teachers of their children, and as religious chamberlains.[130] The proximity of Muslims to this influential class of people was significant for the further spread and growth of Islam in later years.[131]

Also, the Muslims began to organise themselves. The leadership of the community now rested with the Imām, or Chief Imām, as he came to be called in a few places. The leadership of the Imām is important in many regards. First, this was the office which, thanks to the increasing knowledge of Islamic institutions, came to supplant the earlier leadership of the Parakoyi.[132] Henceforth, the office of the Parakoyi remained a junior one in the Yoruba Muslim community. Also, by the tradition that was being re-established in this period, the office of the Imām was not, as was wont to be the case elsewhere, a temporary and elective office possessing only the religious significance of leading the various Muslim congregational prayers.[133] In Yorubaland the Imamate was to become a permanent and institutionalised office which had both religious and political significance for the Muslim community.

Holding his post for life, the Imām was the head of the Muslim community; he conducted the traditional congregational prayers; and he directed, in concert with other titled officers mentioned below, all the affairs of the community.[134] In essence, the Imām was within the Yoruba Muslim community what the Ọba or the Balẹ was within traditional Yoruba society, although he did not possess any of the sacerdotal aspects of Yoruba kingship.

There was also for the community some skeletal organisation designed to assist the Imām in the management of the affairs of the community. At its simplest, this organisation comprised, in addition to the office of the Imām, those of Onitafusiru, Balogun and the *Ladani* (Muezzin). Like the Imamate, these offices were held for life. To qualify for the Onitafusiru, a candidate was expected to possess considerable knowledge of Islam and other relevant studies. For the other offices, there was less regard for scholarship; and they were conferred mainly for reasons of age, status, piety and devotion to the welfare of the Muslim community.[135] The Balogun was expected in addition to have the virtues and leadership qualities analogous to those of his traditional counterpart: intrepidity, strength of character and so on.

Two observations need be made here about this organisation. First, in quite a number of towns such as Ibadan, Abẹokuta and Shaki, the top offices were, by the grace of the community, still being held by non-indigenous Muslims. In Ibadan, Gunnugun and Uthman Kasumu b. Abī Bakr, who were the Imāms in this period, were from Hausaland.[136] In Abẹokuta, a non-Ẹgba muallim, Afa Fulani, was the Onitafusiru and he remained so for many years. It should also be pointed out that the presence of non-Yoruba or settler Muslims in the administrative hierarchy of the Yoruba Muslim community reflects how much they accepted the concept of the equality and universality of the single community of all believers. At the same time, it points to the paucity of indigenous knowledgeable men who could properly perform the duties of these high religious offices.

Secondly, this institutionalised hierarchy was still embryonic, far from the complex organisation that developed later.[139] Yet it contained within it sufficient life and force not only to cope with the present demands of the nascent community but also to readjust and develop as the circumstances of the Muslim community changed. But even at this stage of its development, the Yoruba Muslim community drew upon Yoruba, especially Ọyọ, communal organisation. From this source was borrowed the title of Balogun;[138] more significantly, it was the Yoruba (Qyọ) traditional pattern and rules that surrounded the appointment to and tenure of these offices. This Qyọ influence is to be expected. The Muslim refugees and settlers were mostly from Qyọ-speaking areas, and when they reinforced or established Islam in their new abode, they did so in the light of their own traditions and past experience.[139]

In its organised form, the community tried to, and did, perform corporate functions. Regardless of whatever 'quarter mosques'[140] existed, the Muslims together erected and worshipped at the central mosque (*Mọṣalasi Jimọ*). Even where the central mosque was still 'a hut' as in Lagos of 1860,[141] or a mud building 'with blackened walls and a thatched roof of mat and leaves' as in Abẹokuta of 1860,[142] its pre-eminence over all the other mosques in the towns was acknowledged by all. It derived this unique position partly by virtue of being the oldest mosque but largely by virtue of being the work of the whole community. It, therefore, served as the focal point of the Muslim community and the mosque where the Imām (Chief Imam) led the prayers.

It was also as a body that the community chose and installed its officers. It held communal prayers both at the stipulated times such as '*Īd al-Fiṭr*, '*Īd al-Kabīr*, and at Mawlīd al-Nabī. Such occaof communal activity were festivals, notable for their pomp and show. In 1850, Gollmer observed how at the time of '*Īd al-Fiṭr* in Abẹokuta the Muslims, who were 'a numerous powerful party' came out 'in great show and kept up an incessant noise with drums and muskets'.[143]

A review of the nature of Islam in this period thus shows how much it achieved by way of organising and establishing itself. In spite of its efforts and achievements, however, Islam in Yorubaland could still develop stronger roots. Sir Richard Burton observed, after he had been to Lagos and Abẹokuta between 1860 and 1861, that Islam was 'still under a cloud in these regions: the young and vigorous creed [had] still the proportions of a child'.[144] This observation was only partially correct: young *some* of the communities were but they were generally strong, active and with considerable growth potential.

Notes

1 S. Johnson, *The History of the Yorubas*, pp. 285–9. See also B. Awe, *The Rise of Ibadan as a Yoruba Power*, pp. 126–7.

2 For the Ilọrin wars in Ekiti, the resistance of Ekiti and Ibadan, together with the politico-military repercussions, see B. Awe, *op. cit.*; B. Awe, 'The Ajele System: A Study of Ibadan Imperialism in the Nineteenth Century', *JHSN*, vol. iii, 1, December 1964, pp. 221–30; S. A. Akintoye, *Revolution and Power Politics in Yorubaland, 1840–1893: Ibadan Expansion, and the Rise of Ekitiparapo*, Longmans, 1971, especially Chapters 2, 4 and 7.

3 The population in some of these towns had been diverse before, consisting of the Awori, Egun and some Ọyọ. Fur further details about the heterogeneous peoples, see K. Folayan, *Egbado and Yoruba-Aja Power Politics, 1832–1894*, Chapter 1. These refugees penetrated as far down as Badagry; see CMS CA2/082 Smith to Sec., CMS 25 March 1848; CMS CA2/031 b, Crowther's Journal for 16 and 18 February.

4 Interview in Ilaro with al-hajj Lawani Adewumi (about 80), Muhammad Mustafa Adewumi, the Chief Imam of Ilaro, and others, June–July 1963.

5 *Ibid.*

6 Interview with Adewumi, Chief Imam of Ilaro. The *Khutba*, for example, was obtained and first proclaimed by him in Ilaro.

7 Interview at Shaki with the Chief Imam and *Jamā'a* of Shaki, 4 April 1965.

8 *Ibid.* Afa Asumo was 'Ọmọ ọjọ mẹjọ'. This information was confirmed in an interview with the family, which is still Muslim.

9 *Ibid.* Mọmọ, the Balogun, was said to have been a Sarumi at Old Ọyọ. On his arrival at Shaki, the reigning Ọkẹrẹ of Shaki built a house for him and his retinue at Isalẹ Aganmu.

10 He settled at Lọsi Street, Shaki, which is the abode of the family.

11 It was very common for small nascent Muslim communities in Yorubaland to use this for their communal worship. The *girigiri* persists today with little change in some streets or by-way places in Yorubaland. It consists of a small rectangular area, cleared and filled with white sand. It can be marked off by fairly big stones or stakes arranged round the periphery. It is sometimes under the shade of a large tree. (This word is of course quite different from *grigri* in Hausa, which means talisman.)

12 Interview with the Chief Imam, Alimi Sadiku, and others at Ede, May to June 1965. This is the Imale Family or Compound (Yoruba: *Agbo ile Imale*) which generally provides the Imam for Ẹdẹ up to today.

13 Interview with Afa Maruf Abegunde, the Chief Imam, and other members of the Muslim community, Ogbomọṣọ, May 1965.

14 Iseyin was well defended by mountains, two walls (the outer one about 15 miles in circumference) and well-kept trenches. Carter, on

his visit to this town in 1893, was much impressed by this fortification; see *PP*, 1893 Report by Carter on the Interior Expedition, C.7227. This Report is hereinafter cited as *PP*, C.7227.

15 Al-hajj Suraju in Ijẹmba Quarter, Isẹyin: interview at Isẹyin, April 1965.

16 *Ibid.* The location of this town is not yet identified. But it is believed by the Ijẹmba people to be 'on the way to Shẹpẹtẹri' (Yoruba: 'lọna Shẹpẹtẹri').

17 This was the first mosque to be built in Ijẹmba. It could have provided accommodation comfortably for about 100 people to worship at the same time since it is affirmed that it had '20 safu with about 8 people in each'. Yoruba *safu* means row, i.e. each line of worshippers which is formed behind the Imam at the time of prayers.

18 This is the *masjid jami'* where the Friday *salat* is held. The Yoruba Muslims used to believe that the Friday public prayer must be conducted only in this one mosque. Compare the belief of the Shafi's; see *EI*, article on 'Masdjid'.

19 CMS CA2/031 b, Crowther's Journal for the quarter ending 25 March 1848. See also P. A. Talbot, *The Peoples of Southern Nigeria*, vol. 1 (London, 1926), p. 135. He quotes Campbell, and is quoted by S. O. Biobaku, *The Egba State and its Neighbours*, p. 205.

20 *Tukuru Papers*, vol. I.

21 *Ibid.*

22 CMS CA2/031 b, Crowther's Journal for the quarter ending 25 March 1848. Crowther bemoaned the fact that the one Christian chapel in this quarter was sandwiched between the two mosques.

23 S. O. Biobaku, *op. cit.*, p. 25.

24 CMS CA2/031, Crowther to Sec., CMS, 3 November 1849. See also *CMI*, v. 1, May 1850, p. 305.

25 It has been shown that this great concourse of people was composed not only of refugees from Ọyọ areas but also of adventurers and victims of vicissitudes from all parts of Yoruba country; see B. Awe, *op. cit.*, Chapter III *et passim* (p. 81 'almost every Yoruba town lost a son to Ibadan').

26 R. Ola Oke speaks of the early converts in Ibadan being 'ostracised, persecuted and tortured', and ridiculed; see R. Ola Oke, 'Islam in Ibadan', *Ibadan*, 1949.

27 I. B. Akinyele, *Iwe Itan Ibadan*, p. 50.

28 *Ibid.* Part of his praise-name (Yoruba: *oriki*) preserves this fact:

> 'Baba Ogunjumọbi, Baba Imoru
> O kọle kan ribiti, o ni ki gbogbo ọmọ kewu
> Ki o ma wa f'oju kan ara wọn.'

lit.

> 'Father of Ogunjumobi, father of Imoru
> He built a certain round house for all Muslims
> To come and commune among themselves'

'Imoru' is a Yoruba Muslim version of "Umar". The house referred to here may be the mosque which was erected on the plot he gave the

Muslims, or a building he put up in his own quarters for the use of Muslim mallams.

29 I. B. Akinyele, *op. cit.*, p. 49.

30 *Ibid*. See also S. Johnson, *op. cit.*, p. 307, for further information about other Yoruba immigrants who rose to prominence in Ibadan. See B. Awe, *op. cit.*, pp. 81–2, 106.

31 I. B. Akinyele, *op. cit.*, p. 50. Today the central mosque is on the site of this mosque.

32 He is sometimes referred to as Imam Igun Olọrun. See Oluko Mudasiru Aliyu, *Bi Esin Islam sede Nigeria Apa Kini*, Iwo, 1974. Both Parrinder and El-Masri refer to him as 'Gunnugun', and there is no doubt that he is one and the same person.

33 Parrinder does not mention him at all, listing Ismail Basunmu as the second Imam; but El-Masri records him. He is sometimes referred to as Sunmonu (Yoruba form of Uthman), as Aliyu does.

34 H. Childs and E. J. Gibbons, *A Report on the Administrative Reorganisation of the Epe District Native Treasury Area* 1939. This report deals thoroughly with the early history of Epe. This is probably the total number of all who came.

35 *Ibid*. It is to be noted that some of the followers came in successive waves. Posu and Ajenia, for example, came over only in 1853. In the mistaken belief that the Kosọkọ group was a party of slave raiders, this report describes them as 'desperadoes' and 'gangsters'. For a more sympathetic view, see NAI, C.14 E/Confid./2/1934: *Epe Reorganisation Report*, 1934.

36 Interview with Mallam Salia Tukuru (aged about 55) in July 1965. He was a grandson of one of Kosọkọ's followers, and he possessed much information on the settlement of Ẹpẹ.

37 See below, pp. 69–70.

38 The Yoruba liberated slaves in Sierra Leone were called 'Aku' largely because of their form of greetings (E ku). The 'Akus', however, belonged to various sub-ethnic groups of the Yoruba: Egba, Ijẹbu, Ọyọ, etc. See S. W. Koelle, *Polyglotta Africana*, and J. F. Ade Ajayi, *Christian Missions in Nigeria, 1841–1891*, p. 25.

39 C. Fyfe, *A History of Sierra Leone*, pp. 187, 215, 228, *et passim*; J. E. Peterson, *Freetown: a study in the Dynamics of Liberated African Society, 1807–1870*, pp. 293–7. Two of the most distinguished Aku Muslims in Sierra Leone were Muhammad Sanusi and Ligali Savage, who were leaders of reform. Bassir affirms, with reference to modern times, that the Akus in Sierra Leone are mostly Muslims; see O. Bassir, 'Marriage Rites among the Aku in Freetown', *Africa*, 1954. See also L. Proudfoot, 'The Fourah Bay Dispute: an Aku Faction Fight in East Freetown', *Sierra Leone Bulletin of Religion*, iv, 2, December 1962; C. W. Newbury, British Policy Towards West Africa: Select Documents, i, pp. 191–2, 198, 223 ff.

Many of the Aku became Christians, and some retained their traditional religion; see J. F. Ade Ajayi, *op. cit.*, p. 25.

40 See pp. 29–30.

41 CMS CA2/o31 b, Crowther's Journals, particularly the Journal for the quarter ending 25 March 1845.

42 Dada Agunwa, *Iwe Itan bi Ẹsin Imale ti ṣe de Ilu Ọtta*, p. 1.

43 C. Fyfe, *op. cit.*, pp. 186 *et seq.*

44 *Ibid.*

45 These two groups were reported to have been distinct, even dressing rather differently from one another; C. Fyffe, *op. cit.*, p. 394. Up till now, the Aku Muslims in Sierra Leone keep closely to themselves; for further details see L. Proudfoot, 'Mosque Building and Tribal Separation in Freetown', *Africa*.

46 CMS CA2/o31 b, Crowther's Journal for the quarter ending 25 March 1845.

47 *Ibid.*

48 C. Fyfe, *op. cit.*, p. 228.

49 CMS CA2/o31 b, Crowther's Journal for the quarter ending 25 September 1845. Some of these reportedly boasted to Crowther that if they, the Sierra Leone Muslims, could not read the Arabic Bible none could except people from the East.

50 CMS CA2/o31 b, Crowther's Journal for the quarter ending 25 June 1854. See also his Journal for the Quarter ending 25 September 1845.

51 This is the father of Shitta Bey who built the famous mosque in Lagos; see Chapter 3. See also J. B. Losi, *The History of Lagos*, article on 'Shita'.

52 *Lagos Weekly Record*, 19 May 1894.

53 *Ibid.*

54 Saro is a Yoruba word, a variant of Sierra Leone.

55 Various sources; notably interviews. See Note 39.

56 *The Comet*, 15 April 1944.

57 *Ibid.* This recalls their Sierra Leone (particularly Fourah Bay) origins and connections. Sometimes this mosque is described as 'mọsalaṣi awọn ara Saro', i.e. 'a mosque of the Sierra Leonians'.

58 There are scraps of evidence about the life of these Muslims in Brazil right till today. See notably, H. H. Johnston, *The Negro in the New World* pp. 94–5. These Muslims, he says, 'speak a dialect of Yoruba', and have taken part in some slave revolts.

For information about African, especially Yoruba, culture in the New World, see P. Verger, 'Notes sur le culte des Orisa et Vodun à Bahia', and in *Les Afro-Américaines*.

59 The Yoruba word 'Aguda' primarily refers to Brazilians; and it does mean 'Catholics' as well – the religion of many of the Brazilian repatriates.

60 NAI, CSO 1/1, Moloney to Holland-Bert, 20 July 1887.

61 *Ibid.* These numbers are probably a little exaggerated in view of the size of their settlements in Lagos.

62 Interview with Al-hajj Muhammad-Lawal B. Agusto, 27 September 1970. By 1869 many streets were named after them, for example, Pedro, Martin, Tokunbo etc.

63 *Ibid.* See also Y. A. Safi, 'The Early Mosques of Lagos' (ms.). I am grateful to him for allowing me to use it.
64 *Ibid.*
65 NAI, CSO 1/1, Moloney to Holland-Bert, 20 July 1887.
66 NAI, CSO 1/1, Glover to Sheppard, 7 September 1871. Encl. 1. At Ibadan were Atere, Abudukadiri, Rufayi and Sulemonu. In 1855 Hinderer noted that there were about sixteen Sierra Leone emigrants in Ibadan; CMS CA2/021, Hinderer's Journal, 30 June 1855.
67 D. Agunwa, *op. cit.*, pp. 1–2.
68 *Ibid.* lit.:
    When he arrived, his people did not know him again, because they have taken their minds off him as if he had died long ago, and the period of mourning was over.

    But when he saw his people, he recognised them, and described himself to them before they came to know him; but when they did, they began to weep as if a death had just occurred.

    But after this, they again began to make a great rejoicing, and ask where he settled, and he told them that it was at Akanni Street in Lagos. . . .
69 *The Lagos Weekly Record*, 19 May 1894.
70 *Ibid.*
71 J. B. Losi, *op. cit.*, p. 8. He gave generous help in the building of the Otta central Mosque.
72 Fyfe, *op. cit.*, pp. 498–9. Shitta was reported to have financed the roof of the Fourah Bay mosque when it was rebuilt in 1892.
73 Y. A. Safi, *op. cit.*
74 This parallels the influence of the Christian repatriates; see J. F. Ade Ajayi, *op. cit.*, p. 51. It should be noted, however, that while their Christian counterparts introduced Christianity, the Muslim repatriates did *not* introduce Islam into the country.
75 Interview with some descendants of the Muslim repatriates. Very helpful was L. B. Agusto, a man of over 80, who was the first Muslim lawyer in Nigeria.
76 This was reportedly owing to 'some misunderstanding between the contractors and their Muslim employers'. *The Torch Bearers of the old Brazilian Colony in Lagos*, Lagos, 1943, p. 7. (This work gives no author, but the preface was written by a certain Laotan.)
77 *Ibid.*
78 *Ibid.* See also Y. A. Safi, *op. cit.*
79 J. A. O. Payne: *Table of Principal Events* . . ., p. 21. See also *Times of Nigeria*, 10 January 1921. It is believed that Kosọkọ was influential in effecting the return of Muslims to Lagos around 1840.
80 Sir Alfred Moloney, 'Notes on Yoruba and the Colony and Protectorate of Lagos', *Journal of the RGS*. He notes that Hausa and Bornu people were 'prominent' among the Lagos Muslims. See also *Times of Nigeria* 10 January 1921. Here Dr Sapara perhaps exaggerates the case: Islam was brought to Lagos by Hausa slaves. Nowadays oral evidence insists that the early Muslims in Lagos were 'alejo'

(strangers) or 'Hausa', 'Gambari'. ('Gambari' is what the Yoruba sometimes call the Hausa.)

Strictly speaking, the tribal composition of this nascent Muslim community in Lagos is diverse, containing a few Yoruba, some Hausa and not a few Nupe. The first obvious religious leader was Idris Gana – a name, I am informed, that is common in Nupe. The occasional absence of nice distinctions within an ethnic group would explain in a sense why the word 'Hausa' is used compendiously for the non-Yoruba from the 'North'. 'Ibo' and 'Fulani' tend to be used in the same way.

81 *Ibid.*
82 A. Moloney, *op. cit.* He describes them as an 'intellectual and respectable class of citizens'.
83 J. A. O. Payne, *op. cit.*, p. 21; J. O. George, *Historical Notes on the Yoruba Country and its Tribes*, p. 55. He confirms this. He, however feels that this was due to the influence of Christianity. Plausible as this view is, it is obvious that Kosoko and the immigrant Muslims would have won by themselves this right of freedom of open worship.
84 Interview with Al-hajj A. W. Elias, the Baba Adini of Lagos. See also 'Short History of Lagos Central Mosque' in *Lagos Central Mosque: Golden Jubilee Celebrations*, Lagos, 1963.
85 Chief Aguda, *A Brief History of the Central Mosque, Lagos* (Lagos, n.d.) in NAI. See also I. A. Animasaun, 'Historical Truth about Islam in Lagos', *Times of Nigeria*, 17 January 1921.
86 R. F. Burton: *Wanderings in West Africa . . .* Vol. II, pp. 223–31; J. A. O. Payne, *op. cit.*, p. 6.
87 See Dr Sapara, in *Times of Nigeria*, 10 Jan. 1921 and I. A. Animasaun, *op. cit.*
88 I. A. Animasaun, *op. cit.* Burton met this Imam around 1860; R. F. Burton, *op. cit.*, p. 226; and he gave his name as 'Muhammad Ghana'. Chief Aguda puts this Mallam's name as 'Nofiu' but Animasaun calls him 'Sule Gana'. Dr Sapara (*op. cit.*) describes him as 'one of King Akitoye's Hausa slaves'.
89 R. F. Burton, *op. cit.*, vol. II p. 226. He feels that the estimated number of 2,000 was exaggerated. See also his *Abeokuta and the Cameroons Mountains*, vol. I, pp. 8–10.
90 See Chapter 6.
91 See Chapter 6. See also G. O. Gbadamosi, 'The Establishment of Western Education among Muslims in Nigeria', *JHSN*.
92 See Chapter 6.
93 There is a common saying among the Yoruba: 'Ijẹbu-Ode, ajeji ko wọ ọ, bi ajeji ba wọ ọ la arọ, a fi ṣẹbọ lalẹ', that is: 'Ijẹbu-Ode is a town where foreigners don't go, for if a foreigner enters it in the morning, he is sacrificed in the evening.' This exclusion of the non-Ijẹbu adversely affected the white missionaries and officials until the British conquest of Ijẹbu-Ode in 1892. For further information, see Chapter 5.
94 See Chapter 4. This is only to be expected since the Ijẹbu themselves went out to Ijẹbu to trade and wage wars and thereby involuntarily

came back to Ijẹbu with outside experience and ideas. And more significantly still, some of the Ijẹbu warriors had slaves of non-Ijẹbu origin, and the Ijẹbu traders also harboured them.

95 The case which the Ijẹbu had against the Christian missionary or his minions has been put in a forceful way by E. A. Ayandele: 'Once let in the missionary . . . it seemed to the Ijẹbu . . . all traditional social laws and institutions would break down'; E. A. Ayandele, *The Missionary Impact on Modern Nigeria, 1842–1914, A Political and Social Analysis*, p. 35.

96 Ijẹbu cloth travelled as far as Ardra; see J. Adams, *Remarks on the Country extending from Cape Palmas to the River Congo*, pp. 89–90, 96–7.

97 The use of horses in Ọyọ and in the Savannah areas of Yorubaland accounts, in some measure, for the presence of many Hausa slaves, most of whom were Muslims. J. F. Ade Ajayi has drawn attention to the fact that Hausa slaves were many in the old Ọyọ Empire because they knew best how to care for the horses; see his 'Narrative of Samuel Ajayi Crowther', in P. Curtin (ed.), *Africa Remembered*, pp. 298–316.

98 Akintoye contests the popular notion that the Ibadan forces came to assist the Ekiti against the Ilọrin aggressors. He draws attention to economic, political and even altruistic motives behind the entry of Ibadan forces into Ekiti and Ijẹsa. See S. A. Akintoye, *The Ekitiparapo and the Kiriji War*, pp. 37–41.

99 For a full discussion of these invasions, see K. V. Elphinstone, *Gazetteer of Ilorin Province*, London, 1921, pp. 16–17; S. A. Akintoye, *op. cit.*, pp. 35–75.

100 For the peace moves and settlement, see S. Johnson, *op. cit.*, Chapter 24.

101 A. K. Ajisafe (E. Moore), *History of Abeokuta*, pp. 56–7.

102 S. Johnson, *op. cit.*, pp. 275–7 and 280. Atiba, according to Johnson, once owed his life to him. This was not necessarily a consideration for his holding this office.

103 S. Johnson, *op. cit.*, p. 277. It is possible that Atiba did take a Muslim name under Ilọrin pressure.

104 Obviously, the Muslims joined their towns in fighting their wars. A Muslim in Abẹokuta once boldly led out the Abẹokuta forces against the Dahomey. He was one of the first to fall. Crowther often noted this Muslim role: see CMS CA2/03 b, Crowther's Journals for the quarters ending September 1850, June 1853, and September 1853. Compare the attitude of withdrawal by the Christians and the reaction of the town rulers to it. The chiefs and people of Abẹokuta, Crowther noted in the Journal for June 1853, 'saw no advantage at our [Christians] being among them, we would not help them to fight their battle, their children who could fight, we keep at home to learn book and worship God.'

105 What was said in 1857 of Osundina, a Muslim who was the Osi Balogun of Ibadan, was true of most of them: 'As for the chief of war, he is more for the Mohammedans for he is bound by them, and

it seems they have much influence over him'. See CMS CA2/021, James Barber's Journal for 22 May 1857.

106 See Chapter 1.
107 See Chapter 7.
108 Many missionaries such as Crowther and Bowen met a number of them and described them. See particularly Bowen to Taylor, 28 February 1852. Here Bowen describes some of his own encounters with Ilọrin Muslims at Biọlọrunpẹlu and Awaye.
109 R. F. Burton, *op. cit.*, vol. II, p. 225.
110 CMS CA2/085, Journal Extract for October–December, 1856. Townsend reports meeting at Ijaye 'some Mohammedans from the interior' in the 1850s. See also the Journals of Crowther in CMS CA2/031 b.
111 CMS CA2/043 b, Gollmer's Journal for quarter ending December 1847.
112 Bowen to Bro. Taylor, 10 November 1852. Bowen was in fact sought out by these Ilọrin Muslims, who had heard of him and were anxious to enquire about his doctrine. He preached to them. See also R. F. Burton, *op. cit.*
113 See Chapter 7, p. 207 about this word.
114 R. F. Burton, *Abẹokuta and the Cameroons Mountains*, I, p. 256. The Arab was possibly a Shuwa Arab.
115 In various interviews held with members of the Muslim community, I found that people do not remember the very early itinerant *mu'allim*. Often the effort would be given up in dismay, 'Oh, we can't remember . . . some came . . . but, you see, they never stayed long.' The difficulty of recollection may stem in part from the remoteness of time, but there was less difficulty in recalling fairly contemporary figures such as the Imam, the titled officers and the 'resident itinerant' mu'allim. Consequently, it can be conceded that the lack of recollection may have been due to temporary residence and lack of impact.
116 Ahmad al Rufā'i, *Tārīkh al-Islām fī Ibadan.*
117 *Tukuru Papers*, vol. 1.
118 R. F. Burton, *Wanderings in West Africa . . .*, vol. II, p. 222.
119 E. P. Skinner, *The Mossi of the Upper Volta . . .*, p. 135. He notes how these 'travel-wise counsellors' were also much valued among Mossi chiefs.
120 R. F. Burton, *Abẹokuta and the Cameroons Mountains*, vol. I, pp. 8–10. See Chapter 3 also, pp. 61–2.
121 CMS CA2/051, Hollinghead's Annual Letter, Isẹyin, 28 February 1858.
122 Interview with the Muslim community, Isẹyin, April 1965. For further details see Bibliography: Oral Evidence.
123 R. F. Burton, *op. cit.* vol. I, pp. 8–10.
124 For further information about these and other works popular with the Yoruba Muslims, see Chapter 4, pp. 100–3.
125 The Yoruba call this *Waaṣi* (Arabic: wa'iẓ) or *Nasia* (Arabic: Naṣiha).

126 A Yoruba word literally meaning he who does the Qur'ān commentary (Tafsîr). He was an officer in the Muslim hierarchy, the *Mufassir*. See pp. 56–7 below.

127 CMS CA2/069, Meakin's Quarterly Report ending September 1858. Meakin was so informed by a Hausa Muslim who spoke Yoruba perfectly.

128 See J. F. Ade Ajayi, 'How Yoruba was reduced to Writing', *Odu*.

129 This is what the Yoruba call *anjẹmi* (Ar: *A'jamī*). There is a Yoruba saying popular particularly among the Muslims that the Yoruba–Arabic (anjẹmi) is intelligible only to the writer (Yoruba: 'Alanjẹmi ni anjẹmi nye').

130 It was fairly common for these people to engage on a permanent basis the services of *afas* (Muslim clerics). Compare the situation among the Ashanti in the second half of the nineteenth century. Lochmann reported that 'Ashanti Kings . . . always keep one or two Mohammedan magicians at court and never undertake a war without having first secured their consent'; see H. D. Debrunner and H. Fisher: 'Early Fante Islam', *The Ghana Bulletin of Theology*. In these articles the authors edited Lochmann's Report.

131 See Chapter 3, pp. 68–71.

132 See Chapter 1, pp. 6–7.

133 *EI*, article on 'Imām'. See also Chief Aguda, *A Brief History of the Central Mosque, Lagos*.

134 See Chapter 4 for detailed discussion about this.

135 Interview with Chief Imams in various Muslim communities – at Ibadan, Abẹokuta. See Bibliography: Oral Evidence.

136 Interview with Chief Imam of Ibadan 1965. See also G. Parrinder, *Religion in an African City*, p. 201. Uthman was stated as having come from Katsina.

137 See Chapter 4.

138 This parallels the nature of the political development in the new towns of this period. See S. O. Biobaku, *The Egba and their Neighbours, 1842–1872* p. 43 *et passim*. He stresses the fact that Ọyọ titles were borrowed in Abẹokuta. See also A. K. Ajisafe (E. O. Moore), *op. cit.*, p. 28.

139 See Chapter 3 for fuller discussion about this.

140 See Chapter 3 for more about quarter mosques and their leadership.

141 R. F. Burton, *op. cit.*, vol. I, p. 8. Chief Aguda, *op. cit.*

142 R. F. Burton, *Wanderings in West Africa* . . . vol. II, p. 165. The walls were black possibly because of the use of cow-dung paint. Interview with Chief Imam, Abẹokuta, June 1963.

143 CMS CA2/043 b, Gollmer's Journal for quarter ending 25 September 1850.

144 R. F. Burton, *Abeokuta and the Cameroons Mountains*, vol. I, pp. 8–10.

3 The era of consolidation, 1861-1894

It was during the period 1861–94 that the position of Islam in both old Ọyọ-speaking towns and the towns being founded was consolidated.

Even in an era of consolidation the continuing wars and conflicts of the period could not fail to leave scars on the socio-religious history of certain parts of Yorubaland. This point is well illustrated in Ifẹ area during this period. Since the Ọyọ diaspora of the eighteenth and early nineteenth centuries, Ife had had a substantial population of Ọyọ-speaking refugees, better and later known as Modakẹkẹ.[1] Initially settled at Ka-Ọyọ, these migrants had lived fairly amicably with their Ifẹ hosts, and themselves played host to strangers from Ilọrin, Nupe and the like. Some of the latter and indeed some of the Modakẹkẹ were Muslims, and were allowed to practise their faith and worship. Among them, some names have been remembered – Afa Kannike, Saliu from Sare-Ilorin, Daniyan, Bakare, later Balogun of Imale of Okeowu in Modakẹkẹ, Gbadamọṣi of Alagbayun, and a number of others. They later worshipped together in the Ọyọ section where the Muslim community was larger and stronger.[2] The central Mosque was first at Ita Akogun.

The outbreak of the Kiriji war in 1879 in which Ibadan, supported by Ifẹ (and Modakẹkẹ), was actively engaged introduced its jarring notes[3] and the peace and harmony of socio-religious life of Islam in Ifẹ were immediately affected. Sermons and open religious campaigns were disallowed, and able-bodied men left for the war camp. The situation was not rendered any better by the latent conflicts and tensions between the Ifẹ hosts and their more numerous and powerful 'guests', a relationship made complex by the war situation of the 1880s. Ifẹ changed sides and supported Ekiti against Ibadan, while Modakẹkẹ remained loyal to Ibadan, and Modakẹkẹ became a new theatre of war facing Ifẹ and its allies, Ekiti and Ijẹsa. Between the two communities, there was no love lost. The point of narration here is the effect on the Muslim community of this breakdown of relationship between Ife and Modakẹkẹ, resulting in the second sack of Ifẹ town itself. Modakẹkẹ became a separate area at the time of Oni Adegunle Abeweila. The life of the Muslim community, which in other places developed, was here hamstrung, hindered by the socio-military developments of the era. Indeed, after the uneasy peace introduced by the Treaty of Peace of 1886, such were the exacerbated relations between Ifẹ and Modakẹkẹ that the position of Islam in Ifẹ was uncertain if not insecure. Each community pulled its own way, and in spite of the efforts of Afa Daniyan, Imam Kasumu Adeosun and others to ensure common communal worship and joint harmonious relations, it would be difficult to describe either community as being strongly or securely established, as others were. Some people, Muslims not excluded, were already leaving Modakeke for other towns such as Odeomu, Ipetumodu, Ikire, Gbongan Ago-Owu and other areas in Ifẹ country long before the compulsory exodus of 1908, thereby thinning further the insecure and conflict-torn communities. Here then, the deleterious effects of war, social conflicts and commotions on the healthy growth of Islam in some parts of strife-ridden Yorubaland can be perceived.

The situation in Ifẹ area notwithstanding, the history of Islam in many other places during this period reveals noticeable progress and consolidation. In many Yoruba towns where a Muslim community had been established, such a community remained, to all appearances, a virtually autonomous unit. The history of each unit shows that considerable development and local adaptation were going on during this period, but despite the local and ostensibly separate nature of this development, there was also sufficient general uniformity to justify the treatment of Islam in Yorubaland as a single historical movement with its own definite features.

Analysis shows that this growth of Islam was multi-sided, with each aspect of growth necessarily involving changes and sometimes strains and stresses within the Muslim community.

A significant aspect of the position of Islam in these towns was the numerical growth of the Muslim community. Once the Muslims had been allowed to establish, each Muslim community began to expand, increasing its membership quite considerably. The case of Lagos, as indicated at least by available statistics, amply proves this point. Late in September 1862, the Muslims, at a conservative estimate of Burton, numbered about 800, out of a total population of about 30,000.[4] By 1871, they were about 10,600 out of a total population of about 60,200.[5] And by 1891, the figure had risen to 14,295, representing some 44 per cent of the entire African populationof 32,508[6] of the town and harbour of Lagos.[7]

In step with this numerical growth of the adherents of Islam, there was a substantial increase in the number of mosques built and used by the community. In the preceding decades there were in Lagos only a handful of them; one of which, the Animasaun Mosque at Shitta Street, served as the central mosque until about 1864 when the Mọsalaṣi Jimọ at Victoria Street was built.[8] By 1881, however, there were, in addition to the eight open spaces which also served as places of worship, no fewer than twenty-one mosques.[9] Six of these were built 'with good materials and covered with corrugated iron sheets'.[10] By 1887 the number of mosques had risen to thirty-six.[11] The size, architectural style, etc. of these mosques are not precisely known. Neither do we have much information about their actual capacity. But we can say that their proliferation was an indication not only of the spread of the religion but also of the enthusiasm and dedication of the builders. This development of the religion continued and, as will be seen presently,[12] reached a landmark not only in Lagos but indeed in the whole of Muslim Yorubaland when in 1894 the famous Shitta-Bey Mosque at Martin Street, Lagos, was formally opened.[13]

The case of Lagos appears special, in view of the constant migration into the town of traders and other people, especially from the Yoruba hinterland.[14] However, this does not detract from the fact that there was a considerable expansion of the Lagos Muslim community, all the more so since most of the migrants tended to settle down permanently.

The situation in Lagos Colony and hinterland did not show any weakening of the Muslim position. With regard to the Colony, its Muslim population was estimated at about 10,595 in 1871;[15] but by 1881 it had risen to 12,023[16] and the number soared to 21,108.[17] The accuracy of the figures may be open to doubt in view of the small staff of enumerators, poor calculation and other difficulties. Furthermore, these raw statistics cannot show the nature and quality of the faith of these believers. But as the figures stand they can be taken as reflecting the growth of the Muslim community, especially since the numerical increase was attested by both contemporary Christian and Muslim observers.

With regard to the towns in the Lagos hinterland, it is rather difficult to obtain any figures for the period before the British occupation. But oral and circumstantial evidence strongly suggests that there was considerable expansion and consolidation of Islam in the towns where it had been introduced in the earlier part of the century. The case of Iseyin, which is fairly well documented, may serve to illustrate the growth of Islam in the Lagos hinterland. In June 1878, when it was visited by the Rev. James Johnson, Iseyin was recorded as having only twelve mosques.[18] Seven years later, the Rev. J. B. Wood recorded seventeen,[19] It is remarkable that in spite of the frequent fire outbreaks which destroyed mosques, houses and the palace in the 1880s, the number of mosques in Iseyin still stood, at least, at sixteen in 1893, as Sir Gilbert Carter noted on his visit there in that year.[20] During the regime of Chief Imam Momodu Egberongbe, the ninth Imam of Iseyin, the central mosque was pulled down and rebuilt into a larger one roofed with corrugated iron sheets.[21]

The increase in the number of mosques and, in particular, the rebuilding and expansion of the central mosque, are a fair indication of the further growth of Islam. As the Muslims increased in number, social status and presumably even in wealth, they built more mosques in the town; they rebuilt the central mosque not only to accommodate the increasing Muslim community but also to reflect its growing status.

This development was also evident in other towns such as Abeokuta, Ibadan, Iwo and Osogbo. In these cases, although there are no regular or very precise figures, the rebuilding of the central mosques and other contemporary evidence testify to this general expansion. In 1877, Ibadan alone had no fewer than twenty-four mosques, by contemporary report.[22] And it was observed in 1895 with some possible exaggeration that the Muslims in Abeokuta numbered many thousands.[23]

The consolidation of the Muslim position in this period was remarkably evident in Ibadan, where the stature of Islam seemed to have been personified in Muhammad Latosisa, the Are-Onakakanfo. Before attaining this eminent military post, he had become confirmed in Islam when his prayers for a son were realised in the birth of Sanusi.[24] A young and able warrior, Latosisa soon rose rapidly within the ranks as he scored one success after another. In 1871, he took the title of Are and became the supreme authority in Ibadan, at a time when that city was engaged in war with Ekiti, Ijẹbu and Ẹgba. It was he who raised the military fame of Ibadan to its highest pitch of glory. But the remarkable point about this intrepid military giant was his religious policy. Tolerant towards Christians,[25] he was, by all contemporary accounts, a 'Strict Mohammedan'.[26] While engaged in the Ekiti Parapọ war, he ensured that the large military camp of the Ibadan had a clearing nearby for prayers. He together with his followers said the *'Id* prayers every year at 'the praying ground which is outside the gate at the eastern end of the Ibadan camp', at the risk of coming under fire from the mocking Ekitis.[27] It was under such a leader that Islam grew rapidly in Ibadan.

Concurrent with the expansion of the Muslim community in Ibadan and other Yoruba towns, there was a noticeable tendency to form associations or societies (Yoruba: *Ẹgbẹ*) within the community. The first observable one in Ọyọ, Oṣogbo and a few other towns was the association called *Ẹgbẹ Binukonu*[28] In Ọyọ, this association was very old, probably dating back to the time of Old Ọyọ; it certainly lingered on in the new site before the advent of more Muslim associations such as *Ẹgbẹ Ilupeju, Ẹgbẹ Iyaniwura* and the like.[29] In Oṣogbo there was also an *Ẹgbẹ Binukonu*, and this appears to have existed during the reigns of Ọbas Fabọde, and Bamgbọla (1891–3).[30]

Among the womenfolk, perhaps the most enduring association that has emerged is the *Ẹgbẹ Alasalatu*. This was to be found in various places, although membership was small initially, and consisted largely of Muslim housewives. But their ardour and dedication to the cause of Islam was unmistakable; and under the direction of their leader, *Iya Suna* or *Olori Alasalatu* or *Iya Ẹgbẹ Alasalatu*, this Ẹgbẹ was a strong religious force among women, since it concerned itself mainly with religious education and activities.

These early associations were organised very simply, their main official being the *Giwa*, the president-cum-secretary of the association. It was in his house, or in the mosque, that meetings of the association were normally held. The meetings were irregular, dictated solely by the nature of the affair with which the association was concerned from time to time.

The aims and objectives of the societies were basically the same: to promote contact and co-operation among the members; to foster mutual help; and to propagate Islam. In pursuit of these aims, the societies organised series of activities. They participated

53

fully and actively in whatever social activities any of their members were involved in, such as naming ceremonies, marriages and funerals,[31] and normally turned out as a group during Muslim festivals. On these private and public occasions the members of the association dressed alike,[32] engaged drummers, and a few of them occasionally rode on horseback. By this turn-out, the association gave colour, glamour and gaiety to their social engagements. As an informant put it, 'Nwọn ma nbowo jẹ lori sunna[33] ati nkan bẹbẹ[34] ('they lavished money on naming ceremonies and the like').

These Muslim societies were not simply inward-looking, but as groups of able young men, often tried to play an active part in the life of the entire Muslim community. For instance, whenever the central mosque was being rebuilt, or a Muslim festival such as the *Mawlīd al-nabī* was planned, or there was a need for labour and money within the Muslim community, they voluntarily came forward to contribute their quota. This was a general practice throughout Muslim Yorubaland.

These early Muslim associations were not highly organised social groups. They later shared the social stage with other Muslim societies which were better organised but still had similar socio-religious aims and functions. In Oṣogbo,[35] for instance, there was formed the first *Egbẹ Alasalatu*[36] at the time of the second Chief Imam, Abdul Kadiri, in the reign of Ọba Fabọde (1870–1). This association had three main officers, *Giwa*, *Morafa* and *Sarumi*, in that order of importance and precedence. The first Giwa was Mọmọdu Esundagba of Oke Akan; the Sarumi was Yisa, who later became the Parakoyi of Oṣogbo; and the Morafa was Haruna, better known as the Afa Oke Gẹgẹ of Ibadan. Composed entirely of the Muslim social élite in Oṣogbo, the association was deeply religious. Under the successive leadership of the first six Giwa (Momodu Esundagba in Oke Akan, Yisa, Haruna, Bello of the family of the third Chief Imam, Anisere Sanusi of Olokuta family, and Sunmọnu at the time of the third Chief Imam), the association grew from strength to strength in Oṣogbo.[37]

Its activities, mostly social and religious, grew and became notable. It turned out in full force and colour during Muslim festivals, visiting the political head of the town, the Ataoja of Oṣogbo, and a few important local personalities. Under the leadership of the fourth Giwa, Sunmọnu, the association obtained the services of a muallim, Gbadamọṣi Adepọju, from Ibadan who coached the group about Islam, while endeavouring to rally more people into its fold.³⁸ So popular did the religious and social activities of this association become that when it made its annual courtesy call on Ataoja Gbeja at the turn of the century, he was so astonished at their large number, estimated at 600, that he asked: 'Ogede awọn ọmọ ilu niyi?' (Are all these Oṣogbo people?).

These societies bore different names in different towns. In Ikirun, there were Ẹgbẹ Ilesanmi, Ẹgbẹ Ajenifuja, Ẹgbẹ Anọbilo-nigba, Ẹgbẹ Alasalatu, each with its own set of officers.³⁹ In Ogbomọṣọ, Muslim associations were generally named after the Giwa, its chief officer; and there were Ẹgbẹ Giwa Oke Agbẹdẹ, Ẹgbẹ Giwa Isalẹ Ọra and Ẹgbẹ Ọba.⁴⁰ By whatever names they were known, the associations existed in every Muslim community in Yorubaland, performing virtually the same socio-religious functions already described.

Their significance for the history of Islam in Yorubaland is obvious. By their activities, they fostered corporate feeling among the Muslims; they helped to raise the tone of religious living especially at the individual level; they promoted community development projects, such as the rebuilding of the central mosque, the clearing of the ground for the festival prayers;⁴¹ above all, they made the Muslim religion fashionable and popular. In this respect, the associations demonstrated the growth, vitality, variety and, above all, the consolidation that was taking place within the expanding Muslim community. As the number of Muslims increased, they formed the associations along the lines of age, social status and wealth. These associations by their remarkable display and performance fascinated and attracted others of similar age, status or wealth into the group and Islam, thus performing the double role of reflecting as well as helping the progressive consolidation of the Muslim community.

In so far as various social groupings and associations were a common feature of Yoruba urban life,⁴² the Muslim societies were also indicative of the way Islam had taken root. The strong Yoruba tendency to form associations to promote various interests had been successfully carried into Islam, to the advantage of the latter. The religion became stronger and popular as it expressed itself in native Yoruba idiom. Above all, these societies became the precursors of more important Muslim societies that came into being later, such as the Ansar-Ud-Deen Society and the Nawair Ud-Deen Society.

Perhaps the most permanent change which the growth engendered within the Muslim community was the elaboration and consolidation of the administrative structure. The growth in numbers and knowledge necessarily rendered the simple communal organisation of the previous decades inadequate for administrative purposes. The three existing officers – Imam, Balogun and Onitafusiru – could hardly be expected to cater efficiently for the expanding circle of Muslims. Besides, two recent developments posed new administrative problems. First, in each town there were more mosques, especially quarter mosques, each under a leader called *Imām Ratibi*[43] (Quarter Imam). The rise of this group of Imams posed a problem as to their place and role in the administrative hierarchy of the town's entire Muslim community. Also, as has been pointed out, there were more local scholars who were not necessarily Imam Ratibi but who, because of their knowledge and prestige, had to be brought into the administrative system.

The emerging scholars were, wherever possible, given some of the existing posts in the community. They were offered the posts of Onitafusiru of the whole town jamā'a. The cases of Afa Aliyu and Afa Haruna of Iseyin and Ibadan respectively have been cited. Some, indeed, became the Imam of the whole jamā'a. In Shaki,[44] Afa Sadiku of Oke Oro, a notable local muallim, became the fourth Iman.

As in Iseyin,[45] new posts were, however, created in order to make room for the new talents. At the quarter level, there were Onitafusiru; and for the whole jamā'a there were *Olori Omokewu* or *Olori Alafa* (Head of the Arabic scholars) and *Ajanosi*. The community chose the Onitafusiru, while the scholars themselves selected some among themselves as their leaders. The Olori Omokewu served as their spokesmen and maintained liaison with the community.

These measures were useful in integrating the rising school of learned men into the administrative structure of the community. But the posts were few; and many of the scholars had to remain unattached to the administrative system. Indeed, they probably preferred to remain simply as private individuals, devoting themselves fully to teaching, and, in some cases, to preaching as well. To this class belonged the innumerable muallims, of whom the following were some of the most notable: Abudu Salami,[46] alias Alalukurani, of Badagry; Afa Bello Oyewole of Ikirun;[47] Abū

Bakr b. al-Qāsim, alias Afa Alaga of Ibadan.[48] Both in their official and private capacities, these scholars were consulted as need be by the community for guidance on religious matters.

As regards the Imam Ratibi, these were almost invariably leaders of their own quarters, being so appointed by the Muslims in that locality. Largely as a result of this, they were integrated into the administrative organisation established for the entire Muslim group in the town. They were consulted by the town's Muslim officials on matters affecting the entire community; and they played, as in Lagos,[49] a considerable role in the process of selecting the Imam for the whole town.

For the entire community, more offices were created, amplifying or supplementing the few existing ones. These new offices were not necessarily created at the same time, but were introduced gradually as the community expanded. They were conferred on such deserving and influential Muslims as emerged within the community. The post of *Noibi* (*Nā'ib*), the Imam's deputy, for instance, went to the next knowledgeable elderly Muslim who could deputise for the Imam. As the community expanded, the Otun and Osi titles of the Balogun (second and third lieutenants of the Balogun) were also created and were conferred on ardent and influential Muslims of advanced age. New titles such as *Baba Adini* (Patron of the Religion), *Asipa Seriki* (officer next in rank to the Balogun and leader of the Youths) and *Sarumi* (a rank below Seriki), came in largely in order to honour some influential Muslims and secure their support for the community. In other words, the organisation of the Muslim community was widened and modified in order to keep pace with the internal developments within the community itself.

At its full bloom, the Muslim administrative system consisted of the Imam, Noibi, Onitafusiru, Baba Adini, Balogun, Otun Balogun, Osi Balogun (sometimes called *Eketa*), Ekerin, Ajanosi, Seriki, Parakoyi, Sarumi, Asipa and Ladani. It was, indeed, a complex hierarchical structure that evolved, but it was common.

It is worthwhile to point out here that some Muslim communities, such as those at Abẹokuta and Ọyọ, were evolving additional titles which were peculiar to themselves. At Abẹokuta, there was once the enigmatic post of Ọba Imale[50] (King of the Muslims), existing side by side with that of the Imam. The Ọba Imale was possibly a secular office maintaining relationship with the secular authorities of the town, while the Imam was generally regarded as the spiritual leader and head of the Muslim community. In Badagry, a Seriki Musulumi[51] existed, as an honorific, colourful title, the personality of the bearer, Seriki Abass, outshining that of the Imam and other officers. In Lagos, there was the unique title of Bey, which, as will be seen below,[52] was conferred on Muhammad Shitta in 1894 and has since remained a perpetual but peculiar feature of Lagos Muslim administrative structure.[53]

These peculiar features could be explained in the light of local circumstances. For example, the title of Ọba Imale was created largely at the instance of such Abẹokuta Muslims as Sule[54] who, on their return to Abẹokuta from Bida where such a post was established, pressed for its introduction in Abẹokuta. Its adoption was much assisted by the fact that there were a number of Ọbas in Abẹokuta over whom Ọba Alake of Abẹokuta was, of course, supreme.

The general pattern of the administrative system was, however, clear to a very large extent. And it was the incumbents of the new offices, general or otherwise, together with the Imam Ratibi, the scholars and the Giwas of the various Muslim associations who assisted the Imam and the older officers in the general administration of the affairs of the Muslim community. They looked after the central mosque, made necessary arrangements about the festival prayers, welcomed important visitors, and settled disputes such as might concern Muslims. In the performance of these and other communal duties, it was not essential that all Muslim title-holders be present although they were normally contacted as deemed necessary. The Imam, together with such important town officers as were at hand, sufficed. But they were, in the eyes of the community, jointly responsible for the general welfare and development of the community as a whole.

Three points need be mentioned as regards this developing organisation. First, although there had by this time emerged no central organisational system for the entire Yoruba community, the general pattern described above existed.

In this general pattern, there was strong evidence of local adaptation and influence. As the various Yoruba Muslim communities expanded and tried to tackle their administrative problems, they had no other administrative model at hand besides their own Yoruba traditional system which they were, perforce, to adopt and modify for the purposes of their religious community. In this exercise, the Yoruba Muslim community was helped further by the fact that there were no large non-Yoruba Muslim groups at hand to provide a different example of Muslim organisation. Non-Yoruba Muslims such as the Hausa, Fulani, Kanuri Nupe and the Arabs resident in Yorubaland, were either too few or isolated to serve this purpose effectively. Besides, they had too varied a background to enable them to exercise a decisive influence on the nature of the organisation of the Yoruba Muslim community. Some local influence on the evolution of the Yoruba Muslim organisation was to be expected especially as the greatest single group of their Muslim mentors as well as the foreign-trained Yoruba Muslim pupils were from areas, such as Ilọrin and Bida, where the idea of adaptation of Muslim organisation was acceptable.

It is a particularly remarkable feature of this local adaptation that it was the Ọyọ system of communal organisation that became generalised. Ọyọ influence on the Muslim system is hardly surprising, in view of the preponderance of Ọyọ-speaking Muslim within the entire population of Yoruba Muslims.

However, there was no wholesale adoption of Ọyọ-Yoruba custom; local variations intervened, and borrowings from local tradition were given an Islamic outlook and form. A good illustration of this local adaptation is provided in Abeokuta, where the conferment of titles in the Muslim community, as well as mobility within the hierarchy, closely follows the traditional pattern of distribution of titles along township lines. Largely as a result of historical circumstances, it is only certain sections of the town, in a set order of priority, that can take particular titles. Thus the Chief Imam comes from Ake section, while the other constituent parts of the town – Oke-Ọna, Gbagura and Owu – take the next important titles in that order of seniority. Consequently, the graded vertical mobility present in the Ọyọ-Ibadan system was absent here, giving way to a sort of horizontal distribution and mobility indigenous to the area.

Worth noting here also is the fact that even the older offices of Imam, Balogun and the Onitafusiru were also undergoing some evolution. There had in the course of time been a number of successions to these offices. The nomenclature of the Imamate was changed to that of Chief Imam (*Imām al-Jami'*), as a result of the proliferation of the former title of Imam. The Chief Imam necessarily took precedence over the other Imams (Imam Ratibi), just as much as all the other community officers took precedence over the quarter ones. As there had been in the course of time a pattern of successions to these former offices, some traditions were being created. Three examples may be cited.

First, it was becoming an established practice to give the post of the Onitafusiru to the seemingly most knowledgeable Muslim scholar around. Secondly, as regards the Imamate, there seems to have been a tendency in many towns to make it hereditary in rotation among the families of the first few Imams.[55] It can be argued, perhaps, that this was accidental, the chief considerations for appointment as an Imam being Islamic knowledge, age, comportment and the ability to lead. But the essential point was that, even when judged by these criteria, successive appointments often emphasised further the strong position and claims of the families concerned. Even in places such as Iseyin and Abeokuta, the Imamate seems to have been occupied in rotation among the component quarters of the community and among the lineages of the established families.[56] Lastly, these offices were being arranged in some form of structured hierarchy, although the base line, as well as the line of promotion up the ladder, might vary from place to place. From the lower rungs of the system a titled officer could climb up to reach in some cases the topmost post of Imam. This vertical mobility was best practised in Ibadan, patterned as it was on the promotion system of the traditional civil authorities. The practice was also largely current in the Ife and Osun towns. In Osogbo, for example, the line of advance was from Onitafusiru to Noibi, and ultimately to Imam.[57] In Iwo, Ikire and Apomu there was a progression from Ekerin to Eketa, and thence to Noibi and Imam.[58]

On the strictly religious side, an aspect of the development of Islam in the period under study was the beginning of sufism[59] in Islam in Yorubaland. The *turūq* themselves were unobtrusive, and often they faded out for lack of consistent leadership by the *Mukadamu*.[60] As a result, their history has been rather elusive; but in some of the established centres of Islam, there now emerged a few Muslims who practised the *dikr* or *wird* (Yoruba: *wiridi*). In Epe, the Tijaniyya *dikr* was introduced by certain Sierra Leonian Muslims who came to Epe at the time of the Chief Imam Alaru (*c.* 1866–70).[61] In Iseyin also, through the influence of Haruna, a certain Amadu Tijani introduced the Tijaniyya *tarīqa*.[62] It was this order that was replacing the Quadriyya which had previously been followed in a few places.[63]

In connection with this spiritual consolidation of the Muslim community, we should also note the beginnings of pilgrimage in the greater part of Yorubaland. To the Yoruba Muslim, pilgrimage was proof of piety and wealth, which enhanced his social status.[64] He therefore aspired to it even though the *hajj* was arduous and, in theory, an obligation that could be performed once in a lifetime.[65] The earliest recorded reference to pilgrims in Yorubaland was in the 1860s, when it was observed that in Lagos and possibly in its environs 'there were however several of the same faith who had pilgrimaged to Meccah, and one man a servant of the Carboceer, Kosoko, had resided a dozen years at Medina and had returned to infidel Ekko. Many had also travelled over the northern line from Kano and Sokoto to Tarabulus of Tripoli'.[66] In 1877 it was also observed that there were in Lagos 'several followers of the Mahomet wearing green turbans, to which they are entitled from having performed the pilgrimage to Mecca'.[67] They were joined on 31 August 1884 by two Lagos Muslims – Isau Onipede and another man – who had just returned from the holy journey,[68] after an absence of about seven years. This indefinite number of Yoruba pilgrims – 'alajis'[69] – must have remained fairly steady, increasing only by ones and twos during the immediately subsequent years.[70]

It is not surprising that very few Yoruba went to Mecca during the nineteenth century, if one considers the circumstances of that age. The pilgrimage route was overland; the sea route was not used to any noticeable extent until later in the century. The overland route to Mecca was long, the journey taking no less than eighteen months;[71] and it was perilous, considering the general insecurity in war-torn Yorubaland. Not surprisingly, intending pilgrims would set out as a group or join a caravan. Even then, of those who left for Mecca only very few returned. The Ibadan party which set out on pilgrimage under the leadership of Shaikh Abu Bakr Quasim, for example, was a considerable one, but only very few if any returned.[72] Indeed, as the case of two Lagos pilgrims demonstrated[73] in 1884, the return of such men sparked off hilarious merriment and interminable thanksgiving. In short, the pilgrimage was to the Yoruba Muslim fascinating but perilous; and few were they who performed the Odyssey.[74]

A corollary to the issue of pilgrimage was the small but steadily growing international connections of the Muslim community. There is some scant evidence during this period that there were a few Muslim Arabs in a number of places; some were probably traders, and one or two, like Khalid Sheldrake Effendi,[75] might want to exploit a local favourable situation.[76] But a proportion was probably also around to strengthen religious links as well with their co-religionists. In September 1862 Burton met in Lagos a certain Shaikh Ali b. Muhammad al-Mekkawi, a revered man of fair complexion, who had travelled through Tripoli southwards.[77] He also observed that occasionally there were 'white Arabs', one of whom had recently died in Ẹpẹ. In 1870 the Administrator Simpson drew attention to a certain Muhammad ibn Muhammad, 'a sheriff or Mohammedan missionary', who had recently arrived in Lagos from Seid Okuba in Sham (Damascus), Syria, and he hinted that many of his friends, travellers and traders at Kano, might come down to Lagos about which they had heard such good information.[78] 'Several Mohammedans' from Egypt and Arabia interviewed Mr Kennedy in Lagos around 1870.[79] In addition to Arabs, there were a number of other Muslims from outside Nigeria. The case of 'Abdallah Quillam from Liverpool is well known and will be dealt with later. But mention can be made here of a noticeable number of Sierra Leonian Muslims such as Umar, a teacher, and al-hajj Harūn al-Rashīd, a distinguished Muslim, who later influenced the educational development of Muslims.[80]

Another important aspect of the development of Islam in this period was the growth in Muslim scholarship. This may be properly appreciated if one were not unduly influenced by reports of such missionaries as A. F. Foster and James Johnson or those of casual travellers who were rather fond of portraying Yoruba Muslims as ignorant superstitious 'followers of the false prophet'.[81] Such observations must be treated with some scepticism, if only because they come from biased people little qualified to pontificate on Islamic scholarship. Although initially, the amount of knowledge possessed by the generality of the people was limited, the level of their knowledge of the religion increased over the years. This enabled them to tackle Christian controversialists and earned them respect from informed quarters.[82] This increase of knowledge is naturally evident less among the laity than among the 'clergy', which demonstrated a definite growth of scholarship.

There was a proliferation of Muslim scholars; and one remarkable feature of this was the increasing number of Yoruba scholars. In the previous decades, scholarship had been almost exclusively monopolised by the itinerant muallim or the resident 'aliens'. Similarly, leadership of the Muslim community in some areas such as Ibadan and Abẹokuta was virtually in 'alien' hands. But it was remarkable that among these scholars there emerged a larger number of local men, who had trained 'abroad', and who, on returning home, had set up as preachers, teachers and, in not a few cases, as Imams and religious leaders. These scholars together with others were eminent as the Muslim educators who raised the level of prevailing knowledge. For example, in Isẹyin, there were Isẹyin scholars such as Afa Aliyu,[83] Mọmọdu Ẹgbẹrongbe, Afa Muammad of Imale f'alafia[84] who, after they had been educated 'abroad' for many years, especially in Ilọrin, returned to Isẹyin to become towers of learning educating many others from far and wide. In Ibadan, there was Imam Haruna of Oke Gẹgẹ, who attained a widespread reputation for learning and teaching.[85] In Ikire, Iwo, Ẹpẹ and Abẹokuta there were many others such as Afa Gbadamosi of Alagba Compound and Raji Omolaiye of Olota Compound of Ikirun; Afa Ile Amin of Iwo, Afa Abu of Ẹpẹ, many of whom were probably of less reputation, but who played their own role as teachers in the Qur'anic Schools or as preachers to their own people.

In their role as educators, the local scholars endeavoured to raise the general level and tone of religious activity. Under the influence of Mọmọdu Ẹgbẹrongbe and Afa Aliyu in Isẹyin, for instance, the use of Jalalain as tafsir[86] was started to the greater edification of the Muslim community.[87] The scholars also helped the various communities in introducing such Muslim ceremonies as *Mawlīd al-Nabi*,[88] *Lailat al-Qadr*[89] and so on. In Oke-Iho, for instance, it was the fifth Imam, Abudu Rahman Ajani, alias Arikewusola, who began the celebration of the Mawlīd there.[90] This was possible partly because of the influence which the scholars enjoyed and partly because the scholars were knowledgeable in the Qur'ān exegesis, Hadith literature, theology, Islamic law and history, in addition to Arabic grammar and poetry.

There was a tendency for each local community to appoint the local scholars as the Onitafusiru or even as the Imam.[91] Examples can be multiplied, but three will suffice. In Ibadan, Afa Haruna became the Onitafusiru just as Afa Aliyu was so appointed in Isẹyin; Mọmọdu Ẹgbẹrongbe himself later became the Chief Imam of Isẹyin, and both Afa Gbadamọlṣ and Raji Ọmọlaiye successively became the Imams of Ikire.

It must be emphasised that, in spite of the increase and the role of local scholars, scholars of non-indigenous origin were still very welcome, and enjoyed as much respect as their local counterparts.

In Apomu[92] the leadership of the Muslim community remained essentially in the hands of non-Apomu Muslims for many years. Following a certain Abullahi who was virtually the first Imam, the next three Imams were from outside Apomu, and because of the paucity or inadequacy of local men, they had to rely on non-indigenes: Imam Saidu was from Bida; this successor, Imam Oseni, was a product of Iseyin and was assisted much by a certain Afa Baba Ilọrin; and the next Imam was Imam Lawani, son of Apedeoru, an Iwo man, and he again received much help from a non-Apomu mallam, Afa Aiyegbo. The mother of Imam Lawani was from Apomu; but it was not until Imam Lawani Aiyegboyin of Oke-Jago compound that Apomu first had a full Apomu indigene at the head of Muslim affairs.

The case of Ibadan, however, illustrates in a different manner how non-indigenous scholars were welcome, useful and respected. Here, many non-Yoruba scholars came and went; they held open-air preachings and conducted classes which were attended by many people, irrespective of their ethnic affinity. Ibrahim Gambari remained the Chief Imam of Ibadan until his death in 1892.[93] The renowned Ilọrin Muslim evangelist, Muhammad Salisu, alias Afa Kokewukobere, was much welcome, admired, and respected in Ibadan, as elsewhere.[94] The Ibadan scholar, Afa Haruna of Oke Gege, often studied under, and played host to a large number of scholars who came to Ibadan,[95] not only to Afa Kokewukobere of Ilọrin but also to Afa Jibril, alias Kafahimta,[96] and al-hajj Muhammad al-Wazir of Bida. These non-Yoruba scholars were everywhere received and respected by the local Muslims as educators and preachers who were helping to raise the level and tone of religious life and knowledge.

The presence of the local and 'alien' scholars signified emphasis on scholarship and the mutual contribution to knowledge. In effect, it marked out towns such as Iseyin, Iwo, Ẹpẹ, Ibadan and Abẹokuta as important Yoruba centres of learning. In the organisational control of the Muslim community, however, the influence of the alien scholars generally seems to have given way to that of local men. The major reason for this was that these local scholars understood best the local Muslim environment in which they lived.

Evidently, then, there was considerable growth within the Muslim community – growth in numbers, spiritual life and knowledge. These aspects of the growth of Islam resulted in certain important changes and tension within the community itself. The growth in knowledge, for example, created a split between the literary men who wanted to reform and purify the practice of Islam, on the one hand, and, on the other hand, the more conservative group which desired to stick to the old established but, from the point of view of strict Islamic orthodoxy, sometimes erroneous ways. The split was evident in Ogbomọṣọ in 1876 over the issue of the *Ṣalāt* for *Īd al-Kabīr*.[97] As this festival (20 October) fell on a Friday, many of the Muslims, in accordance with established practice, demanded that it be shifted to Saturday so as to obviate the 'evil' of reciting two *khutba* in the town on the same day. But the well-informed *'ulamā'*, including the Chief Imam Muse, felt otherwise; and they were hard put to it to persuade the community that there was nothing ominous in celebrating the festival even on a Friday.

However, antagonisms between the reformist literary men and the traditionalists did not always end in victory for either side. Lagos dramatised the tension and conflict which accompanied the process of growth and consolidation. In August 1875 a distinguished Hausa Mallam, Sulaiman,[98] arrived in Lagos. As the Ramadan approached, there began in Lagos, as elsewhere in Yorubaland, the series of customary open-air lectures during which learned Muslims expounded on the Qur'ān. This exposition was often done with the aid of the *Ḥadīth*, the popular *Zabūr* of Dawūd and, in particular, Jalalain, the commentary of the two Jalals which had become widely revered throughout Yorubaland.[99] Sulaiman must have attended some of these open-air meetings; and he was evidently struck by the free and sometimes erroneous interpretations the teachers gave to the Qur'ān.

Not surprisingly, therefore, he began to preach some reform. Contrary to current belief and practice, he insisted that the Qur'ān was all-adequate, and he lifted his voice high and clear against the time-honoured use of the *Ḥadīth* and the commentaries of scholars such as Jalalain.[100] This doctrine of the all-sufficiency of the Qur'ān was new to the Lagos Muslims and, indeed, to the entire Yoruba Muslims who knew no other important *Qur'ān tafsīr* than that of Jalalain. The doctrine could not be ignored: so distinguished was the learning of the teacher and so powerful and devastating his lectures. The doctrine shook Lagos, and split the community permanently into two groups, the Qur'anic section (Alalukurani)[101] under his leadership, and the other, Jalalain, under the Chief Imam of Lagos. The 1875 division in Lagos was theological; but the doctrinal division was to a great extent the consequence of the growth of knowledge and criticism.

In spite of these internal changes and tensions, it was quite clear that Islam in Yorubaland grew fast and in various directions, reaching a climax in 1894, with the erection in Lagos of the Shitta Bey Mosque. The building and opening of this renowned mosque properly dramatised the whole process of the consolidation of Islam in Yorubaland.

Begun in 1891, the mosque had been the sole individual enterprise of the renowned Muhammad Shitta, the successful Muslim merchant-prince and philanthropist.[102] While it was still under construction, its fame had spread all over the Yorubaland, and across the seas to Sierra-Leone, England and Turkey. On completion, the mosque had a capacity for over 200 worshippers and, which was unique, provided quarters for the *Imām* and muezzin. Altogether it cost about £3,000 at that time.[103] It was a magnificent building, and its formal opening on 4 July 1894 was a grand occasion attended by high-ranking government officals and representatives of Muslim communities and societies throughout Yorubaland.[104] The Governor, Sir G. T. Carter, was present, and so was a special representative of the Sultan of Turkey in the person of 'Abdallah Quillam, the President of the Liverpool Muslim Association. The mosque was formally opened by the Turkish representative who, at the behest of the Sultan, conferred upon Shitta, the Muslim benefactor and stalwart, the honorary decoration of the order of the Medjidie of the third class with the title of Bey of the Ottoman Empire.[105] It was not only a personal distinction it was also Islam's debut and stature in Yorubaland that was being granted international recognition.

The record of progress was impressive, involving more converts, the emergence of local scholars, the elaboration of organisational structure and the erection of better and bigger mosques. Important as these aspects were, they represented no more than a reflection of the general progress of the whole Muslim community *vis à vis* the rest of the Yoruba society. However, the picture will be incomplete without a consideration of the political growth of the stature of Islam.

It has already been noted how in the previous decades, the Muslims could count on some of their co-religionists within the administrative hierarchies in towns such as Ibadan, Ọyọ, Abẹokuta and Iwo. In the period 1861–94, a most striking feature of the development of Islam was the further entrenchment of Muslims in the political set-up of many of these towns, and the corollary movement towards the establishment of an Islamic state.[106]

In Isẹyin, up to 1895, there was no Muslim Asẹyin.[107] Nevertheless, there is evidence to show how Muslim political influence at Isẹyin grew, especially in the court of the Asẹyin. Even Asẹyin Adẹyẹmi Afemiagbajoye, who was believed to have been a great friend of the Christian mission,[108] obtained the services of 'a very respectable, polite and hospitable elderly Mohammedan' as a tutor to one of his princes.[109] His successor, Adeyanju Ologunebi, though not a Muslim, was no less pro-Islam. The association between the court and Islam seems to have been fairly close. In the palace in 1881 there was a resident mallam, the King's priest, by name Noo;[110] and the Aseyin himself joined in the customary Muslim fast of 1881.[111] It became an established custom for the Muslim community to call on the Asẹyin at his palace every Friday to offer prayers for him, the Kakanfo and other public officers.[112] The Rev. Foster, the CMS pastor resident in Isẹyin, often reported that seldom did he visit the Aseyin without meeting in his court, either by accident or design, the Imam and some Muslims.[113] Undoubtedly, the influence of the Muslim community continued to grow at the court and among the chiefs[114] even though the Asẹyin had not yet formally embraced Islam. Similar developments were taking place in other towns, for example Ogbomọṣọ.[115]

More remarkable was the political advance of the Muslims at Ibadan. Here, the position of the Muslims progressively improved in the second half of the century, as Muslims climbed up the administrative ladder. In the 1830s there was no Muslim in the state's political hierarchy; but towards the middle of the century Ọṣundina became the Osi Balogun[116] (third rank senior war chief and his praise name has preserved a picture of him as the Muslim titled officer who wears his turban right to the battlefield and performs his ablutions even under a hail of arrows. About two decades later, Ọṣundina's brother Alli Laluwọye[117] and Mọmọdu Latosisa became the fourth and fifth officers respectively in the political hierarchy.[118] Alli Laluwọye rose to become the second in command by October 1871.[119] And it was this same Mọmọdu

Latosisa who, as Arẹ-Ona-Kakanfo, became the supreme authority in Ibadan in the period 1871–85.[120] Quite apart from the presence of Muslims among the titled men, the Muslims as individuals or as a group could exert considerable influence upon those that officially wielded political power.[121]

There were places, however, where Islam had virtually captured the political power in the towns. In Iwo, for instance, most of the civilian and military chiefs became Muslims[122] during the period under study. On top of this the Ọba who ascended the throne around 1860[123] was a Muslim[124] – Mọmọdu Lamuye, the son of Anide, the previous Oluwo. The circumstances surrounding his adherence to the Muslim faith demand some explanation. When he was young, Ifa divination was obtained in order to find out his future life. It is reported that Ifa declared he was destined to be a Muslim.[125] The question of people 'destined to be Muslims' will be treated more fully a little later.[126] The important point here is that this Prince Mọmọdu (who also bore the name of Lamuye, the traditional name) remained a Muslim, even if a nominal one.

His accession to the throne in 1860 provoked some misgiving, at least in the royal household. Appreciating the fact that he had necessarily been a Muslim by divine decree, the traditionalists and some members of the royal families were sincerely puzzled as to how the king-elect would, in practice, carry out the non-Muslim and royal traditional practices such as sacrifices to the gods, which were normally incumbent on traditional rulers. Yet it would be patently unfair and even dangerous to deny him his divinely-decreed religion, or urge him to forgo his right to the throne. Before he was installed as the Oluwo in 1860, a compromise solution had to be reached: he was to keep his own religion (Islam), but assist the necessary officials in the performance of the traditional rites.[127] Ọba Mọmọdu Lamuye may have wanted to reconcile the irreconcilable: but events showed that he definitely leaned more towards his religion which, divinely-prescribed, attracted him. He stood for Islam, and many chiefs in Iwo became Muslims.[128] Until his demise in March 1906, Iwo remained under his leadership, and has since been a stronghold of Islam, in which political power remained largely in the hands of Muslims.

As in Iwo, there were at Ẹdẹ[129] and Ikirun[130] Ọbas who were Muslims largely as a result of their having been declared predestined Muslims by Ifa before their accession to the throne in the second half of the nineteenth century.[131] Timi Abibu Lgunju of

Ẹdẹ and Aliyu Ọba Oyewọle of Ikirun were both strong supporters of Islam in their respective areas. Indeed, Ọba Oyewọle probably went further than any of the Yoruba Muslim Ọbas, so far that he was popularly eulogised in his *oriki* as a friend of Muslims, and a helper of Muslims.[132] He had a *Qadi* in Mallam Bako from Ilọrin.[133]

In the movement towards a Muslim state, Lagos was not left behind. It however had a special difficulty since it was the seat of government. But it was not dismayed. At a meeting of Muslim elders and scholars, it was decided to petition the government about the manifest wishes of the Lagos Muslim community. Accordingly, they forwarded a remarkable petition to the Governor of Lagos in July 1894[134] demanding that they should be made subject thenceforth to Islamic law and custom, and that they should be judged in regard to their civil rights and grievances according to the law and usages of their faith. The petition, how-ever, failed, primarily because of the Government's policy to rule according to native law and custom. The significance of the petition lay in its being an index of the extent that Muslims were willing to stretch themselves for their religious faith. The petition may have been ineffective as a subtle criticism of British policy and rule. It was, however, a clear indication of Islamic consciousness and Muslim solidarity and growth.

It was, perhaps, in Ẹpẹ that the movement was most successful. Ẹpẹ, it will be recalled, was virtually transformed into a Muslim settlement in 1851 with the migration there of Kosọkọ and his many Muslim followers.[135] But it was some time before the new settlers became fully established, for Kosọkọ still nurtured the hope of returning to Lagos, and Ẹpẹ was bombarded twice, in 1861 and 1863. In 1862, a political settlement was negotiated by Glover with Kosọkọ, whereby the latter and such of his Ẹpẹ followers as so desired could return to Lagos to settle. This was the Glover Resettlement Scheme,[136] for which an area at Isale-Eko was set aside.[137] Many of Kosọkọ's followers took advantage of this political settlement and returned to Lagos; but a substantial number, almost entirely Muslims, decided to settle permanently at Ẹpẹ. They were known as Eko Ẹpẹ in contradistinction to the Ijebu-Ẹpẹ.

Following this agreement, Ẹpẹ began to witness a period of peaceful development and growth. The Chief Imam, Idris Salu Gana, returned to Lagos with Kosọkọ,[138] leaving the leadership of the remaining Muslims with Chief Imam Awudu of Oke Balogun who can thus be regarded as the first permanent Chief Imam of Ẹpẹ.[139] From his time onwards, Islam began to thrive. Ẹpẹ gradually became Muslim, under the ardent leadership of Ajeniya, the Muslim Balogun,[140] and it was near his house that the central mosque was built.[141] On his death around 1875, some definite organisation began, by which Eko-Ẹpẹ had a Muslim Balẹ, and a political set-up entirely composed of Muslims.[142] Here, probably more than anywhere else in Yorubaland, Islam became the way of life of the majority of the people.[143] The people had Muslim rulers; their cases were tried according to Maliki law by these rulers in concert with the Chief Imam and their lives were guided by the Muslim code of conduct.

Thus a survey of the political situation in this period reveals how much Islam had gained in political stature. A town like Abẹokuta still had its Ogboni, the citadel of civil political authority, dominated by non-Muslims. Oro, with all its 'pagan' embroidery, was still an established arm of the political system in many places. Yet the political stature of Islam had risen considerably in many big towns such as Ibadan, Ikirun, Isẹyin, Iwo, Ogbomọsọ and Ẹpẹ. In Lagos, the Muslims had unsuccessfully sought, by means of a petition, to establish some Islamic law; but in places like Iwo, Ikirun and Ẹpẹ, the establishment of an Islamic state had been virtually won *de facto*.[144]

The existence of a large number of Muslim rulers and chiefs was in itself of great significance. It underscored the change in the status of Islam; it was a far cry from the time when the community was composed of people who were not titled men in traditional society: floating refugees, domestics and returning liberated slaves. It was also a far cry from the period when, suspected and repressed, Islam had a cloud hanging over it. By 1894 Islam was in the ascendant.

However, if one were to ask why the Ọbas, the Baloguns and the important chiefs became Muslims, one may find an answer in the socio-political situation of the day. Some were doubtless won over from traditional religion to Islam in the genuine belief that the latter was a better religious system. Some of the notable people became Muslims because they heeded Ifa divinations which prescribed Islam for them as their 'divine' religion, while there were, too, many conversions made abroad before the incumbents' attainment of public office. Besides, there is the fact that Islam naturally seeks to convert rulers. But allowance must be made for political discretion or acumen as well. Political rulers of a society such as in Iwo, Ọyọ, Ibadan and so on, where Islam was a rising dominating movement, must have found it judicious to associate with the new force in order to buttress their political and religious power.[145] And Muslim assumption of political offices and titles was facilitated by the fact that in a number of cases such titles were at least relatively less attended by pagan sacrifices and rituals which as Muslims they would obviously have found embarrassing. In other cases, holders of ritual-saturated offices managed to evolve some working formula to assuage their own consciences as well as appease the traditionalists.

The growth in the political stature of Islam was also in a sense a natural development from the position of Islam in the previous decades. The Muslims had been favoured by the military men and courted by the royalty for their knowledge, experience, advice and ability to make powerful charms. This position they easily exploited in order to entrench themselves, winning further support and thereby consolidating the position of Islam among these upper echelons of Yoruba society.

The possession of political power proved to be a great asset to the Muslim community. Although very few of Muslim public title-holders were scholars or clerics, nevertheless many of them such as Arẹ Latosisa of Ibadan, Mọmọdu Lamuye of Iwo were practising Muslims. Arẹ Latosisa and Osi Ọṣundina, for instance, did not neglect their prayers even in the war camps, as already indicated; and in order to enable them and their co-religionists to perform the *ṣalāt*, they made special arrangement with the enemy war-leaders.[146]

The Muslim leaders did much to promote the cause of Islam in their own areas, for elders and titled officers normally had considerable influence in Yoruba society.[147] In Iwo, the Oluwo Mọmọdu Lamuye was a tower of strength; and by virtue of his being a Muslim, many of his chiefs soon became ardent Muslims, thus further consolidating the position of the Iwo Muslim community.[148] The most remarkable case was Ẹdẹ.[149] Partly because of Ifa divination and partly because of his long sojourn at Gambari Quarter in Ilọrin,[150] he became a Muslim, taking the name Abibu. On ascending the throne of Ẹdẹ, Timi Abibu Lagunja played a significant role in consolidating the Muslim community there.[151] He invited to Ẹdẹ many knowledgeable Ilọrin Muslims, such as Afa (later *al-hajj*) L'Oke Imale, in order to help Islam. He also invited others to Ẹdẹ from elsewhere, such as Afa Rufai Ajomole, a scion of Olupo from Igbomina. He actively encouraged people, including his chiefs, to become Muslims. By an ingenious system of giving his daughters' hands in marriage to muallims, particularly those from outside Ẹdẹ, he strengthened the external Islamic bonds of Ẹdẹ. For example, he married one of his daughters to the first Chief Imam in Ẹdẹ; another to Gbamolada in Isale Osi, Ibadan; and yet another to Afa Lawani in Shaki. All this provides some insight into how in the major centres of Islam in Yorubaland, particularly in towns like Iwo, Ẹdẹ, Ẹpẹ, Iseyin and Ibadan, the Muslim rulers used their positions to consolidate the influence of Islam.

Although much attention has been devoted to a consideration of the multi-sided growth of Islam in established communities of the big towns, it must be noted that Islam also made headway in other towns. Inseparable from the growth of Islam in the big towns was the spread of the religion to the outlying districts. And, indeed, it was the growing and established communities of the big towns that nurtured the younger ones in the surrounding villages, or smaller towns.

Apomu and Ikoyi, for example, used to come to Ikire to worship till the former areas could stand on their own. From the established centres in Lagos, Badagry and Ilaro, Islam spread to the small towns and villages in the south-western district of Yorubaland. At Okokomaiko in Badagry area, Islam was established through the agency of Badagry Muslims such as Mọmọ, alias Atari Obo.[152] Further inland at Idogo, it was introduced by Muslims from the surrounding towns – Badagry (Seidu Adelakun), and Lagos (Buraimọ Komosan, later the first Imam of the area), and by other individuals, such as Audu Raufu.[153]

Also from Ẹpẹ, Islam radiated to outlying districts such as Odo-Ẹgiri, Ibọnwọn and Odo-Ragunsen,[154] largely through the efforts of Badiru Adebogun.[155] As a young man, he was a 'pagan'.[156] He went to Ẹpẹ to learn a trade and for many years he served as a tailor-apprentice to Sule Fọlami of Oke-Balogun in Ẹpẹ. However, shortly before becoming a master-tailor, he was converted to Islam, partly through the influence of his master and the social context of Ẹpẹ. On returning home, he kept to his new religion, in spite of jeers and opposition.[157] Soon, he had a nucleus of co-religionists, such as Seriki Asani, Yesufu Bade, Bakare Moibi and others, all drawn from neighbouring villages. These Muslims came to worship together at Odo Adegbajo and later at Ibọnwọn under the inspiration of Badiru. Actual leadership rested with Sunmoila Ibọnwọn who was the oldest of the early Muslims. The nascent community, which was drawn from more than one village, sustained itself, thanks to the help offered by the Muslims in neighbouring Ẹpẹ. Sule Fọlami and the renowned Afa Abu of Ẹpẹ were especially remembered as having persuaded many to join the community, which continued to grow until each of the Muslim villages was able to fend for itself, endowed with a mosque, an Imam, etc.

The case of Badagry and Ẹpẹ illustrates the general trend of the expansion of Islam to outlying areas.[158] This was also facilitated by the city–village relationship between the towns and the outlying areas. From the latter, people went to the towns to trade, acquire skills and perform various social functions and if in such towns Islam was particularly well established, the 'immigrants' might well be converted in the course of their continual contacts with the Muslims in the towns. Conversely, some townspeople had farms in the districts, and attended periodical markets there; they were, by definition, cultural agents of Islam particularly to the countryside.

With Islam established and becoming fashionable in such areas, it was but a short step, and indeed, largely a matter of time, before it was accepted, with little or no difficulty, in the outlying districts. The role of the Yoruba towns as pace-setters should not be underestimated in any study of the expansion of Islam in Yorubaland.

Contemporaries were greatly impressed by the growth of Islam during the period 1861–95. As early as 1878, James Johnson, who exhibited much interest in Islam, commended Muslim energy and spirit of self-help, adding that Muslims 'have covered the country with mosques [and] their number is very large and steadily increasing'.[159] The editor of *The Lagos Times* in 1881 gave vivid expression to the position of Islam in Yorubaland in the following memorable words; 'Yoruba Mohammedanism walks, trots and gallops about with the vigour, nobleness and energy of independent manhood.'[160] In a similar vein, another newspaper observed very aptly: 'silently but eloquently, Mohammedanism is declaring itself a power among us'.[161]

Notes

1 Much dependence has been put here on S. Johnson, *The History of the Yorubas*, pp. 230–3, 475–8, 505–7, 514–27 *et passim*.

2 Information on Muslim history is derived largely from the oral evidence collected from various members and leaders of Ifẹ/Modakẹkẹ Muslim community in 1965. Among those interviewed were Chief Oyewusi, Balẹ of Modakẹkẹ, Chief Salami Oyedoyin, Balẹ of Odeomu, and Chief Imam of Ife, al-hajj Hassan.

3 Much dependence has been put here on S. Johnson, *loc. cit.*

4 R. F. Burton, *Wanderings in West Africa* . . ., vol. II, p. 222. Some credibility can be given his reckoning largely because he was a close observer. He was in Lagos some time between 21 and 24 September 1862 and moved closely and amicably enough within the Muslim community. He was doubtful of the estimated population of Muslims being 2,000, and he settled for the very conservative figure of 800 which has been used here. See also *Colonial Report, Annual*, 1887, p. 27, where he was quoted by the government.

5 *Colonial Report, Annual*, 1887. The Colonial Report definitely put the Muslim population figure at 10,595 and that of the entire population at 60,221. See also *The Lagos Times*, September 1881.

6 The figures used here refer to the Town and Habour of Lagos; and are taken from J. A. O. Payne, *Table of Principal Events* . . ., p. 30.

7 J. A. O. Payne, *op. cit.* Christians numbered 8,996, forming about 28 per cent of the population. The 1891 census covered four areas: the Town and Harbour of Lagos; Central District; Eastern District and Western District.

8 Chief Aguda, *A Brief History of the Central Mosque Victoria*. Mss. in the NAI Mosalassi Jimo: Central Mosque.

9 *The Lagos Times*, 14 September 1881. But J. A. O. Payne, *op. cit.*, p. 70, put the number of mosques in Lagos at 27. Payne's figure looks rather exaggerated to me; the more modest estimate of *The Lagos Times*, is corroborated by subsequent developments described below.

10 *Ibid.*

11 CMS G3A2/05, Report on the Yoruba Mission by W. Allen. See also *Colonial Report, Annual*, 1887, p. 30. The latter's evidence was based on the report by Ibrahim, the Chief Imam.

12 See pp. 66–7.

13 *The Lagos Weekly Record*, 7 July 1894.

14 *Colonial Report, Annual*, 1891. Lagos as a flourishing port attracted many traders, and people seeking fresh hopes in the city. See also CMS CA2/056, James Johnson's Annual Letter, 1874. He noted that some of the Muslims in Lagos who celebrated the Muslim festivals, especially the ʿĪd al-Fiṭr, were from the Lagos hinterland.

15 *Colonial Report, Annual*, 1887.

16 *Ibid.*

17 *The Lagos Weekly Record*, 1896. See also J. A. O. Payne, *op. cit.*, p. 30.

18 CMS CA2/056, James Johnson to Sec., CMS, 20 June 1878.

19 CMS G3A2/04, Wood to Sec., CMS, Annual Report 1885.

20 *PP*, C.7227, p. 12.
21 Interview at Iṣẹyin with the Muslim community. See Bibliography: Oral Evidence.
22 CMS CA2/056, James Johnson to Sec., CMS, August 1877.
23 J. O. George, *Historical Notes on the Yoruba Country and Its Tribes*, p. 55.
24 S. Johnson, *op. cit.*, pp. 502–3. He has so far given the fullest biography of this remarkable man.
25 Daniel Olubi, journal extract for the half year ending December 1879. He was impressed by 'the kindness of the Mohammedan head chief to us and our religion'.
26 CMS G3 A2/03 Wood's Report of his mission to interior for peace 30 September encl. in Wood to Lay, 16 December 1884.
27 *Ibid.*
28 Chief Imam of Ọyọ, oral evidence taken in March 1965. This Society literally means the Society of Close Friends. See Bibliography: Oral Evidence.
29 Lit: Egbe Ilupeju: Society of All-in-the-Town.
   Egbe Iyaniwura: Society of Mother-is-Gold.
30 Interview with the Chief Imam of Oṣogbo, and others at Oṣogbo, mid-May 1965. See Bibliography: Oral Evidence.
31 See notes 28 and 29.
32 This was and still is a favourite habit of Yoruba association and a marked feature of Yoruba social life (Yoruba: wọ anko; aṣọ ẹbi etc) *anko* is a Yorubanised version of 'and company'.
33 'Sunna' is the Yoruba word for Muslim naming ceremony. On that occasion the child is given an orthodox (Sunna) Muslim name. The word is pronounced differently from 'Sunna' (Yoruba: sunna) meaning orthodox.
34 Interview with Nā'ib of Oṣogbo, mid May 1965.
35 Information on this society is based partly on the evidence of the Nā'ib of Oṣogbo Muslim community, who was a member of this association. His evidence was corroborated by other elderly men. See Bibliography: Oral Evidence.
36 Lit: Society of those who perform the Muslim prayer – *Ṣālat*. This is now generally a society of Muslim women in Oṣogbo.
37 Interview with Nā'ib of Oṣogbo and a few surviving members of the association, mid May 1965.
38 *Ibid.* 'A wa nfiṣe pe ki a le pọ nibi adini . . . Ẹgbẹ na gbajumọ dada.' (lit.: we were trying to become many in the religion . . . the society was very famous).
39 Ikirun Muslim community: *History of Islam in Ikirun* (unpublished MS.). The Muslims, interested in their own history, set down much of it here. My interviews at Ikirun in May 1965 show its reliability.
   Ẹgbẹ Ilesanmi: Society of the-home-is-good-for-me;
   Ẹgbẹ Ajenifuja: Society of wealth-is-power;
   Ẹgbẹ Anọbilonigba: Society of the-Age-of-the-Prophet.
40 Interview held with Ogbomọṣọ Muslim community in May 1965. See Bibliography: Oral Evidence.

41 The Yoruba Muslims call this *Yidi*, or *Yindi*, a word obviously derived from *Id* (festival).

42 For a discussion of these associations in Yoruba society, see Ọkediji and Ọkediji (eds), *N. A. Fadipe: The Sociology of the Yoruba*, Ibadan, 1970, ch. 7; and Eva Krapf-Askari, *Yoruba Towns and Cities*, Oxford, 1969, pp. 82–130. Fadipe states that '*Ẹgbẹ* was a convivial association which ministered to the traditional desire of Yoruba for gregariousness, good fellowship and mutual assistance'; *op. cit.*, p. 258.

43 Sometimes he was called *Lemomu Ratibi* (Arabic: Imām Rātib). This means, to the Yoruba, an Imam lower in rank to the Chief Imam.

44 Interview with Afa Lawani of Idi Agbẹdẹ, the Chief Imam and the Muslim community, Shaki, 4 April 1965. See Bibliography: Oral Evidence.

45 Interview with the leaders of Muslim community, Iseyin, April 1965. See Bibliography: Oral Evidence.

46 He was a notable Badagry Muslim teacher. Among his students in Badagry were those who later became the Chief Imams of Badagry, namely, Sanni and al-hajj Tijani. See Appendix I.

47 *History of Islam in Ikirun* (unpublished MS.). Interviews held at Ikirun in May 1965 also confirmed this.

48 Interview with the Chief Imam and others, Ibadan. Abu Bakr was called 'Alaga' (Chairman) because of his pre-eminence over other Ibadan scholars of his age.

49 To get elected as the Chief Imam of Lagos, a candidate *inter alia* has to obtain a majority vote among the *Imam Ratibi* of Lagos; see Bello Odebode and others v. Idris Ashaka 17 NLR 84. In this court case over the Imamate of Ebute-Mẹtta, this point about majority support of the congregation and the Imam Ratibi was clearly put.

50 *Tukuru Papers*, vol. I. This was confirmed at the interview held with the Chief Imam and others at Abẹokuta. Nowhere else throughout Yorubaland was there an Ọba Imale. In fact, the Abẹokuta title soon lapsed, for it was difficult to have it along with that of the Imam.

51 This title has remained since in Badagry. It is taken as hereditary in the family of Abass.

52 See p. 66.

53 This title is now hereditary in the family of Muhammad Shitta.

54 *Tukuru Papers*, vol. I. He was the only Ọba Imale of Abẹokuta.

55 Compare the situation in Hausaland where, according to Dry, 'the right to provide an Imam is in most villages and wards vested in a particular family'. See D. P. L. Dry, 'The Place of Islam in Hausa Society'.

56 Lineage structure is, of course, important in Yoruba society, especially as regards seniority and appointment to posts such as Ọba, Balẹ and so on. See P. C. Lloyd, 'The Traditional Political System of the Yoruba', *South Western Journal of Anthropology*. See also his 'The Yoruba Lineage', *Africa*, and his *Yoruba Land Law* (Ibadan, 1962), p. 41 *et passim*. Welldon agrees also that among the Yoruba the lineage is 'the unit within which chieftaincy titles are held'. R. M. C.

Welldon, *The Human Geography of a Yoruba Township in South Western Nigeria*, pp. 70–2.

57 Interview with the Afa Hafsir of Idi-Ako, the Chief Imam of Oṣogbo, and officers of the Muslim community, Oṣogbo, mid-May, 1965. Afa Hafsir (over 50) is a descendant of the first Imam and had been a Nọibi before becoming Imam. See Bibliography: Oral Evidence.

58 Interview with al-hajj Akinlade, the Chief Imam, and officers of the Muslim community, Iwo, Ikire and Apomu, June 1965 and 1968.

59 About Sufism in Islam, see A. J. Arberry, *An Introduction to History of Sufism*; R. A. Nicholson, *Studies in Islamic Mysticism*, and his *The Mystics of Islam*.

60 The Yoruba Muslims refer to the Sufi leader as *Mukadamu* (Arabic: *muqaddam*).

61 *Tunkuru Papers*, al-hajj Salia Tunkuru, the Chief Imam of Ẹpẹ. See also the File of Population Census at Ẹpẹ Divisional Office, 1965. About the spread and influence of this *tariqa* in Western Sudan, see Abun Nasr, *The Tijaniyya*, pp. 101–56; and J. S. Trimingham, *Islam in West Africa*, pp. 94–101.

62 Interview with al-hajj Kasim, the Tijaniyya Mukadamu in Iseyin, April 1965.

63 Interviews collected at Iseyin, Ọyọ, Oṣogbo and other places. See Bibliography: Oral Evidence. Information is scanty about the time and circumstances of this replacement.

64 This explains why the title 'al-hajj' is generally prefixed to the names of those who had returned from the *hajj*. They are generally accorded greater honour and respect than other Muslims. This, of course, is fairly general in the Sudan; see J. S. Trimingham, *op. cit.*, p. 88.

65 cf. Qur'an P, 197. See also *EI*, article on 'The Islamic *Hadjdj*'.

66 J. Whitford, *Trading Life in Western and Central Africa*, p. 89. He added that they were 'crossing and re-crossing the continent of Africa, from Lagos to Egypt, over the Nile and across the Red Sea to Jida the port of Mecca'. This casts doubt on Losi's statement on p. 67 of *The History of Lagos*, that the first pilgrims from Mecca returned in 1884; quoted by H. Fisher, *Ahmadiyya*, p. 92.

67 Whitford, *Trading Life*, p. 89. Green was a favourite colour of the Holy Prophet and Islam. The 'green turbans' might have been what the Yoruba Muslims call 'malcawiya' – a special cap bought in Mecca sometimes with green cloth neatly wrapped round it.

68 J. B. Losi, *The History of Lagos*, pp. 53–4. The other pilgrim unnamed was simply described as 'an elderly man residing at Olowogbowo'. The pilgrims were said to have been 'the first to go from Lagos to Mecca and to return safely'.

69 Yoruba variant of al-hajj. See Chapter 7.

70 C. R. Niven deals briefly with this rising swell of Nigerian pilgrimage in his 'Nigerian Pilgrimage to Mecca', *Corona*, 2, 11, 1950.

71 In practice, and in popular belief, this lasts for upwards of six years. The route, as described by the Yoruba Muslims at a later date, was from 'Kano – Kukawa – Forolomi – Wadai – Morosali – Fashir – Nahot – Kubaiya – Arotuni – Sawaki – Jedda – Mecca'. See NAI

C.20, 26, Resident of Oyo to S.S.P., Lagos. 5 April 1923 (File No. 06790).

72 Al-Jalil al-hajj Ahmad al-Rufāʻi, *Tārīkh al-Islam fī Ibadan.*

73 J. A. O. Payne, *op. cit.,* p. 15.

74 See G. J. Lethem and J. Tomlinson, *The History of Islamic Propaganda in Nigeria,* London, 1927, on stranded Nigerian pilgrims.

75 He claims to have been unanimously appointed by Lagos Muslims as their representative. See CO, MI 20498, enc. in Gov. 20078.

76 There is considerable respect for the descendants of the Holy Prophet; and some unscrupulous people come down to this area, posing as such and collect money.

77 R. F. Burton, *op. cit.* vol. II, p. 225–6.

78 CO 11451. Administrator Simpson to Kennedy, 13 September 1870, enc. in Kennedy to Earl of Kimberley, 107 of 4 October 1870.

79 CO 11451, Kennedy to Earl of Kimberley, 107 of 4 October 1870. They asked him about facilities, time, cost etc. of getting from Lagos to Alexandria via England.

80 *Lagos Weekly Record,* 28 April 1894. Described as a young man 'hardly over 30', he had spent about 3 years in the University of Fex in Morocco, and was later a tutor of Arabic in Fourah Bay College, Sierra Leone. Widely travelled, he had made extensive journeys in the interior of Africa, performed the pilgrimage to Mecca, and had been to England a year before arriving in Lagos on 20 April 1894.

81 See Chapter 5.

82 Sir Alfred Moloney, 'Notes on Yoruba and the Colony and Protectorate of Lagos', *Journal* of the R.G.S. See also Chapters 5 and 6.

83 Interview with Al-haaj Suraju, Ijẹmba, Isẹyin, April 1965.

84 Interview with the Muslim community, Isẹyin, April 1965. See Bibliography: Oral Evidence. He was believed to have been a man of God (Yoruba: *Wolii Olorun*; Arabic: *waliyy Allah*).

85 Interview, Chief Imam, Ibadan. See also Ahmad al-Rufāʻi, *op. cit.*

86 The use of this Qur'ān commentary later gave rise to a theological dispute in Lagos in 1875. See pp. 65–6.

87 Interview with the Muslim community, Isẹyin, April 1965.

88 This is the birthday of the Prophet Muhammad – Rabī I. For further details see *EI*, article on 'Mawlid'.

89 The Night of Power. This is the 'blessed' night on which the Qur'ān was revealed; see Qur'ān, chapter 97, 94 v. 2. It is taken to be one of the last ten nights of the Ramadan. See *EI*, article on 'Ramadan'.

90 Interview with Chief Imam and Baba Onisu of Oke-Iho and others, Oke-Iho, April–May 1965. See Bibliography: Oral Evidence.

91 Compare the treatment given to other scholars (see pp. 56–60).

92 Interview with the leaders of Apomu Muslim community including Chief Imam, al-hajj Garuba Oyedokun Ajawesola, al-hajj Yesufu Alapomu (Aro Compound), al-hajj Yesufu Naibi (Akoda Compound).

93 Ahmad al-Rufāʻi, *op. cit.*

94 *Ibid.* Interview with the Chief Imam of Ibadan, Ibadan. For more information about this veteran Ilọrin evangelist see Chapters 4 and 7.

95 *Ibid.*

96 The nickname comes from his constantly asking his audience whether they understood his preaching: *Ka fahimta (mā aqul)*?

97 Interview with Afa Maruf Abegunde, the Chief Imam of Ogbomọṣọ, May 1965. See also B. A. Agiri, *Development of Local Government in Ogbomoso*, pp. 89–91.

98 Some records describe him as having come from Kano or Nupe; see Chief Aguda, *A Brief History of the Central Mosque, Victoria* (unpublished ms) in NAI. Others simply but vaguely describe him as having come from 'the interior of the country'; see CMS CA2/o56 James Johnson to Sec., CMS, 6 March 1876. The Yoruba often tend to regard virtually all non-Yoruba from the 'North' as Hausa or Gambari.

99 See Chapter 4 for details about these works.

100 Chief Aguda, *op. cit.* See also al-hajj Muhamad Raji Bakrin Ottun, *Islam in Nigeria* (unpublished ms.) in his private possession.

101 Sometimes this group is called 'Shakiti', a term which, as al-hajj Muhammad Raji Bakrin Ottun explains, is derived most probably from the dryness of their Qur'anic interpretation; see his *Islam in Nigeria*. Another name is *Ahl al-Qur'an*. For further discussion see Fisher, *Ahmadiyya*, pp. 93–4.

102 J. B. Losi, *op. cit.*, article on 'Shitta'. He had helped in the erection of mosques outside Lagos, for example, at Otta. See Dada Agunwa, *Iwe Itan bi Ẹsin Imale ti ṣe de Ilu Ọtta*. See Chapter 4.

103 *The Lagos Weekly Record*, 19 May 1894. This was the most expensive mosque in Yorubaland at the time. Later accounts tend to exaggerate the cost to £5,000; see *The Times of Nigeria*, 10 January 1921.

104 *The Lagos Weekly Record*, 7 July 1894. It provides details of the formal opening.

105 In Turkey, this was the highest distinction that could be bestowed on a civilian. In Lagos, the title has since been hereditary in the family of Shitta Bey. See *Macaulay Papers*, II, 2, in UIL.

The Sultan of Turkey was 'Abd al-Hamid II (1876–1909). A very firm ruler, 'Abd al-Hamid tried to maintain his authority by relying on Islamic sentiments. He promoted Pan-Islamic ideals abroad, and under him Constantinople became the political capital of Islam, See *EI*, article on 'Turks'; G. L. Lewis, *Turkey*, pp. 37–42; B. Lewis, *The Emergence of Modern Turkey*, pp. 174–5.

106 This was natural for Islam; see S. H. Nasr, *Ideals and Realities of Islam*, pp. 97–118; A. A. Maudūdī, *Islamic Law and Constitution*, pp. 2–10. About Islamic law generally see such works as J. Schacht, *An Introduction to Islamic Law*; N. J. Coulson, *A History of Islamic Law*, pp. 9–61; L. Millot, *Introduction à l'étude du droit Musulman*, pp. 32–96. A. A. Fyzee, *Outlines of Muhammadan Law*, pp. 21–5.

107 Wale Adeleke, *Iwe Itan Ilu Iseyin*, p. 7.

108 *CMI*, 1892, p. 682. Wale Adeleke, *op. cit.*, p. 7. This Asẹyin indeed gave one prince for Christian instruction, but the prince soon left it.

109 CMS CA2/o56, James Johnson, Journal for 20 June 1878.

110 CMS G3 A2/o2, A. F. Foster, Journal for the half year ending June 1881. Foster later wrote that this King's priest 'said plainly that the Mohammedans are liars'! Whatever his views, this 'priest' continued

in his post, symbolising the close relationship of Islam and political authorities. 'Noo' might have been a mis-spelling for 'Nuru(din)'.

111 CMS, G3 A2/02, A. F. Foster, Journal for quarter ending Dec. 1881.
112 CMS G3 A2/01, A. F. Foster, Journal Extract for the half year ending December 1880. See also CMS GA2/040, Foster to Sec., CMS, 14 May 1874.
113 CMS G3, A2/03, A. F. Foster, Journal Extract for year ending 1883.
114 Bishop Oluwole found in 1894 that the 'present king and many of his chiefs are more favourable towards Mohammedanism'; see *CMI*, 1894, p. 682. Bishop Oluwole spent a week in Iṣẹyin, during his first confirmation tour in 1894.
115 *CMI*, 1894, p. 681.
116 His praise-name enshrines his devotion to Islam; see I. B. Akinyele, *Iwe Itan Ibadan*, pp. 282–3. He was the Osi Balogun to Balogun Ibikunle.

Imale 'badan, on la ba ki,
Imale 'Badan, on la ba yin;
A ko r'eni a o se 'Madai fun mo,
A s'aluwala nibi ofa nrojo
Osi 'Badan ti we lawani re k'ogun loju.

lit.: 'The Ibadan Muslim, we salute you,
The Ibadan Muslim, we praise you.
We've missed the person we can honour
You who perform your ablutions even in a hail of arrows;
The Ibadan chief warrior who goes to battle wearing his turban.'

117 Alli Laluwọye was a brother of Oṣundina, and he assumed the post of Ẹkẹrin under Baṣọrun Ogunmọla (1859–67); see S. Johnson, *op. cit.*, p. 316. See also B. Awe, *The Rise of Ibadan . . .*, pp. 180 *et seq.*
118 S. Johnson, *op. cit.*, pp. 366, 424.
119 I. B. Akinyele, *Outlines of Ibadan History*, p. 32.
120 *Ibid.*, pp. 10–11, 33–4.
121 See Chapter 6.
122 CMS, CA2/069, G. Meakin, Journal for the quarter ending September 1859. He found on 28 April 1858, when 'the King had gathered all the chiefs and Baloguns together to hear what I had to say that the chiefs are all Mohammedans'.
123 This Oba who died in 1904 was believed to have been 'very old'. Indeed, the Ibadan historian wrote that he reigned for one hundred and forty years; see I. B. Akinyele, *Iwe Itan Ibadan*, pp. 202–3. But this Oba must have ascended the throne between 1859 and 1860 – possibly the latter – because his predecessor was reported dead only in 1859; see CMS GA2/049. Hinderer's Half Yearly Report ending September 1859.
124 Interview with members of the Royal Household, Iwo, June 1965. See Bibliography: Oral Evidence.
125 See Chapter 4.
126 *Ibid.* 'Ifa ni Imale lo ba wa saiye. Nwọn si sọ ni Orukọ Imale – Mọmọ (Mọmọdu).' (Ifa says that he is to be a Muslim. They therefore gave him a Muslim name – Mọmọdu.) Mọmọ or Mọmọdu is a Yoruba variation of Muhammad.

127 *Ibid.* 'O ni oun yio ma ba wọn bọ (oriṣa) wọn, ṣugbọn oun yio ma sin Ọlọrun ti o da oun' ('He promised to help them in the worship of their gods but he would keep to the worship of his God who created him'). This information is also corroborated by the evidence of local Muslim historians in Iwo (see Bibliography: Oral Evidence).

128 *Ibid.*

129 *Private Papers* of Timi of Ẹdẹ, particularly his address to Islamic Congress at Ẹdẹ on 3 August 1963.

130 *History of Islam in Ikirun* (unpublished MS.). Evidence confirmed by interview at Ikirun with the Muslim community, May 1965. See Bibliography: Oral Evidence.

131 Precise dates of their accession are difficult to fix. Carter met a Muslim Ọba at Ẹdẹ in 1893, after an absence of fourteen years; see *PP*, C. 7227, p. 28.

132 Part of his praise-name (*oriki*) as given during the
'Aremu Agbe
O ko le kan gbagada ko onimale si;
O wo Alufa ba sore;
O wo ọmọkewu se l'ore.'
lit.: 'Precious Aremu,
Who erects an open and big building to house Muslims;
Who engages Muslim clerics as friends;
Who chooses Muslims as beneficiaries.'

133 See note 138. He, Mallam Bako, was regarded as an Ajẹlẹ, and his house as 'ile Ajẹlẹ Ilọrin'. This may also have been due to the fact that Ikirun had come under Ilọrin.

134 *The Lagos Weekly Record*, 21 July 1894, published the petition.

135 See Chapter 2.

136 See *Epe Reorganisation Report*, 1934.

137 *Ibid.* This area is also called Epetedo (lit. a place founded by people of Ẹpẹ).

138 Y. A. Safi, *op. cit.*

139 *Tukura Papers* (Malam Salia Tukuru, the Chief Imam of Ẹpẹ): 'The event during the Life Time of each Chief Imam of Ẹpẹ from the year 1851 upward.'

140 *Epe Reorganisation Report*, 1934.

141 T. Ola Avoseh, *A Short History of Epe*, p. 24.

142 *Epe Reorganisation Report* 1934. See also H. Childs and E. J. Gibbons; *A Report on the Administrative Re-organisation of the Epe District Native Treasury Area*, in Ijebu-Ode Provincial Office.

143 Interview with the leaders of the Muslim community, Ẹpẹ, July 1963; see Bibliography: Oral Evidence. 'Esin Islam la ntele nibi' ('We follow Islam here'). The principle of this statement is borne out by the high regard which Yoruba Muslims have for Ẹpẹ, as a Muslim citadel in Yorubaland. Ẹpẹ is, indeed a coastal Ilọrin in this regard.

144 Lewis comments that in West Africa, as opposed to East Africa, Islam strongly emphasises law in the society; I. M. Lewis (ed.), *Islam in Tropical Africa*, p. 18. Contrast the view of others, particularly

Trimingham, that Islam is only a 'department' of life in Yorubaland; J. S. Trimingham, *op. cit.*, p. 22 *et passim*.

145 Skinner says of Mossi rulers who became Muslims that 'it was by being Moslems of this kind that Mossi rulers managed to retain the allegiance of their Moslem subjects'. See E. P. Skinner, *The Mossi of the Upper Volta*, p. 138; see also his 'Diffusion of Islam in an African Society' in *Annals, New York Academy of Sciences*.

146 CMS G3 A2/03, Wood's Report of Mission to the Interior for Peace. Wood observed that the Are was 'a strict Mohammedan'. The *ṣalāt* must have been the *'Īd al-Kabīr*.

147 See, for example, James Johnson's observations in his 1877 Report in CMS, CA2/056; and E. G. Parrinder, 'Divine Kingship in West Africa', *Numen*. Some scholars noted the influence of chiefs in promoting Islam in the Western Sudan. See particularly N. Levtzion: *Muslims and Chiefs in West Africa*, pp. 189–91 *et passim*. For other areas in Africa where the acceptance of Islam by the court militates against its spread, see I. M. Lewis (ed.), *op. cit.*, pp. 36ff.

148 I. B. Akinyele, *op. cit.*, p. 198: 'gbogbo awọn Ijoye rẹ fẹrẹ ba kirun tan . . .' ('almost all his chiefs worshipped with him as Muslims').

149 Interview with the Muslim community, Ẹdẹ, May–June 1965. The evidence here given is corroborated by that provided by the family of Abibu Lagunju in Ẹdẹ. See Bibliography: Oral Evidence.

150 He was said to have spent about 30 years in Ilọrin.

151 Compare the role of Lat-Dyor, the Damel (King) of Kayor in promoting Islamisation of the Wolof; see V. Monteil, 'Lat-Dyor, Damel du Kayor (1842–1886) et l'Islamisation des Wolofs du Senegal', in I. M. Lewis (ed.), *op. cit.*, pp. 342–7.

152 T. Ola Avoseh, *History of Badagry* (unpublished MS.).

153 Interview with the Chief Imam and others at Idọgọ.

154 Information derived from interviews conducted in Ẹpẹ in 1963.

155 *Ibid.*

156 His pagan name was Osonaike.

157 'Gbogbo awọn enia nigbayẹn lo binu si' ('Everybody was angry with him at that time'). Same interviews. He and, later, the other early Muslims became the object of abusive songs such as:

'Oso didu, e r'owo se'fa
O deyin Imale o.
Imale a tan niyan, afowo jona o
Aiye re o, awon Onimale'.

lit.: 'You black hearts can't afford money to get Ifa
You therefore troop to Islam
Muslims deceive people, and will get their fingers burnt,
Behold, you Muslims.'

158 This belies a common belief that Islam appealed only to 'the detribalised young man in the city'. See particularly J. Mendelsohn, *God, Allah and Juju*, pp. 130–1.

159 CMS, CA2/056, Annual Letter of James Johnson, 1878.

160 *The Lagos Times*, 14 September 1881.

161 *The Lagos Observer*, 3 and 24 September 1887.

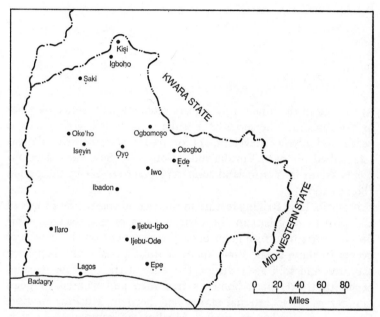

The spread of Islam in Yorubaland 1861–92

4 The zenith of Islamic expansion, 1892-1908

At the end of the nineteenth century momentous events took place in Yorubaland. The series of Yoruba wars ended, giving way to peace and further development of trade; also, British rule was established all over Yorubaland. Alongside these new developments Islam in Yorubaland took very great strides in the period 1892 to 1908.

A particularly striking feature in this period was the rapid spread and growth of Islam in the eastern parts of Yorubaland. This development was, to a great extent, consequent on the course of events in these areas. First, many Yoruba people who had been captured and sold away during the wars of the previous decades began to trickle back home as free men and women. A good number of these internal slaves had become Muslims in Ẹpẹ, Ilọrin, Iwo, Ibadan or similar Muslim environments. As they returned home they proved very useful in spreading their faith in their respective areas.[1] Furthermore, from about 1870, the Yoruba eastern (trade) route[2] was again put to active use. This route took off from Ilọrin and Ekiti, passed through Ọwọ, Akure and Ondo and, before it terminated in Lagos, touched various points on the coast, notably at Ẹpẹ, Makun, Ajuẹrẹ and Itẹbu.[3] Although this route was at first mainly used as a highway for transporting, among other things, ammunition to the war centres in Ekiti area,[4] nevertheless it served another immensely useful purpose. It promoted contact and trade between Ẹpẹ, Ilọrin and these eastern areas,[5] thereby further encouraging, in the latter areas, the ingress and establishment of Muslims.[6]

It is largely in the context of this increasing volume of contact and trade between the Muslim areas and the eastern parts of Yorubaland that one can view the rise of Islam in places such as

Akurẹ, Ile-Ifẹ, Ondo and Ọwọ. It was not until the 1870s that some Muslims infiltrated Ondo, for example. The earliest record[7] of a Muslim in Ondo was made by the Rev. Charles Phillips, who observed that one of the six women he baptised in July 1880 had been converted to Islam during the time when she had been in slavery in 'Yoruba country'.[8] On her return to her home-town, Ondo, in 1877 she still kept to her new religion and it was probably her feeling of isolation as a Muslim that impelled her to change to Christianity in 1880. But by this time the Islamic infiltration was steadily increasing. The Rev. Charles Phillips continually ran into a group of Lagos Muslims with whom he used to dispute theological issues.[9] Several Ondo long-distance traders such as were typified by Lawal Okoigi returned home as Muslim converts.[10] A core of Muslim residents[11] soon developed in Ondo, their numbers increasing to such an extent that, early in the reign of Ọba Jimẹkan (1881–94),[12] they were able to form a Muslim community[13] under the leadership of Afa (later al-hajj) Muhammad Alimi,[14] who was chosen as their Imam.

The Imam was from Erinmo.[15] As the leader of the nascent Ondo Muslim community, he endeavoured, throughout his tenure of office, to propagate the religion. He encouraged the converts to stand firm in their faith, and tried to woo and attract others to Islam.[16] Together with a few indigenous Ondo converts, he gave private and open lectures on Islam to would-be converts, and also offered various inducements, in form of clothes and money, to win people over into the Muslim fold.[17] This propaganda proved a considerable success and the number of Ondo Muslims rose. A central mosque was erected at Oke Ọtunba about 1888. Built by communal labour and with mud and palm-leaves, this modest mosque served for the next thirty-two years the needs of the Ondo Jama'a. The community continued to expand, and early in the twentieth century it could boast of certain important Ondo leaders, such as Abu Bakare Ajao, Sadiku Oyenẹyin, Alli Akin-yoyenu, Sadiu Adefisoye; and some of them became important town chiefs, for example Chief Lijoka Muhammad Kuteyi, Chief Logbosere Saidu Akinfolarin, Chief Sara Abdul Kadiri Ọladapọ and High Chief Sasẹrẹ Abubakare Ayọdeji.[18] With such reinforce-ments, the Muslim community was strongly established. By 1906 the Muslims were already keeping themselves 'prominently before the people' and had three mosques in different parts of the town.[19]

It was largely during the tenure of office of the first Imam,

Muhammad Alimi, which continued till 1918, that the Ondo Muslim community became firmly established and organised. In addition to the post of Imam, other posts were created and filled in order to facilitate the administration of the affairs of the young community.[20] The offices were generally given to the elderly and most influential Muslims within the community. Abdul Kadiri Oladapo became the first Muslim Balogun, Saidu Fawẹhinmi the Seriki; Sadiku Oyenẹyin, the Ọtun Balogun; Yusuf Akinnibosun, the Osi Balogun; Lawal Okoigi, the Baba Adini; and Saidu Adefisoye, the Baba Isalẹ.[21]

The religious life of the community was looked after by the Imam assisted by the Onitafusiru, who was Afa Yahya from Ilọrin. The religious functions of these officials were often supplemented by those of the itinerants muallims who came mostly from Ilọrin and Lagos. One of them unnamed was persuaded to stay for a while, and was held in high esteem by the local Muslim population.[22]

In Ilẹsa, the rise and growth of Islam was more remarkable than in Ondo, even though the pattern of development appeared similar. As far back as the early 1860s Ilẹsa had begun to see the return of some of its sons who had been converted to Islam during their sojourn outside Ilẹsa.[23] The most notable of these was Sedu Ogun of Oke-Ẹsa, who returned to Ilẹsa from the colony in the 1860s. For a long while, he was virtually alone and not much could be done until other Muslims trickled back to Ilẹsa in the 1860s and 1890s. He then assumed the responsibility of organising the few available Muslims into a community. Distinguished as the 'father of Islam' in Ilẹsa, he was assisted in the work of organisation by many other returning Ilẹsa Muslims, such as Afa Suaibu of Oke-Ẹsa, Afa Amodu Farise of Egbe-Idi, Afa Kanomodi Iwere, and Afa Salami Baṣọrun of Egbe-Idi. These early Muslims got together and, after gaining the consent and sympathy of Ogedengbe, the Obanla of Ilẹsa, they erected two mosques, one at Oke-Ẹsa under the leadership of Sedu Ogun, and the other at Egbe-Idi, under Amodu Farise. Sedu Ogun made available to the community the services of Afa Parakoyi, a native of Ilọrin, whom he brought to Ilẹsa from the coast. As the leading Mu'allim and Lemomu Ratibi of Oke-Ẹsa, the largest Muslim quarter, Afa Parakoyi occasionally led the entire Ilẹsa community in prayers.[24] He was, however, not formally installed Imam for Ilẹsa.[25]

Thus, for some time, this young and tender community was

without a Chief Imam, and was still denied the opportunity of conducting the Friday congregational services. But its position improved shortly afterwards on the return to Ileṣa of two princes, Ajimoko and Abubakare Orimogunje, a converted Muslim.[26] The princes used their positions to establish the religion and enhance its position. Prince Abubakare Orimogunje, in particular, was outstanding for his notable contribution in this regard, sparing neither effort nor money.[27]

During the reign of Ajimoko I (1896–1901),[28] Abubakare, who was his relation,[29] strove to consolidate the position of Islam. Largely by his exertions, the Friday congregational services were started. Land was acquired on which a central mosque was erected, and very many people were encouraged to join Islam, which soon became so respectable that it was publicly practised and proclaimed without fear or shame. For the leadership of the entire community, Abubakare Orimogunję secured for Ileṣa the services of Afa Disu Kannike, who became the first Chief Imam of Ileṣa. Non-Ileṣa knowledgeable Muslims, particularly Afa Parakoyi and the Chief Imam, established some Qur'anic and *'ilm* schools in which they taught the people more about the Qur'ān and the tenets of the religion. By 1910, when Obanla Ogedengbe, a staunch supporter of the Muslims, died, Islam had been solidly established in Ileṣa.

Farther north, in Ekiti area, Muslim communities were also being formed. The development of Islam here at first encountered the normal traditional opposition to new ideas and systems, but in Ekiti more than anywhere else in Yorubaland at this time, the anti-Islam attitude was very pronounced. It arose from the historical circumstances of the Ekiti, for their first experience of Islam was mainly through Ilọrin which, as a militant Muslim post, had spread its belligerent activities to Ekiti for the greater part of the nineteenth century.[30] The Ilọrin wars and raids in Ekiti no doubt exposed Ekiti to Islam in a dramatic way. There were captives on both sides; and either way, some Ekiti people changed to Islam. But more serious was the repercussion of the Ilọrin wars on the cause of Islam in Ekiti: they generated considerable opposition against Ilọrin and the religion with which it was associated.[31]

Anti-Islam feeling among the Ekiti died hard. In 1894, Bishop C. Phillips noted that 'the Ekitis were influenced by resentful feeling against Mohammedanism'.[32] Up till the first decades of the twentieth century, this antagonism persisted.[33] Largely because of this, some people, such as the Ajero of Ijero who had been converted abroad, renounced Islam.[34] Those who did not were obliged to worship in secret.

Gradually, however, the light of Islam began to shine once again. Although a former Ewi, Ali Atẹwọgboye (1836–85),[35] had been a Muslim, yet Islam was far from being established during his reign, thanks to the above-mentioned feeling and the series of wars in which Ado was involved.[36] But the reduction of the scale of war, and the faint dawn of peace in the last decades of the nineteenth century brought fresh hopes.

In the 1880s some people, such as Yakubu, a son of Ewi Ali Atẹwọgboye, and Bello Olokodana, his maternal half-brother, returned to Ado. They were later joined by other Ado people who had been carried away into Muslim areas and now began to trickle back, bringing their new faith with them.[37] Bello of Idemo family, who was believed to have been the first Muslim to return to Ado, came back as a convert during the reign of Ewi Aladesanmi Ajimudaoro (1886–1910). Saliu Ayemi of Odofin family, who had been taken away into slavery in a French-speaking country,[38] eventually returned home a Muslim with a fair knowledge of Islam. There was also a woman who had been taken captive to Ẹpẹ where she was converted to Islam and married to a certain Abass. It was this small group of returning Ado Muslims who formed the early Muslim community in Ado-Ekiti. The total number is believed to have included about twelve men and one woman.

The Muslims took counsel together but it was not until in the reign of Ewi Aladesanmi Ajimudaoro, *c.* 1892–1910,[39] that they could form a community, under the leadership of Saliu Ayeni who, alone, had a fair knowledge of the Qu'rān. They constituted 'the sprinkling of Mohammedans' as Bishop Charles Phillips discovered in 1894.[40] In the face of strong local traditions and a general antipathy towards Islam, however, this small group encountered many difficulties in their effort to establish their community, but had 'a very strong footing' by 1908, as a certain clergyman testified in his annual report.[41]

Ikẹrẹ-Ekiti provides a different example of the early formation of the Muslim community.[42] A fortified town, Ikere had served as a refuge for many people cast adrift by, and fleeing from, the raids, the war and threats of war that disturbed the peaceful atmosphere of this period. The immigration led to the foundation of a quarter in Ikẹrẹ for the Ọyọ-speaking refugees. The Muslims among them, such as Aliu from Ilọrin, Bamgbola Aba-Ọyọ, and Osabiyi, gathered a few others together for joint worship under Aliu, later Balogun Eyin Ogan.[43] The small mosque was situated in their quarter at Eyin Ogan. At that time in Ikẹrẹ, Islam was essentially the religion of the alien, though Yoruba, settlers.[44] The community was later disorganised as a result of the series of battles and conflicts[45] that were together known as the Ado–Ikẹrẹ War of 1881–93, which on some occasions disrupted the whole town.[46] Later, the few who survived – Babajide, Odunlami, Yesufu Abe – were reorganised, this time by an immigrant Nupe mallam, Afa Abudu Karimu; and they worshipped once again at the Eyin Ogan Mosque of the Ọyọ Quarter.[47]

The small number rose slightly with the trickling in of some Ikere people who had been converted to Islam during their sojourn abroad in Ẹpẹ, Ilọrin and other Muslim centres. For instance, Bakare of Ile Bariba, who later became the Ọtun Imale of Oke-Ikẹrẹ, returned from Ẹpẹ where he had been won to Islam.[48] The reconstituted group was small, still largely Ọyọ-speaking, and far from being assertive. For many years, all it had to show was the joint worship at the Eyin Ogan Mosque under the leadership of Afa Tapa Abudu Karimu, who stayed and lived with them. The latter's laudable exertions were occasionally supplemented by those of passing Muslim teachers and preachers, such as Basuki and Akadiri from Ilọrin. They had no formal organisation until after this period, when the famous iconoclastic Muslim preacher, Afa Kokewukobere of Ilọrin, came to Ikẹrẹ and advised the amorphous group of Muslims to organise themselves better.

In many ways, the position of Islam in Ikẹrẹ was similar to that in many other Ekiti towns and Ọwọ.[49] Islam was embraced by a few people; and the Muslims were largely aliens and mostly Ọyọ-speaking. There were few local Muslims, and most of these had been converted abroad. In spite of wars, contempt and other indignities, they worshipped together but had little or no organisation. Nevertheless, it is true to say that by the close of this period, Islam had spread noticeably into the eastern parts of Yorubaland. Although the new communities were in varying stages of consolidation, there was little doubt that they were developing roots.

The question then can be raised here as to the factors aiding the establishment of Islam in these new areas. This establishment cannot be explained adequately by reference to the presence of

Muslim settlers and returned local sons and daughters. For by this period, Islam was more strongly established in Ondo than in Ado-Ekiti, which had more Muslim repatriates. Also, notwithstanding the existence of an Ọyọ quarter in Ikẹrẹ, the religion was less established there than even in Ado-Ekiti. An important factor here assisting the establishment of the religion was the social status of the Muslims.

Initially, the social status of the Muslims in most of the new areas was humble – the Muslims were 'aliens', returning local slaves in Yorubaland, and shifting traders. They were also almost ignored by their own society. After a while their social status was, in some areas, transformed, so transformed, indeed, that their early humble status became no more than a dim recollection. As the circle of Muslims widened and began to include notable people, Islam became strengthened and fashionable. An analysis of the history of Islam in these new areas shows that this process of transformation at the time was slower in Ekiti than elsewhere. Thus, Muslims remained few and their position weak, whereas in some towns in the eastern part of Yorubaland, such as Ondo and Ilẹṣa, Islam soon outgrew its humble social origins, and became fairly popular and respectable.

It was Ijẹbu area that provided the most notable accession to Islam in this period, dramatising the social transformation of the position of Muslims. Until late in the nineteenth century Islam was little known in Ijẹbu, most of the entire area holding fast to their traditional religion. The relative absence of Islam, as already noted, could be attributed not merely to the little external contact which the area had with the outside world, but also to the virtually closed nature of the society.[50] In the last two decades of the nineteenth century, however, Islam began to filter rather unobtrusively into Ijẹbu area. Present in Ijẹbu country were a few domestic and Hausa slaves who had been brought by the Ijẹbu themselves. Some of these domestics were Muslims, and constituted the staunchest adherents of Islam in many parts of Ijẹbu, such as Ipẹru, Ṣagamu, Ikẹnẹ and Ijẹbu-Ode.

At Ipẹru, a sizable market town,[51] local tradition is particularly strong about the role of Muslim 'Hausa' slaves in the first phase of the establishment of Islam there.[52] They had been brought to Ipẹru at various times and belonged to certain families such as Odufote, Oluwo Isale and others. They were fairly substantial in number, and seemed to have enjoyed the favour of their masters.

Consequently, they were allowed to clear and use an open space in the town as their prayer ground and mosque.[54] There was, however, a limit to the religious toleration granted them – no celebrations or services were permitted. Nevertheless, it was this core of northern Muslims who kept alive the light of Islam right down to the time when they were joined by converts from among the local people. In 1878, the Rev. James Johnson noted that in Iperu the adherents of Islam were largely Hausa slaves, and that though many had run away, 'Islam is still represented by very few slaves and a few free born'.[55]

When the present site of Makun Ṣagamu was being founded in 1869, some notable families who came along from the old site brought with them a number of Hausa Muslim domestics[56] from areas north of Yorubaland. There were Awodu of Oduname family, Jato of Odumala family, Igbesi of the family of Osi Makun; and, most important, Afa Ibraimọ, nicknamed Kodurogbọjẹ.[57] He was an ardent and intrepid Muslim domestic from the interior, belonging to the Oduname family. This small group of 'Hausa' Muslims constituted for some time virtually all that there was of Islam and they were under the leadership of Afa Ibraimọ, who is now said to have been one of the first people to begin Islam in Sagamu. It was at this new site that the number of Muslims soon began to increase and, more significantly, to include some indigenous people.[58]

But perhaps in most other big towns of Ijẹbu, it was the 'Hausa' Muslim slaves who introduced the religion.[59] Some of the northern Muslim slaves are still remembered for various reasons. One of them was Alli, said to have been 'from Ilọrin', who was much richer than his master, Tubogun, so that the latter's name became better known through the slave;[60] Liasu, an Ilọrin slave of Sanni Oboromboro, was well known for his exertions in the cause of Islam in Ijẹbu.[61] These slaves with a sprinkling of free-born indigenes had an open space for worship, thanks to the liberal policy of their masters.

It could thus be seen that in these places it was the non-Yoruba Muslim domestics who first openly practised Islam in Ijẹbu for a number of years. They enjoyed some religious toleration, but their number was unstable though fairly considerable.[62] In occupation they varied from clerics of the Liasu type to warriors and medical advisers of the Afa Ibraimọ type. In social status they were a humble and a fairly restricted circle of people; and largely because of this, the religion was treated with an indifference that almost amounted to contempt, if not hatred. As a local Ijẹbu historian puts it: 'Isin yi ko ja ma nkankan loju Ijẹbu.'[63] Nevertheless, they were the early nucleus of non-Ijẹbu Muslims, who brought to the Ijẹbu the first intimate awareness of Islam and, indeed, helped to lay some basis for the expansion of the religion in Ijẹbu.

It was not long before the position of Islam was transformed from a lowly and uncertain one to one that was firm and respectable. This transformation started when the free-born Ijẹbu began to accept and practise the new faith. In this process, three main agencies were at work. The first striking one was the existence of people who were believed to be 'predestined'.[64] How did this come about? When some parents sought out a diviner, to predict the future life of the children,[65] they were informed by some of these Ifa diviners that such a child was predestined to be a Muslim.[66] The parents were then taught by the diviner the proper steps to take to ensure the well-being of the predestined Muslim. On being so informed, the Yoruba parents, true to Yoruba custom, hardly queried Ifa predictions, and followed such divinations strictly. They prepared in the house a small enclosure of the size of the 'girigiri',[67] held parties[68] for the child once every week, especially on Fridays, and cut for the child a number of white dresses. This was continued until the child came of age. As soon as any mallam appeared, the parents called on him to 'surrender the child to him'. The child was then given a Muslim name and, as a protégé of a Muslim, was brought up in the true Muslim way. There were many examples of these 'predestined Muslims' in Ijẹbu area.[69] For instance, there was at Ipẹru Asana the mother of the Chief Imam, who lived until 1957; in Idowa[70] there was Kasumu Ojeneiye.

It is pertinent to ask how Yoruba Ifa diviners, whose divination constitutes such an important element in Yoruba traditional beliefs which they were expected to preserve, could thus divine that certain Yoruba children were to belong to a different system of belief. An answer could be sought here not in their 'treachery' – for they were being faithful to Ifa corpus – but in the fact that the Ifa corpus itself had been undergoing some internal change. It evidently incorporated a few stanzas[71] which prescribed Islam for certain people to whom such stanzas appeared when Ifa was divined. This goes to show the vitality and adaptability of Ifa, and confirms the point that the Ifa priest (*babalawo*) indeed 'occupies a focal point'[72] in Yoruba cultural system, channelling sacrifices and people to different cults and worship.[73]

If Ifa is taken as a body of knowledge accumulated by the Ifa diviners, then it will not be difficult to accept this incorporation into it. With the expansion and acceptance of Islam in Yorubaland, it needed but little imagination to predict that some people would be Muslims, *ceteris paribus*. The Ifa diviners were seldom persecuted for such divination, and their verdict was accepted as valid as much by the individuals for whom it was divined as by the people in general.

Vital here is the point that in the process of the transformation of the position of Islam, the existence in various places of 'predestined Muslims' served as an immensely useful catalyst. To the Muslims they were more than a numerical accession, for in all circumstances they, as 'predestined Muslims', stood firm and unwavering in their faith. By their existence also, they and others were able to sustain and propagate their faith either by pointing out how Ifa itself had decreed it or by silencing their potential persecutors with the unquestionable divinations of Ifa.[74]

A considerable reinforcement to the 'predestined Muslims', was the significant number of home-returning Ijẹbu traders who had been converted abroad.[75] By far the most important of these were the long-distance Ijẹbu traders. Many of them were to be found in almost all Ijẹbu towns – Ipẹru, Ṣagamu, Ijẹbu-Ode, and so on. Their conversion abroad may well have been in the interests of their trade, since by being Muslims they could mix freely with Muslim traders and enjoy protection in such market towns as Ilọrin and Iseyin, where Islam had been firmly established. Possibly their closer acquaintance with Islam in those towns made them more favourably disposed towards the religion which, at home, they had little understood or even looked down upon or ignored as alien and contemptible. Still others might have been influenced to take to Islam because of local political and social alignments. But whatever motives inspired their conversion abroad, on their return home they assisted their community in no small measure, not only with their wealth but also with the varied experience they had acquired at the Muslim towns where they had traded.

A third important accession to the cause of Islam in Ijẹbu was the conversion in the town itself of free-born and indeed well-placed indigenous people. Largely as a result of the presence of converted Ijẹbu traders, and of the presence and influence of the Hausa Muslim domestics in the homes of influential and wealthy Ijẹbu men, many of such indigenous free-born adults were converted in due course.[76] Consequently, the process of the establishment of Islam went apace in this period. In Ṣagamu[77] the early local converts such as Akeredolu Oyefeko, Idowu Jinadu Jobayo, Alli Pedo, Bello (later the Otun Imale), Bakare Ogunlesi (later Seriki Makun), combined to form a community, having an enclosed piece of ground[78] for their prayer meetings. Prayers were led by the renowned Afa Ibraimọ, who acted as the Imam until his death some years after the 1892 Magbon War.[79] The organisation of the community was simple, consisting only of two other officers, the Nọibi and the Ladani, who were Sanni Sotimiren of Offin quarter, and Suberu, a Nupe man, respectively. The nascent community was fairly respectable and enjoyed religious liberty. Ṣagamu to some extent illustrates a fairly general pattern in Ijẹbuland: joint worship of all Muslims, non-Ijẹbu Muslims, traders and converted adults combining to form a community with a simple common organisation.

Ipẹru differed from Ṣagamu. Soon after its establishment in 1879, it had a Muslim community which included Hausa Muslim slaves, 'predestined Muslims', such as Asana, returning Ipẹru Muslim traders, such as Oyeti Bello,[80] and locally converted notables, such as Hassan son of Bisuga, the Apena of Ipẹru. In the simple organisational set-up, the leaders were almost entirely locally-recruited men. The Imam was Oyeti, an Ipẹru long-distance trader, who had been converted abroad and had some wealth and knowledge of Islam. The Balogun was the intrepid Hassan of the Apena family. Under this local leadership the community organised itself, using for some time the same prayer ground as the Hausa Muslims had been using before. At the start, they were all ridiculed and jeered at by the non-Muslims as worshippers of *esin Gambari* (the Hausa religion). But the community stood firm and progressed. The Ramadan was observed as were the other Muslim festivals such as *Lailat al-Qadr*, *Mawlīd al-Nabī*, *'Id al-Fiṭr*, *'Id al-Kabīr* and *'Ashūrā*. Above all, a new and larger mosque was built.

Ipẹru also provides a good illustration of the reaction and opposition of traditional Ijẹbu authorities to the growing community. In spite of and perhaps because of its local leadership, the community suffered the harassment of Oro worshippers and local masqueraders such as Olisigun Adeoro and Jobielu. It was a most excruciating time for the Muslims. As informants put it:

Awọn Oloro ko fun wọn laye rara. Awọn Musulumi fori laku si. Ẹniti ko ba le duro dada, ti ko kọ iku, ti ko kọ 'kia'[81] fun nkan ki i le ṣe Musulumi. Akoko naa le gan.[82]

To construct their new mosque they had to resort to the trick of building side walls on one single night, to the intense fury of the traditionalists. Their angry protest at the court only drew forth from the sympathetic Ọba[83] a classic Herodic reply; he pleaded his helplessness and remonstrated with them that it was not customary to pull down a mosque once it had been erected.

The Muslims' survival as a community as well as their subsequent expansion owed much to the support of their rich members, who financed the work of the community,[84] and of such notables as Hassan who braved many dangers on their behalf.[85]

As in many other towns, the religious nurture of the Ipẹru Muslim community came essentially from outside Ipẹru. Through the services of the informed Ipẹru Muslim traders a mallam, Afa Kuranga,[86] came down from Iseyin. The community put him up with a leading Muslim, Hassan Odufote, and the Afa virtually made Ipẹru his home. It was he who instituted the *'Īd al-Fiṭr* and *'Īd al-Kabīr* prayers. Through his open-air teachings, religious propaganda songs[87] and organisation of a Qur'anic and *ilm* school,[88] he greatly raised the tone of religious life in the community, to the great joy of the local Muslim community.

The course of events at Ijẹbu-Ode was, perhaps, the most dramatic and crucial for Ijẹbuland. In some respects, the early phase of Islam here was similar to that of Ṣagamu and Ipẹru. The community consisted essentially of Hausa slaves; and largely because of their humble origins, the religion was looked down upon and, perhaps, even hated. Again, the community here received the reinforcements of 'predestined Muslims', traders and converted adults. But within a very short time, the religion outgrew its humble beginnings to become really fashionable and popular. As already noted, some of the slaves, such as Alli, became wealthy; and some of the slaves' masters, such as Tubogun, Sanni Oboromboro, were converted to Islam, together with several notables, such as Lawani (later Nọibi), Afa Idi Agbon, and Abudu Tokunbo. One notable member of this group was Alli Akayinode from Isale Iwade in Ijẹbu-Ode. A well-travelled trader, Alli had become a

Muslim in the course of his business tours, and gained some knowledge of Arabic. When he tried to introduce open worship, together with the ill-liked call to prayer, he incurred the displeasure of the traditional authorities and had to flee to Ṣagamu to save his life. It was he who on his return to Ijẹbu-Ode some years later became the Imam of the town. It was under these circumstances, however, that Ademiyewo Awujalẹ Afidipọtẹ had little hesitation in granting the Muslims the use of a piece of land at the outskirts of the town for a mosque.[89] Local opposition, by contrast to Ipẹru, was virtually stilled, thanks to the growing number of prominent free-born men within the Muslim fold and, above all, some royal patronage. Indeed, the influence of the religion had grown so much that even before 1879 the Ijẹbu-Ode notables were among mounted colourful celebrants on the occasions of Muslim festivals.[90] The laying of the foundation stone of a new mosque in 1891 was a great occasion, involving virtually the whole town. Generous contributions, for prayers, were made by many people, including the Awujalẹ, Aboki Tunwase Arojojoye (1885–86).[91] On that day many people were converted publicly to Islam, including Prince Alli Ogunnaike, who later became Awujalẹ Fibiwoga (1929–33). Open call to prayer was permitted to be made after a number of influential officials such as Odunlami and Aroboto, Odi Ọba, had successfully mediated with the reigning Awujalẹ, Adesimbo Tunwase (1885–6)[92] who probably saw no practicable alternative. The growth of Islam soon became rapid and mosques were springing up at Isale Iwade (Etimoro) and at Iyanro (compound of Etimoro). 'There was a great rush to the religion', which in 1896 became, by all contemporary evidence, 'the religion favoured by the chiefs'.[93] The process of expansion and consolidation of Islam reached a climax around 1902[94] when Balogun Kuku dramatised his triumph and conversion to Islam. Balogun Kuku was an energetic, able, intelligent and adroit man who, however, had weathered much persecution. He had formerly resided at Oru, where he as the Seriki had been sent by the Awujalẹ to assist Balogun Nafọwọkan in managing the Ijẹbu military camp.[95] At Oru his power and wealth grew out of a brisk trade in salt and ammunition, to the extent that it was generally feared he would make himself independent of Ijẹbu-Ode.[96] Indeed, when he was ordered to return to the city, he refused and had to be forcibly turned out. He took refuge at Ibadan, since he had ingratiated himself with them at Oru through trade and fair treatment;[97] he stayed in a splendid house in Madame Efundunke's compound. When the pressure to leave became insupportable, he returned to Ijẹbu-Ode where he stayed for a brief while. Involvement in local partisan politics, especially his support for the Awujalẹ against the powerful 'party of young men' clamouring against trade and friendly relations with Ibadan and the colonial government[98] forced him again to resume his journeys, this time to Ifẹ[99] where he was when the Anglo-Ijẹbu war of 1892 broke out. His support for Ijẹbu forces appears to have been nominal for his forces were present at Magbọn but apparently took no part in the engagement.[100] He was allowed to return to Ijẹbu-Ode, and he sought to win the favour and recognition of the colonial government. The latter was only too willing to obtain his loyal support and recommended him for an annual stipend. Henceforth his position at Ijẹbu-Ode was strengthened, and the capable and rich man first consolidated his position by building a house, as the Ijẹbu had destroyed his former house.[101]

It was in 1902 that this renowned Balogun Kuku, of Oru fame, a Muslim sympathiser a few years back,[102] formally opened his house called Ọlọrunṣogo (Glory to God), at Ijẹbu-Ode, to which he had attached a good mosque.[103] He turned the event into a grand occasion, inviting people from far and wide – Lagos, Ibadan, Abẹokuta and Ẹpẹ, and on this occasion he publicly declared for Islam, taking the name of Mọmọdu Bello.[104] He was joined by scores of people who were also converted.[105] Among these were influential and highly placed Ijẹbu men, such as Prince Isaka Dawodu, the son of Fidipọtẹ, Abass Odejai, and Abass Oduni.[106] A certain prominent Muslim wrote jubilantly in 1902 to His Honour Abdallah Quillam Effendi, Shaikh ul-Islam of the British Isles, about this wholesale conversion of important chiefs at Ijẹbu-Ode:

> Kuku one of the leading men of Ijẹbu Ode: and over 600 of his people declared their belief in the one and only eternal God and His Glorious Prophet (eternal peace and rest be upon Him) and have been received into the holy Islamic faith.[107]

The impact of the 1902 incident on the course of Islam throughout Ijẹbu was considerable. Henceforth, Balogun Kuku became a champion of the religion to Imuṣin, Ijẹbu Igbo, Ago and indeed throughout Ijẹbu,[108] and many more people, inside and outside Ijẹbu-Ode, began to turn to Islam. The religious tide swelled.[109]

The Christian missionaries who were still trying to make a niche in Ijẹbu-Ode were dismayed; for while, by their own frank testimony, they were having only 'a few inquirers after the truth', Islam appeared to be sweeping all before it.[110] Indeed, 'perhaps the Ijẹbu had come to associate Islam with greatness',[111] due obviously to the influence of these socially-high Muslims. And as elsewhere, the Ijẹbu Muslim chiefs and elders used their influence with their people;[112] and by 1907 the position of Islam in Ijẹbu was such as to elicit from eye-witness missionaries comments that Ijẹbu 'could be said now to be a Mohammedan nation'.[113] The people all flock to Mohammedanism which has become the popular and dominant religion.[114]

By 1908 Islam had been introduced into virtually all the major towns in Yorubaland: Abẹokuta, Ado-Ekiti, Ẹdẹ, Ẹpẹ, Ibadan, Ijẹbu-Ode, Ikẹre-Ekiti, Ikirun, Ilaro, Ilẹṣa, Isẹyin, Iwo, Lagos, Ogbomọṣọ, Ondo, Oṣogbo. The size of the community cannot be determined precisely; but it can be gauged from contemporary official and Christian missionary records. Isẹyin, which in 1893 had sixteen mosques, could boast in 1899 of an additional six.[115] In Ibadan in 1900, Muslims formed, at least 10 per cent of the population,[116] and had about seventy mosques in 1908.[117] Ijẹbu-Ode in 1908 was at least half, if not almost wholly, Muslim, with twelve mosques;[118] Ogbomọṣọ had about 1,000 Muslims using thirty-seven mosques.[119] Muslims in Lagos were reckoned in 1901 to have been about 50 per cent of the population.[120] In 1908 they formed about 60 per cent of the Lagos population, having 'thrice as many mosques as churches of all [Christian] denominations'.[121] There was hardly any doubt that Islam in Yorubaland had made 'an astonishing success',[122] as Mr F. C. Fuller, the Resident at Ibadan, had reported in 1901. This was corroborated by the Rev. A. W. Smith, who in 1908 declared, in the light of his own independent enquiry, that Islam in Yorubaland 'has grown from a small stream into a mighty river'.[123]

As if to crown this remarkable spread and growth of Islam, two significant events took place. First, contrary to a former belief echoed in 1878 by Bishop James Johnson that 'Mohammedanism does not sit on the throne of the Yoruba (Ọyọ)',[124] a Muslim Alafin, Lawani Agogoja, came to the historic throne of the 'New Ọyọ Empire'[125] in July 1905.[126] Secondly, among the newly-Islamised areas, Ijẹbu-Ode in 1906 had a Muslim ruler in Awujalẹ Adeọna Fusigboye (1906–15).[127] The significance of the establishment of Islam in these major centres was clear: Islam had virtually captured Yorubaland.

The planting of Islam in these major centres of Yorubaland was also significant for the future expansion of the religion among the Yoruba. The Yoruba town has always been an important nodal point,[128] serving as the capital and the largest market for the neighbouring villages and farms with which it is in close contact. It has been also a social focal point, the place where the important festivals were held and the people set the social pace and fashions. In these capacities, the Yoruba town has exerted a considerable influence on its immediate environs.[129] As far as the history of Islam in Yorubaland is concerned, it was particularly portentous for its future development that the major towns had accepted Islam. This acceptance admirably paved the way for its future expansion into the outlying districts.[130]

The rapid spread of Islam in Ijẹbu and some towns in eastern Yorubaland was no doubt due to certain factors already enumerated. But the role of a veteran missionary, such as Afa Muhammad Salisu, better known as Kokewukobere, must be mentioned in this context. An Ilọrin preacher,[131] and a teacher as well, he was by far the most outstanding figure who achieved mass conversions of people all over Yorubaland and particularly in Ijẹbu and Ekiti. Indeed, when he was leaving Ijẹbu-Ode finally after many fruitful years of preaching and teaching there, he allowed his name to be used by one of his more brilliant pupils, Sanni Janiyandanwo. Rechristened Sanni-Kokewukobere, this pupil always tried to live up to the standard of his illustrious master and patron whose memory he tried to perpetuate. Nevertheless it is because of his exertions in the cause of Islam, as well as for his brief religious duties,[132] that he is remembered everywhere today.

Afa Kokewukobere was, however, only one of the many people who not only preached but also maintained the Muslim system of education in Yorubaland. At the bottom of that system was the *ile-kewu*, founded by the early Muslims around the persons of their mallams. Apart from enforcing the study by rote of the Qur'ān, the *ile-kewu*, as already mentioned,[133] was largely an orientation school, directing the young wards as well as the older ones along the straight path (*Sirāṭ al-mustaqīm*).[134] As proficiency at this primary level was gained, some people began to emerge ready for further work. The second stage was '*Ilm*, which involved translating the Qur'ān into Yoruba and a more meaningful study of its text. This was generally accompanied by a supplementary study of allied subjects such as Arabic grammar, *Tafsīr*, *Ḥadīth*, etc. At this level, study was evidently deeper; and often it was the inadequacy of locally available scholars that compelled the Muslim Yoruba students to travel out to Ilọrin, Bida and such places in order to acquire knowledge. Abroad, some of these pupils went beyond accomplishment in the basic Islamic studies, and also tried to study Islamic law, poetry, *Tawḥīd* and other subjects, so long as they could find qualified teachers. It was essentially these advanced scholars who, on returning to their towns or some other Yoruba towns, set up as teachers not only at the secondary but also at the advanced level of Arabic studies in Yorubaland.

During the period under study there were quite a number of such scholars especially in the big Muslim cities of Yorubaland. We can mention only a few here: in Abẹokuta, Afa Erumbe and Afa Musulumi Dindi were prominent; there were Afa Egberongbe of Idiose and Alaji Agbaji in Isẹyin; Afa Sunmonu and Badiru in Iwo; and Ẹpẹ had scholars in their Imams, Afa Onitafusiru and others of the type of Braimah Edu, an influential Balẹ and Muslim stalwart. But perhaps Ibadan had the pride of scholarship in such distinguished people as Imam Qifu, Shaikh Abu Bakr b. al Qasim and Shaikh Omo Alaga. Particularly noteworthy were Muhammad, alias Afa Oke-Koto, the author of a number of works on Islamic law; and Ahmad al-Rifai b. Bello, the author of a number of works on *Madh* and history of Islam in Ibadan, who later became the first Mufti of Yoruba Imams and Mallams.

The local scholars were like literary oases, attracting many eager but famished students. They brought Islamic education almost literally to the very doorsteps of the Yoruba Muslim, for around each one of them grew an ever-expanding circle of local pupils, far exceeding the number that could travel outside Yorubaland to slake their thirst for Islamic education.

A large number of subjects was taught – *Tafsīr*, grammar, *Ḥadīth*, law, history, poetry, etc. On each of these subjects there were usually one or two popular books which were current and served as textbooks.

By far the most popular and deeply studied subject was *Tafsīr*. For a long time the study and teaching of *Tafsīr* was based principally on the short ethical work *Mawā'iz bāligha min Zabūr Dawūd*.[135] Divided into thirty sections, the book is filled with religious admonitions and homilies, and had a tremendous influence in shaping the ethical character of Islam in Yorubaland. Later this work was supplemented and virtually superseded by the scholarly and famous *Tafsīr al-Jalālain*[136] (Commentary on the Qur'ān by the two Jalals) which was begun by Jalāl al-Dīn al-Maḥallī, and finished by Jalāl al-Dīn al-Suyūṭī.[137] Extracts from this and other sources were current; for example, *Tafsīr Yāsin li al-Jamā'a*[138] was used and studied.

On the *Ḥadīth*, many compilations were available in various collections but the popular ones were the *Ṣaḥīḥ* of al-Bukhari and Abū Muslim. Fairly well known were the *Ḥadīth* as related by Huraira and 'Abdullāh b. 'Umār. Other compilations of the *Ḥadīths* were contained in the *Maṭīyat al-Zād* by Abdallāh b. Muḥammad[139] and the *Kitāb al-Muntabih 'an al-Isti' dād li yawn al-mi''ād*, a book which warns about the last Day by copious references to *Ḥadīth* and sayings of the four rightly-guided *caliphs* and others.

On religion, miscellaneous other works were available for study. Only a few examples can be given. There were *Shāhadat al-Islām* by Muḥammad b. 'Abd al-Raḥmān b. 'Abdullāh b. Abī Bakr b. Muḥammad b. Salīm al-Awjalī; and *Qawā'id al-Islām* by a notable Maghribī scholar, al-Qurṭubī (c. 1093–1172).[140] The *Qawā'id al-ṣalāt* by Muḥammad Bello was also well known and studied.[141] On *Tawḥīd*, there were such works as *'Ilm al-Tawḥīd* by Abū Bakr b. Muḥammad b. Abī Bakr.[142] Fairly popular were the anonymous works *Kitāb fī Tawḥīd* and the *Kitāb al-Tawḥīd*, the latter of which describes the attributes of God and strongly asserts a conception of Him that is spiritual and not anthropomorphic in a way that easily brings to mind the *Muwaḥḥid* movement of twelfth-century Maghrib.[143] A popular work which taught the pillars of the faith (*arkān al-Islām*) was the poetical composition by Muḥammad b. Nasir.[144] On the Ṣalāt, there were many works. Some were short selections from *Ḥadīth* by Shaikh Abū Al-Walīd;[145] or the *Ṣalāt* by Shihāb al-Dīn.[146] Others were longer and elaborate, such as the *Qawā'id al-Salāt*[147] a work divided into fifteen parts, dealing with various issues about prayer, beginning from *dukhūl al-waqt* to *tark al-kalām*.

For both religious and perhaps literary reasons, many poems were studied.[148] There were straightforward religious poems like *Muniyat al-Murid* by Ibn Bābā al-'Alawī al-Maghribī,[149] or the popular Madḥ poems including the *Qaṣīda fī al-Madḥ* by 'Al Aḥmad b. 'Īsa and the *Durr al-durar fī Madḥ khair al-bashar* by

'Alī b. Muḥammad b. Ḥusain.[150] Many were those in praise of
the Holy Prophet; these were, and still are, generally memorised.
Two of the most fascinating of these were anonymous poems, one
beginning *Hal mā shi'ta fī dārain*[151] (If you wish to be happy in
both worlds) and the short but golden poem by al-Badamāsī.[152]
Fairly popular also were the poems on each letter of the alphabet.
The poems by Shaikh al-Haysubi and Muḥammad al-ḥajj 'Abd
Al-Raḥmān al-Bainani[153] were among the most cherished ones.
Some of these poems are didactic and ethical, praising famous men
in general. For example, there were the popular anonymous poems
Maqāma ladā sidrat al-muntahā;[154] and the poem by Muḥammad
'Abdullāh b. Abī Zaid al-Qairawānī, which seeks to inspire
people to knowledge (*'ilm*) and work (*'amal*) rather than to wealth
(*māl*) and day-dreaming (*āmāl*).[155] Others were simply panegyric
out-pourings about Allāh, religion and so on; for example, the
simple flowing poem, *al-ḥamdu l-Allah Huwa al-wāhid*.[156] But
many of this class of works were anonymous, for example the
Raghba ladā Allāh and the *Kitāb al-Anwār*, and sometimes in
praise of some famous scholars,[157] such as Haruna, Afa Bida, and
Afa Suleiman of Iwo.

These books constituted the basic sources used for instruction
in open-air or special preaching. It was not unusual to draw on
works on law, history and other relevant studies. In particular,
certain short sermons on various themes were sometimes consulted; for example the *wa'ẓ* by a certain 'Abd al-Rahmān b.
'Awf[158] which deals with literature, society, and forgiveness of
sins; and the *Fī ladā al-durr*, in which the author, Muḥammad b.
al-Wardī, dwells on the terrors of the Judgement Day (*ahwāl
yawn al-qiyāma*).[159] There was also the short composition by a
certain Muḥammad b. Jibrīl b. Muḥammad al-Kuqināwī, which
he called *Tafakkur*[160] (Reflections).

On law, the standard work used was the famous compendium,
the *Risāla*, by Ibn Abī Zaid al-Qairawani together with the
Mukhtaṣar of Khalīl b. Isḥāq al-Jundī, a fact which immediately
reveals which school of law was popular among the Yoruba
Muslims. This book was also supplemented by others, such as the
al-'Ashmāwiyya[161] and the *mubtadi fī ba'd al-sharī'a*, an anonymous work[162] dated 1277 A.H. (1860/1). Divided into twenty
sections, this work gives, largely on the basis of the *Ḥadīth*,
rulings on funerals, prayers, marriage etc. and the punishment for
various offences such as adultery, sodomy and taking of alcohol.

Another work bearing on law was the collection of queries and rulings called the *Kitāb Jumlat al-Masā'il wa al-fatāwī* by a certain 'Alī b. al-Ḥusain al-Samidi.[163]

Religious studies apart, Arabic grammar, history, arithmetic and astrology were also studied by the inquisitive pupils. The grammar books were detailed, including the *al-Alfiyya* of Ibn Mālik. There were various books, such as *Milh I'rāb* and *Kitāb al-naḥw*, one by a Maghribian scholar, 'Abdallāh Muḥammad b. Muḥammad b. Dawūd al-Ṣinhājī,[164] another by Shams al-Dīn al-Basrī,[165] and yet another by Muhammad b. Mu'tī b. 'Alī al-Sūdānī.[166] Pertinent to this study also was the *Risāla fī'l-tajwīd* (a Letter on Intonation) by 'Abd al-' Azīz al-Naqshabandī.[167]

The history books used show that there was a tendency to study in great detail the life of the Prophet as well as the history of the Arabs and of Islam; available was even a book on the Pharaohs who ruled Egypt, written by ibn M-n-b-h.[168] Arithmetic (Hisāb) and astrology generally went together, and they were both studied for their divination value. Mentioned late, but certainly one of the most popular, treasured works was that literary showpiece, the *Maqāmat* (Assembly) by Abū Muḥammad al-Qāsim b. 'Alī al-Harīrī.[169] This was available in various selections and compilations.

A survey of these works strongly reveals how dependent the Yoruba scholars and Muslims were on external sources for their Islamic education. Many of the books were famous books from the Maghrib. Many more were from the immediate Sudanese belt, and a few came in from Kumasi. There was also a significant number of compositions by some notable scholars from Bornu, Kano and of course, Sokoto.

The method of studying these subjects requires to be discussed. On each subject, the prospective student chose a textbook, usually the primer, and, furnished with this, he sought a teacher or teachers who guided him through it. On completing this, he took up another text book in the same or a related field; and again he sought out the appropriate teachers. If there were other pupils of the same level of knowledge, then a class was formed at the feet of the particular teacher.[170] It was certainly not unusual to have the same teacher conducting classes on subjects ranging from Arabic grammar to law. Many teachers and students were peripatetic. The process of education had its own logic and system, but has been criticised as being long and laborious; [171] this feeling helps to explain why it took some time for scholars to emerge among the Yoruba Muslims who had attained any high level of proficiency in Islamic studies.

The knowledge which these scholars disseminated to their students was absorbed slowly but surely. However, the social and religious impact of the scholars on the community was more immediate. Under their guidance, most Yoruba Muslim communities could celebrate all the important Muslim festivals and rituals properly: *Mawlīd al-Nabī*, *'Ashūrā'*, *Lailat al-Qadr*, etc. Perhaps none personified this community influence of the Muslim scholar better than Alli of Kishi.[172] As a young man, he was the first Onitafusiru in Kishi to use, in place of the time-honoured *Zabūr* of Dawūd, the commentary of Jalāl al-Dīn al-Suyūtī at the Ramadan lectures. It was he who introduced into Kishi the *dhikr* of Shaikh Tijānī, and the celebration of 'Īd al-Mawlīd. He was first made a Balogun and later became the Chief Imam of the whole community.[173] Many were converted by him and were taught Islam. Above all, since this mallam, preacher, teacher and missioner was the first person in that town to go to Mecca, he again thereby set a new standard for the community.[174] In such ways, scholars stood as the leaders of the religious community. It was largely in appreciation of their services that poems were composed later in their memory.[175]

Besides the remarkable degree of Islamic expansion in this period, there were the noticeable beginnings of a reform movement within Islam. These beginnings had two aspects. First, there was the feeling that the Yoruba practice of Islam could be made 'to look more modern', by accepting such Western ideas as were compatible with Islam.[176] A remarkable illustration of this new development was the novel way in which the *'Īd al-Fitr* was celebrated in Lagos in March 1895, when the Muslims gathered together at various centres in Lagos and held public tea parties.[177] Ordinary as this might seem today, it was spectacular in 1895; as tea symbolised Western habit and taste. The 1895 practice became popular, marking not only the beginning of such Muslim parties but also the percolation into the Muslim community of some 'Western' ideas.[178]

The move to modernise Islam developed, and resulted in the formation of the Killa Society. This society (Ẹgbẹ Killa, as it was generally called) was first formed in Lagos around 1895 possibly in admiration of that impressive Muslim, Abdallah Quillam about whom more will be said later.[179] This society comprised a group of fashionable Muslimmen who, like members of the former

Muslim societies,[180] added colour and gaiety to Muslim ceremonies whether public or private. They also cherished mutual self-help. But this Killa Society differed from the previous socio-religious associations in one very important respect: its members were prepared to bring to their co-religionists such enlightened and progressive ideas as they conceived acceptable to Islam. This society was the most popular, widespread, and colourful among the Yoruba Muslims. It became popular first in Lagos; and afterwards in Abẹokuta, Ẹpẹ, Ijẹbu-Ode, Ọyọ and Ogbomọṣọ, to mention only a few towns. These hinterland societies were each called Killa Society but they were virtually autonomous, being independent of the parent one in Lagos. Nevertheless, they performed functions similar to those of Lagos, whose style they copied.

This modernisation movement later coalesced with the subsequent desire to spread Islamic knowledge and improve the practice of Islam among the Yoruba, together inspiring the formation of the Nigerian Ahmadiyya Movement in 1911 and of Young Ansar Ud-Deen in 1920.

In step with the new Western ideas which were penetrating the Muslim community, there were fresh vistas which opened before the Muslims, largely as a result of administrative changes taking place in the country. There were important Muslim individuals who took up new roles in this changing society; they had seats in the native councils that were being set up at the turn of the century. In the Ẹgba Council of 1899, there were Sule Ọba Imale and a couple of other Muslims, such as Yesufu, who must have owed their seats to their positions as titled Muslims: Osi Balogun and Seriki respectively.[181] In the Ẹpẹ Provincial Council of 1901[182] there were Disu Kujeniya, the Muslim Balẹ, Braimah Edu, Yesufu Waki and Sanusi Alawusa. The Native Council of Ijẹbu-Ode had Muslim members.[183]

Some notable local Muslims were also paid stipends by the government which, apparently realising that Islam was a force to be reckoned with, tried to harness the influence of such men to the machinery of government. In this regard, one recalls the names of Balogun Kuku of Ijẹbu-Ode; Seriki Abass of Badagry; and Sule of Abẹokuta. These Muslim leaders were much respected by the government. Sule, for example, was to Denton 'a man of fine presence and agreeable dignified manners [he was] by far the most intelligent [of the Council members]'.[184] And the government's respect and need for Abass was such that he was later appointed the Senior Chief of Ilaro Division, exercising considerable administrative and judicial authority.[185]

Consistent with this new tendency was the service of Muslims on the larger and more important administrative bodies which were being set up for the country. In 1897 the Native Advisory Board was established by MacCallum in order to meet some French menace along the western borders of the colony.[186] About half its membership was Muslim.[187] When the board gave way in 1901 to the Central Native Council set up by Sir William MacGregor, about half the council's membership was composed of Muslims.[188] Indeed, some of the Muslim members, such as Imam Buraimọ, Yesufu Bey, Kasumu Giwa and Ali Balogun, had been members of the defunct Native Affairs Board. Unlike the membership of the board, the coverage extended beyond Lagos to include the whole colony, and Muslims such as Braimah Edu and Seriki Abass represented Ẹpẹ and Badagry respectively. Throughout the active life[189] of the council, Muslim members, for example Sule Giwa, Ali Balogun and Braimah Edu, took an active part in its deliberations. They participated rather as council members than as Muslims or representatives of their religious group.

It is clear from the above that the Muslims were becoming fairly well represented on some of the early administrative establishments in the country. These new developments were significant for the history of Islam. It is true that this rise of a class of Muslims in the service of the government created some tension between such Muslims and the traditional leaders of the Muslim community. In Ijẹbu-Ode, for example, the Muslim council members complained to the government that on resigning their seats on the council they 'were being subjected to much insult and persecution on account as they said of the progressive and enlightened manner in which they had carried out their duties as members of council'.[190] But internal struggles like the one between Seriki Abass and the officers of the Badagry Muslim community were occasional. More significant was the overall advantage which the Muslim community derived from the appointments and service of these people. As government officers – and particularly as respected officers – their prestige was enhanced and the stature of their religious community was increased. With the authority of the Senior Ilaro Chief, Seriki Abass did assist in the foundation and nurture of Islam in his town of Aiyetoro. He was no less a pillar of strength to the Badagry Muslim community.

Also, the new government appointments opened fresh avenues to Islam. Hitherto, Muslim political efforts had been within the traditional political structure. The establishment of British rule had altered the balance of political authority and influence. That Muslims now took up active service in this changing pattern and that that service was accepted by the Yoruba Muslims, showed how much the Muslims in Yorubaland were also prepared to keep abreast of the new changes in society.

As the Muslims spread into new areas, and moved into fresh avenues, it might well be supposed that they were having the best of both worlds. But the position of Islam faced a great potential threat under the new era of British rule.

Paradoxically, this threat issued from the establishment of native councils and courts. Under the Native Council Ordinance of 1901,[191] Native Councils were set up to enhance the prestige and Authority of chiefs for the purpose of administrative efficiency. They were to serve as a forum for local elders from various aspects of life to meet and discuss local problems in the customary fashion; the local British officer was to govern, with the assistance of the native council. And the Native Courts which were being set up were designed to enforce justice according to native law and custom. The application of the principle of native law and custom was not new in 1901. Before that date, it had been the spirit guiding British administration and had been occasionally given some forceful expression.[192] But by the establishment of the Native Councils and Courts the principle was given a legal force and there was now an elaborate opportunity for expression.

The operation of this system seriously affected the further development of Islam in Yorubaland. Before the introduction of the system, there was no doubt that Islam had been well established among the Yoruba. Where Islam had not arrived at the pinnacle of traditional political power, it had, in fact, permeated the political structure in varying degrees of intensity. Also, Yorubaland was becoming progressively Muslim, containing an increasing number of Muslim scholars.[193] But the introduction of the new system of administration and, in particular, the enforcement of the concept of the native law and custom both in the council and in the courts had some adverse effect on the multi-sided growth and, particularly, the politico-legal development of Islam among the Yoruba.[194] For example, in 1894 the Lagos Muslims had, it will be recalled,[195] petitioned the government that they should be ruled and judged in regard to their civil rights and grievances according to the Islamic system of law and justice. But the bedrock of British administration was the principle of government according to native law and custom which was meant to apply to all, including Muslims.[196] Consequently, the Muslim move was thwarted by the primacy of this fundamental principle of British administration; and the message of 1895 was as clear as its effects on the political development of Islam were final.

In places such as Abẹokuta and Ijẹbu-Ode, where Islam was fairly well established by the 1900s, there were, true enough, some Muslims in the councils and courts established. For example, among the thirty-five members of the Ẹgba Council in the Ẹgba Native Court, there were five Muslims. Two of these, Abudu Fọlami and Badaru Ajisegi, were, indeed, titled officers within the Ẹgba Muslim community, being Balogun of the Ẹgba Muslims and Balogun of the Oke-Ọna Muslims respectively. They were nominated largely because they were Muslims. The other three Muslims were important titled men and officials of the town: Bakare Shodeke, the Agura; Bakare Amusa, the Osi of the Ẹgba; and Aminu Ẹgbẹyẹmi, the Ẹkẹrin of the Ẹgba. But the potential Muslim influence of these five people in the native court was rendered otiose and ineffectual not so much by their small number as by their prescribed duty of enforcing native law and custom.

Even in Muslim towns such as Ẹpẹ, Iwo and Isẹyin, the numerical preponderance of Muslims, as well as their growing dominance in the political hierarchy of the town, was of little significance at this time, since power lay with the new council, which was expected to be guided by non-Islamic principles. This heightened the latent tension in a place like Ẹpẹ, between the predominantly Muslim Eko Ẹpẹ and the not-so-Islamised Ijẹbu Ẹpẹ, both of whom were brought together in the same council, the Ẹpẹ Provincial Council of 1901.[197] In this council there was Ogunbọna, the Ijẹbu Balẹ and a non-Muslim. He was probably expected to represent the non-Islamised Ijẹbu Ẹpẹ. The other five local members were all Muslims; indeed, they were the local leaders of the Muslim Eko Ẹpẹ Section. This council met at the house of one of its members, Braimah Edu, the Muslim Mọgaji (later Muslim Balẹ).[198] In its deliberations, however, the council was expected to guide itself by the principle of native law and custom. As a result, the latent friction between both groups was intensified; and a deadlock was reached which was resolved only by the dissolution of the council in 1904.[199] Each hereafter had its own council; the non-Muslim Ijẹbu one included the Oṣugbos, and the Ẹpẹ one was thoroughly Muslim.

Thus the politico-legal development of Islam in Yorubaland was in a way effectively threatened, though rather unintentionally; and the establishment of Native Councils and Courts marked the beginning of the loss of political power by Islam. Whatever lingering influence Islam could muster necessarily had to be 'backstairs'. This point will be appreciated further when it is realised that the Native Councils and Courts, and the principle of native law and custom, were part and parcel of British rule in Nigeria. It was all part of that 'era of colonial rule' (Yoruba: *aiye Ovinbo*), one of the unintended by-products of which was the part deprivation to Yoruba Islam of the opportunity for full political and legal development.

This checkmating of Muslim politico-legal influence later had wider repercussions for Islam. It will have been noticed that a chief stimulus to the growth of Islam in Yorubaland had been its possession of political influence.[200] With this new political arrangement, the corresponding compromise to the position of Islam can be perceived, even though this was not immediately apparent. Also, the legal development of Islam in Yorubaland was to be forestalled. Wherever possible, Islam endeavoured to install its own system of law and justice. This installation, generally gradual, often depended on the possession of political power. As Islam acquired increasing political influence in Yorubaland, especially from the closing decades of the nineteenth century, the next stage of development that could be expected was the introduction of Islamic system of law. But this stage was to be forestalled, with the establishment of British rule and its corollary enforcement of the principle of native law and custom on all. Thus the further growth of Islam and the introduction of Islamic concepts of government were precluded and undermined. And finding it a little difficult to play any significant public political or legal role, Islam was to restrict itself largely to the personal aspects of life.

The Muslims, meanwhile, never made an explosive issue of this politico-legal blockade. This was due to several factors, such as the localised form of Yoruba Muslim organisation; the paucity of Yoruba Muslim legists and reformers ready to press the issue; and the over-awing power behind British rule, the effects of which had only been recently felt everywhere.

Notes

1 I am grateful to Ajayi and Ayandele, the historians of Christianity in Yorubaland, for the information that liberated slaves constituted an important factor in the spread of Christianity in these areas at this time.

2 E. A. Ayandele, who is doing some work on this route, informs me that it had existed early in the nineteenth century; but it fell into disuse largely because of political disturbances, particularly in Ondo and Ifẹ, about the middle of the century.

3 Akintoye has identified some fairly important road-networks within this eastern route: the Oke–Aye Road (from Atijere–Itẹbu–Iju–Oke–Aye–Ondo); the Igbobini Road (Atijere–Oluwa river–Igbobini–Oke–Aye); Agbabu Road (Atijere–Agbaje Wharf–Agbabu). S. A. Akintoye, 'The Ondo Road Eastwards of Lagos c. 1870–95', *JAH*, x, 4, 1969, pp. 581–98.

4 In so far as this route relates to Ekiti wars, see S. A. Akintoye, *The Ekitiparapo and the Kiriji Wars.*

5 Charles Phillips noted that as the other routes to the coast were closed on account of the war, Ondo trade became very profitable, thanks largely to this eastern route. See his Annual Letter, 26 November 1880, in CMS G3 A2/01.

6 S. A. Akintoye in his article cited above declares the importance of this route for the spread of Christianity into this part of Yorubaland: 'Moreover, it was through the Ondo road that Christian missionary activity spread fruitfully into the eastern Yoruba country.'

7 CMS G2 A2/01, Annual letter of Charles Phillips, 26 November 1880. Out of the six women baptised on this day, five were Ondo by birth and this former Muslim was one of them. I have not been able to trace her name.

8 Phillips probably meant Ọyọ-speaking country here. Some of the early missionaries refer to the Ọyọ as the Yoruba.

9 CMS G3 A2/01, Charles Phillips's Journal for 1887. On 4 March he made the entry that he again 'had some conversation with another set of Lagos Mohammedans . . .'

10 Interview with al-hajj S. O. Oyenẹyin, Ondo, July 1965. Okoigi used to trade as far as Ilọrin, and, on becoming a Muslim, his dress was like that of a rich and typical Muslim of his times, complete with turban, *alikimba* (a short Muslim overcoat), etc.

Al-hajj S. O. Oyenẹyin was the secretary of the Ondo Central Mosque Committee, and has served the Muslim community in

various capacities. Aged about 58, he is the son of Chief Otun
Sadiku Oyenẹyin, an early Ondo Muslim, and displays a remarkable
knowledge of Ondo Muslim history. See Bibliography: Oral Evidence.

11 CMS G3 A2/05, Charles Phillips's Journal, June–August 1887.
Entry for Thursday, 9 June 1887.

12 S. O. Bada, *Iwe Itan Ondo* (Ondo, 1940), p. 62.

13 See Chapter 2 *et passim*, for earlier practices elsewhere.

14 al-hajj S. O. Oyenẹyin (ed.), *The Establishment of Muslim Religion in
Ondo* (MS.) (June 1965). This version of the history of Islam in
Ondo was taken down by al-hajj S. O. Oyenẹyin after a considerable
period of close interrogation with his fellow Ondo Muslims; its
contents were checked, verified and elaborated by the local Muslim
Central Mosque Committee. I am grateful to al-hajj S. O. Oyenẹyin
and the Committee for allowing me to make use of this document,
which is hereafter referred to as *Muslim Religion in Ondo.*

15 Interview with al-hajj S. O. Oyenẹyin, Ondo.

16 *Ibid.* 'O nigbiyanju ati fa enia mọra' ('He tries to draw people to
himself').

17 S. O. Oyenẹyin, (ed.) *Muslim Religion in Ondo, loc. cit.*

18 *Ibid.*

19 *Proceedings of the C.M.S., 1905–6* (London, 1906), p. 44.

20 S. O. Oyenẹyin (ed.), *Muslim Religion in Ondo.*

21 These titles, it will be noticed, are Ọyọ titles, but had become current
in the previous decades. On this, as well as on the structure of
Yoruba Muslim organisation, see Chapter 3, pp. 55–60.

22 CMS, G3 A2/05, Charles Phillips's Journal, June to August 1887.
He does not mention his name. Informants during interview could
only recall many of his type such as Afa Busari, Afa Lawa, and Afa
Kokewu kobere.

23 The Executive Committee of Ilẹsa Muslim Community, *Itan bi
Islam se de Ilesha*, 1965. This history is compiled after long and
detailed investigations among their elders. It was recorded by I. A.
Balogun, a grandson of Afa Amodu Farise of Egbe-Idi. It is hereafter
referred to as *Itan Islam ni Ilesa* (unpublished MS.). I am grateful to
Mr I. A. Balogun and the Committee for allowing me to use this
manuscript.

24 *Itan Islam ni Ilẹsa*, p. 1.

25 *Ibid.* This is quite understandable, in view of the relative instability
of the community at the time.

26 Interview with the Chief Imam and members of Executive Committee
of Ilẹsa Muslim community in June 1965 confirms this. Most helpful
in this interview were Chief A. K. Arowojobe, al-hajj S. A. Famuyide,
Chief Bello Risa Iro and al-hajj Musa Sarumi. They were all above
age 50, and had grown up as active Muslims in Ilẹsa.

27 *Itan Islam ni Ilẹsa*: 'Prince Abubakare Orimogunje yi jẹ ẹlẹsin
Muslim o si ṣe gugugudu meje fun Igbeyo ati isin Ọlọrun lọna Islam
laìsi ibẹru.' lit. 'Prince Abubakare Orimogunje was a practising
Muslim who gave all for the growth and worship of Islam without fear.'

28 J. F. Ade Ajayi, *Population Census of Nigeria, May 1962*, p. 373.

This Owas was a professing Christian. Captured at about the age of 12, he was sold into slavery but liberated and sent back from Sierra Leone. At Lagos he acquired some education until he was called to the throne about 1896; see Rev. F. Melville-Jones, 'Itinerating in Yorubaland', *Niger and Yoruba Notes*, No. 97, vol. v, July 1898, pp. 6–7, Rev. T. J. Dennis, 'From Oyo to the Niger', *Niger and Yoruba Notes*, No. 97, 9, July 1902, pp. 5–6.

29 As a half-brother of the Owa ('Ọba Ajimoko si jẹ ọbakan Abubakare . . .': see *Itan Islam ni Ilesa*), Abubakare evidently used his influence with the Ọwa.

30 For further information about these wars, see notably H. B. Hermon-Hodge, *Gazetteer of Ilorin Province* (London, 1929), pp. 70 *et passim*; S. Johnson, *The History of the Yoruba*, pp. 424ff.; Ahmad b. Abī Bakr, *Tā'līf Akhbar al-qurūn, min umarā blād Ilūrin*.

Some Islamic influence was exerted by Nupe through Akoko area; but this was comparatively small.

31 Interview in June 1965 with elderly members of the Muslim Community Ado-Ekiti such as Afa Jimo (over 50) the Chief Imam, Balogun Sanni (about 60), S. S. Balogun, the Secretary of the NUD, Ado-Ekiti. See Bibliography: Oral Evidence.

32 CMS G3 A2/07, Bishop C. Phillips's Report of a Tour to Ekiti and other areas, 20 June 1894.

33 CMS, G3 A2/0, T. Harding's Report of Visit to Ekiti Country and a few other places.

34 CMS, G3 A2/07, Bishop C. Phillips's Report of a Tour to Ekiti and other areas, 20 June 1894. He was informed by the Ajero that he was so incensed at the ruin of his country by Ilọrin that he had renounced Islam. The Ajero was Oba Oyinyo, *c.* 1867–1901. See J. F. Ade Ajayi, *op. cit.*, p. 379.

35 Father A. Oguntuyi, *A Short History of Ado-Ekiti*, Part II, p. 41. He describes this Ewi as a 'staunch Mohammedan'. He might have been such a Muslim privately; and Oguntuyi probably intends to emphasise here the Ewi's reliance on Muslim charms in effecting, in spite of all opposition, the return of Ado to their former site. He himself gives no evidence of what the Ewi did publicly to advance the cause of Islam.

36 Oguntuyi, *op. cit.*, pp. 52–67. Here he deals with the Ikere wars (1882–6).

37 Evidence given at the interview with the Muslim Community, Ado-Ekiti, in June 1965. Besides the Chief Imam, other leading members of the Muslim Community were helpful: al-hajj Saliu Ajijola, Chairman of Central Mosque Committee; S. S. Balogun, Secretary of the NUD, Ado-Ekiti; Balogun Sanni (about 60), a relation of the second Imam of Ado-Ekiti.

38 His son, the present Chief Imam of Ado-Ekiti, insists that he (Saliu Ayeni) was taken into captivity in *France*, where he became a Muslim. It has not been easy to find corroborating evidence, and caution has been maintained here in describing his foreign sojourn as being in 'a French-speaking country'.

39 J. F. Ade Ajayi has given these dates for Ewi Ajimudaoro, but it is well to note that a local historian, Oguntuyi (*op. cit.*) puts the beginning of his reign in 1886.
40 CMS, G3 A2/07, Bishop Phillips's Report of a Tour to Ekiti, 1894.
41 *Proceedings of the CMS*, 1908, pp. 31–2. This was a report from a certain African clergyman based in Ekiti. He was unnamed.
42 The evidence given on Ikẹrẹ-Ekiti here is derived from the interviews held with the Muslim Community and particularly in *Itan bi Esin Islam se de Ikẹrẹ* (unpublished MS.), prepared by that community. I am grateful to the Chief Imam and the other leaders of the Ikẹrẹ Muslim Community for allowing me to use this document.
43 Interview with leading elderly members of the Muslim Community, Ikere, May–June, 1965. Really informed about Ikẹrẹ history were people like Bakare Otun of Ile Bariba, Balogun Salami Odo-Oja, and Yesufu Adegbite. A committee set up by the community to record their history has produced an *Itan Esin Islam ni Ilu Ikẹrẹ-Ekiti* which, I am grateful to say, I have been allowed to use.
44 *Ibid.*
45 Akintoye says that the Ado–Ikẹrẹ war 'developed into prolonged desultory skirmishing with hostile camps facing each other at Ago, Igirimo, Awajiu in the forests between Ado and Ikẹrẹ'; S. A. Akintoye, *op. cit.*, p. 92. It is probably too much to write off this episode as being a military confrontation in the bush, for the war did have social consequences viewed as serious by the local community.
46 For a full account of this war see A. Oguntuyi, *op. cit.*, pp. 52–67.
47 See Note 43.
48 Interview with Bakare Otun (well over 70 years of age), in May 1965. He spent about five years at Ẹpẹ.
49 About Owo, caution is essential in handling the report of Archdeacon F. M. Jones and the Rev. H. F. Ganes which was published in *Proceedings of the CMS*, 1908, that in 1906, 'about 2,000 and 3,000' people were converted to Islam, and that later as these desired to overthrow the government, the Christian king expelled the Muslim teachers. There is no confirmatory evidence; and this piece may be a subtle Christian plea to overseas patrons for more money and men.
50 See Chapter 1.
51 Ipẹru was a walled town with a large market attended by Ẹgba, Ijẹbu and Ibadan traders. Its population was put in 1878 at 6,000; see CMS CA2/056, J. Johnson to Sec., CMS, 21 June 1878.
52 Interview in August 1963 with the Muslim community of Ipẹru. Present at the interview were the Chief Imam Yesufu Asani and other elders of the community.
53 This Odufote was not a Muslim, but he was the grandfather of an important man – the Chief Imam who was one of my informants.
54 This is the famous 'girigiri'; see Chapter 1.
55 CMS CA2/056, J. Johnson to Sec., CMS, 21 June 1878.
56 Interview with Chief Imam and members of the Muslim Community of Ṣagamu in the July and early August 1963. Present at the interview

and giving valuable information were people, who were sons and grandsons of those who had played some role in the establishment of Islam in Ṣagamu. Particularly helpful was the late Balogun.

57 The memory of this intrepid figure is still vivid. He is reported to have been a hard-fighting warrior ('alagbara ninu ogun'), who took part in certain local wars, such as the Agbete war between Egba and Makun, Gbedeke war, between Gbedeke and Makun, and the Ikene war. He was certainly short of patience, as suggested by his nickname, *Kodurogbejo* (he does not wait for explanations); but this notwith-standing, he was much admired. He spoke Hausa and some Yoruba and had no facial marks.

58 Interview with the Muslim community, Ṣagamu, Friday, 2 August 1963.

59 M. B. O. Apena, *Iwe Ikekuru ti Itan Ijebu*, pp. 28–9. Interviews with some Muslims in Ijẹbu-Ode also corroborate this evidence.

60 M. B. O. Apena, *op. cit.*, pp. 28–9. He writes: 'Olọrun bukun fun Alli yi lopolopo ju Oluwa re lo, tobe to je pe on lo gbe oruko Oluwa re yi ga ti a si npe oruko re ni Alli Tubogun. Bayi la fi npe oruko Alli ki a to daruko ogboni re titi di oni.'

61 M. B. O. Apena, *op. cit.*, p. 29. He was believed to have prepared some Muslim charms to facilitate the spread of Islam in the town.

62 As slaves were sometimes sold away and new ones brought in, the number of Muslim slaves fluctuated.

63 M. B. O. Apena, *op. cit.*, p. 28: 'Isin yi ko ja ma nkankan loju Ijẹbu' (lit: 'this religion meant nothing to the Ijẹbu'). See also CMS CA2/ 056, J. Johnson to Sec., CMS, 21 June 1878. Largely because of the humble status of these early Muslims in Ijẹbu, Johnson writes: 'The Jebus hate and detest the religion . . .' He, however, probably over-states the position and the more restrained language of Apena is here preferred.

64 The case of 'predestined Muslims' was by no means peculiar to Ijẹbu (see Chapter 3). It seems, however, to have been an important factor in some Ijebu towns.

65 Yoruba: 'Gbọ abawasaiye ọmọ'. It is a common practice for some Yoruba parents to do this.
     Scholars of Yoruba culture are all agreed on the familiar use which the Yoruba make of Ifa divination. On this, see A. B. Ellis, *The Yoruba-speaking Peoples of the Slave Coast of West Africa*; S. S. Farrow, *Faith, Fancies and Fetish*, pp. 35–6; J. D. Clarke, 'Ifa Divination', *JRAI*; W. R. Bascom, 'The Sanctions of Ifa Divina-tion', in *JRAI*; and his 'Ifa Divination: Comments on Clarke's Paper', *Man*; R. Prince: 'Indigenous Yoruba Psychiatry' in A. Kiev (ed.), *Magic, Faith and Healing: Studies in Primitive Psychiatry*. They all essentially agree to Idowu's finding that 'at any and all times, *Ifa* is consulted for guidance and assurance. As the saying goes, "Oni l'a ri, a o r'ola, on ni baba'lawo se nd'Ifa l'ororun – It is today we see, we do not see tomorrow, hence the babalawo consults the oracle every fifth day"'; E. B. Idowu: *op. cit.*, pp. 78–9.
     Clarke also writes that this divination is on the third day after

birth; but as already pointed out above, this can also be on the eighth day or at any other time during the tender age of the child.

66 'O ba 'Male wa saiye' (lit. 'he came down to the world with Islam', i.e. destined to be a Muslim).

Other children may be requested to devote themselves to other religious systems; see R. Prince, *op. cit.*, and J. D. Clarke, *op. cit.*

Ajayi Crowther's parents were told that Ajayi would worship '*Ọlọrun*'; see NAI, CMS (Y) 4/3/10, Ajayi Crowther: 'Omode Eru-kurin ti o di Bisopu tabi Itan Samuel Ajayi Crowther' (type-script, 1925).

67 Chapter 2, Note 11.

68 The Yoruba call this *saraa* or *saara*. Strictly speaking, this is not 'charity', as R. C. Abraham translated it in his *Dictionary of Modern Yoruba*. It is simply a party, a free-for-all party.

69 Interview in August 1963 with Afa Idris, the Chief Imam of Idowa, Afa Tijani Balogun Martins, the Onitafusiru, Saliu Yesufu, the Ẹkẹta Adini, and Seidu Ayoku, the Oloriọmọkewu.

70 There are examples of these predestined Muslims all over Yoruba-land, and one or two have been referred to above. It should be noted that information on this issue is often but not invariably given in 'whispers'.

71 The particular *Odu* divining Islam as being the religion for the child is *Otura Meji*.

72 Some writers, such as Prince and Clarke, rightly emphasise the intelligence of these diviners. Prince describes the diviner as 'often a good intuitive psychologist very much in tune with the peculiar stresses of his culture'; R. Prince, *op. cit.*, p. 111.

73 W. R. Bascom, *Ifa Divination*, pp. 11–12. Wande Abimola also describes Ifa as being 'the middle man between other gods and the people' and 'the public relations officer of all the other Yoruba gods'. Perhaps, Islam has now come to be regarded as 'a Yoruba god'. See W. Abimola, *An Exposition of Ifa Literary Corpus*, Ph.D., Lagos, 1969, p. 16.

74 Compare the situation in Mossi, where diviners induced many barren people to become Muslims by attributing their barrenness to the refusal of children to be born except as Muslims. See E. P. Skinner, 'Islam in Mossi Society' in I. M. Lewis (ed.), *Islam in Tropical Africa*, pp. 350–73.

75 For discussion about the other groups – artisans, wives, etc. – see Chapter 7.

76 It was suggested during some interviews that once a few such people adopted Islam, they often tried to convert their friends who were in their age-grade. Age-grades were, of course, popular in Ijẹbu, being formed every three years (see M. B. O. Apena, *op. cit.*, pp. 2–6; and T. B. Bovill-Jones; *Intelligence Report on Ijebu Ode Town and Villages*, May 1941.). Consequently, this factor may well have been important. But it seems to be all of a piece with a common practice of persuading one's friends and colleagues to team up with one.

77 Interview with the Ṣagamu Muslim Community, already cited.
78 This mosque was described as having had a capacity for about 120 people in 8 rows of about 15 each.
79 The exact date of his death is unknown but it was probably around 1895. He is also said to have died about four years after the age group, called Ilelaboye, had been born. He was survived by one Ejimo of the age group of Arobayo (*c.* 1873; see J. F. Ade Ajayi, *op. cit.* p. 153 *et passim*), who married and had a daughter, Olabo, of the same age-grade with the third Imam of Makun, al-hajj Sadiq.
80 Interview with Madame Oyeti, Iperu. The informant belongs to the age group of Obaneye and therefore was born *c.* 1881; see T. B. Bovill-Jones, *op. cit.*, p. 19. She also discloses much information about this Oyeti. His mother was Odute, his father Sobudu, both 'pagans.' He traded as far as 'Ile Oke' (upcountry) and had about ten slaves, some of them Muslims. On his return to Ipẹru he was, to all appearances, a Muslim – in speech, dress and mien (he had a big beard). He took the name of Bello and later became the Imam.
81 In passing, we may note how the English word 'care' becomes *kia* in this Yoruba passage.
82 Interview with the Chief Imam and others at Ipẹru – already cited. 'The Oro worshippers gave them no chance at all. The Muslims dared death on this issue. Those who could not stand very firm, who did not mind death, and who did not care for any consequences, could not be Muslims. So hard were the times.' Simply, this means that only brave people could be Muslims.
83 This was presumably with the connivance of the Ọba Okupe Agbonmagbe I.
84 Two of the three people who paid the workers of the mosques were the rich Muslim traders – Hassan Odufote, Alli, the Ladani, and Abudu Salami, the Seriki.
85 'Hassan gan lo jagun fun esin; awon lo to i ko awon oloro loju'. Lit.: 'This Hassan fought for Islam; only people like him could face the Oro worshippers.'
86 He stayed long in Ipẹru. He stayed with his Iseyin wife and probably one child for about one year with Hassan Odufote, and witnessed the rebuilding of the central mosque. Indeed, he is credited by some as having initiated the *Jum 'a* service in Ipẹru. When he was getting old, he returned home to Iseyin with his four daughters, leaving behind nothing but the admiration and gratitude of Ipẹru Muslims who owed so much to him. He received no pay.
87 Some of the most popular ones are still remembered.
    (i) *'Ejeki a gba Anabi gbo ka ma sonu'*
    (ii) *'Olorun ni ṣ'ola,*
    Anabi lọ nṣogo,
    Ẹnyin o ri ọla Muhamadu
    Bi o ti to bi laiye to.'
    Lit. (i) 'Let us believe in the Prophet so that we do not get lost'.
    (ii) 'It is God who provides wealth.
    It is the Prophet who provides honour,

See how the glory of Muhammad
Is so great the world over.'
88 Many are his pupils today in Ipẹru, notably the present Chief Imam.
89 This was probably about the middle of his reign (1852–82). The
mosque was built around 1891, but mosque-building often took some
time to complete.
90 M. B. O. Apena, *op. cit.*, p. 29, 'O si di asa awon borokini ilu lati
ma ba won gun esin lo si odun'. (lit. 'it became the habit of respectable gentlemen of the town to go on horseback to the festival'). This
was happening before the Ibadan pitched their battle at Oru in 1879.
91 It was this Awujale who granted the Muslim community a plot of land
at the outskirts of the town to use for the '*Íd* prayers. He donated
one pound on the occasion described above.
92 M. B. O. Apena, *op. cit.*, pp. 29–30.
93 CMS G3 A2/P4, Bishop Oluwole, Report of a Tour to Ijebu Ode
and Ijebu Igbo from 9 June to July 29 1896. This is also reported
in *Niger and Yoruba Notes*, iii, 28, October 1896, pp. 30–1.
94 *Ibid.*
95 NAI, CSO 1/1, Carter to Knutsford, Confid. of 14 July 1892.
96 *Ibid.*
97 S. Johnson, *op. cit.*, pp. 607–12. His house was near the Are Ẹgbẹ
Omo market. He writes that at Oru 'in the absence of the Balogun,
Kuku disposed justice to them and fair treatment against the grasping
and greedy Ijebus taking undue advantage' and that 'Kuku the
Seriki of Ijẹbu Ode had done much for the Ọyọ war chiefs and for
his own pocket by selling them rifles and cartridges at very high
prices'. The Ibadans were therefore prepared to repay his kindness.
98 NAI, CSO 1/1, Carter to Knutsford, Confid. of 14 July 1892; S.
Johnson, *op. cit.*, pp. 567, 608–9.
99 Carter to Knutsford, *ibid.*
100 *Ibid.* See also Carter to Knutsford, 266 of 17 August 1892. The
Awujale was granted £200 a year, Chief Kuku £100 a year and
Balogun Nafowokan, aged about 90, £50 a year.
101 *Ibid.* See also M. B. O. Apena, *op. cit.*, p. 33. Governor Carter who,
met Kuku at Ijẹbu-Ode on many occasions, writes in 1892 that Kuku
was rebuilding his house which the Ijebu had destroyed and that
'he has established a mosque in Ijebu Ode'. Carter to Knutsford, 266
of 17 August 1892, and Confid. of 14 July 1892.
102 In 1891, he had come down to Ijebu-Ode from Ife to donate five
shillings towards the building of the central mosque. See M. B. O.
Apena, *op. cit.*
103 M. B. O. Apena, *op. cit.*, p. 33. See also NAI CSO 1/1, Carter to
Knutsford, 17 August 1892.
104 *Ibid.*
105 Interview with various Muslims, notably B. A. Daramola (over 65), at
Ijẹbu-Ode, 1963 to 1967. One informant said that in the distribution of
white pieces of cloth for the new converts, many bales were exhausted.
106 *Daramola Papers*. See also Anon., *History of the Central Mosque,
Ijebu Ode* (Lagos, 1967);M. B. O. Apena, *op. cit.*p. 33.

107 Letter received on 19 March 1902 and quoted in CMS G3 A2/010, Oluwole to Bishop Tugwell, 7 April 1902. He also confirmed Kuku's conversion and its impact of Ijebu. He added that among these converts were schoolteachers and pupils of the Christian schools.

108 Interviews at Ijẹbu-Ode and other towns confirm this. See Bibliography: Oral Evidence.

109 See 'The Needs of the Ijẹbu Country' by Bishop Oluwole in *Niger and Yoruba Notes*, No. 96, vol. 8, June 1902, Bishop Oluwole records that there has been 'recently a very large accession to Mohammedanism in the Jebu country. This has been mainly brought about by a chief of great influence embracing it'.

110 *Ibid.*

111 O. Ayantuga: *The Ijebu and Its Neighbours*, p. 316.

112 Rev. R. Coker noted the preference of the Chiefs and elders of Ijẹbu-Ode to 'see their people embracing Islam'. *Niger and Yoruba Notes*, No. 52, vol. V, October 1898, pp. 30–1.

113 *Ibid.* See also *The Twenty-Sixth Report of the Lagos Church Missions for the Year 1907* (Exeter, 1908), pp. 14–15. Rev. R. A. Coker, who was the Superintendent of Ijẹbu-Ode District of the Lagos Church Mission, used this expression since he observed Islam had 'become the predominant religion'. His observations were confirmed by Bishop Herbert Tugwell in 1910: Ijẹbu 'today . . . appears to be wholly Mohammedan'; CMS G3 A2/013, Herbert Tugwell.

114 *Proceedings of the C.M.S.*, 1908, pp. 31–2.

115 See Chapter 3, p. 52. See also *Niger and Yoruba Notes*, v, 57, March 1899. Here Rev. F. Melville-Jones recorded a first-hand experience at Isẹyin on his way to Shaki. A 1905 government publication estimated Isẹyin Muslims at 500 out of a population of 20,000; see Lagos Colony Government Notices, 7 June 1905. This is dubious in view of overwhelming evidence to the contrary.

116 NAI, CSO 26, F. C. Fuller, *Report for the year 1900 on that portion of the Lagos Hinterland under the control of the Resident*. By independent calculation Rev. A. W. Smith corroborated this evidence: *Report of the Proceedings of the Third Session of the First Synod of the Diocese of Western Equatorial Africa*. A government rough estimate in 1904 put the number of Muslims in Ibadan at 9,000 but did not give the total population of Ibadan; see *Lagos Colony Government Gazette*, 9 January 1904.

117 *Report of the Proceedings of the Third Session of the First Synod of the Diocese of Western Equatorial Africa* (Exeter, 1908). Data were based on enquiries sent out to local missionaries. See Appendix V.

118 *Ibid.*

119 *Ibid.*

120 *Lagos Government Gazette*, 2 November 1901. Muslims numbered 22,080 out of a population of 41,847.

121 *Ibid.*

122 NAI, CSO 26, F. C. Fuller, *op. cit.*

123 Rev. A. W. Smith in the Synod Report already cited. See Appendix V.

124 CMS CA2/o56, Johnson's Report, January–February 1878; and S. Johnson to Tugwell, 20 July 1896, in *Niger and Yoruba Notes*, v, 29, 111, November p. 35.

125 J. A. Atanda has tried to show that in the colonial era, a new Ọyọ 'empire' was created under the Alafin. This empire was larger than the former, although ultimate sovereignty lay with the British Government; J. A. Atanda, 'The New Ọyọ Empire: a Study of British Indirect Rule in Ọyọ Province, 1894–1934'.

126 Lawani was the Aremo (first son) of Adelu (1859–75). His attempt to succeed his father had failed because, according to a contemporary account, 'he had proved himself so cruel and overbearing' (see Enclosure 2 in Higgins Report, C.5144); CMS CA2/o40, A. F. Foster's Journal for the Quarter ending December 1875). As an unsuccessful candidate to the throne, he had to leave Oyo (J. A. Atanda; *op. cit.* p. 132, fn. 1) and he stayed at Ibadan, enjoying the protection of Muhammad Are Latosisa, until he returned to Oyo to ascend the throne in July 1905.

127 This was probably the first Muslim Awujalẹ; the second was Awujalẹ Fibiwoga (Prince Alli Ogunnaike) 1929–33, and the third is al-hajj Sikiru Adetona, Ogbagba 1959 – who is on the throne now. We draw attention here to the statement by O. Ayantuga, *op. cit.*, p. 316, that Awujalẹ Anikilaya, 1895–1905, was a Muslim.

128 B. Awe, *The Rise of Ibadan*, Chapter I shows this inter-relationship. See Chapter 1.

129 For the role of cities and towns in initiating and perpetuating changes in behaviour patterns and institutional changes, see R. Lee, *The City: Urbanism and Urbanisation in Major World Regions*, New York, 1955.

130 That Islam spread as a result of social disturbances (see W. Watt, 'Some Problems before West African Islam', *Islamic Review Quarterly*) obviously is, at best, only partially true.

131 Interview in April 1965 with the present Afa Kokewukobere of Ilọrin (over 60). A nephew of Muhammad Salisu, he also bears the appellation of Kokewukobere and through his father, Muhammad Salisu, this Afa had gathered considerable information about the veteran preacher. He was very useful in providing much information about him, confirming and enriching what I also gathered in my enquiries at the various Yoruba towns where Kokewukobere had preached and taught.

132 By far the most popular one (from which he derived his nickname) was

    'Ko kewu, ko bere,
    Bawo ni yio ti ṣe la?
    Ko kewu, ko bere.
    Bawo ni yio ti ṣe la?'

lit.: 'He does not read Arabic, he makes no enquiries,
    How will he be saved?
    He does not read Arabic, he makes no enquiries,
    How will he be saved?'

This ditty he rendered sometimes in Arabic:
'Lam yaqra,' wa lam yas'alu
Kaifa naja?
Lam yaqra', wa lam yas'alu
Kaifa naja?'
This was intended to spur his listeners to a good knowledge of Islam so that they might practise Islam better and be saved. 'Kewu' or 'Arabic' here is understood by the Yoruba to mean not simply a language but *the* language of Islam as well as Islamic tenets.

133 See Chapter 2.

134 The Muslims believe they follow this 'straight path' mentioned in al-Fatiḥa, the opening *Sūra* of the Qur'ān.

135 This work purports to be selections from the Zabūr (psalms) of David and other 'revealed sources'. Strictly speaking, it is not *tafsīr*; but the Yoruba Muslims found the book useful in their preaching because of its general religious and ethical character.

136 This work was published in Cairo in 1305 and often since then. Among the Yoruba it was copied by hand.

137 Jalāl al-Dīn 'Abd al-Raḥman b. Abi Bakr al-Suyūtī (1445–1505). A distinguished Egyptian scholar, al-Suyūtī showed remarkable versatility in his varied compositions. This particular Qur'anic commentary is one of his compendious world-famed books; see R. A. Nicholson, *A Literary History of the Arabs*, pp. 454–5. See his *Kitāb al-Itqan fī colum al-qur'ūn* (Cairo, 1871).

138 This is a commentary on Sūra Yasīn, Qur'an, chapter 36. Since this chapter is regarded with special reverence by the Muslims, we can understand why this separate commentary on it was popular. We do not know the author of this *tafsīr* on the *sūra*.

139 This may well be the same *Maṭīyat* by 'Abdallāh b. Fūdī – a work cited by D. M. Last in 'Sokoto in the Nineteenth Century with Special Reference to the Vizierate', p. 395. It is available in UIL, as 82/13.

140 C. Brockelmann, *Geschichte der Arabischen Litteratur*, I, 737. The work is not cited.

141 W. E. N. Kensdale, *A Catalogue of Arabic Manuscripts in the University Library, Ibadan*, p. 2.

142 This work was found first with Al-hajj Jimọ Parakoyi of Ọyọ in June 1963. It is available in UIL, 82/258, 325, and 526.

143 This is the movement founded by Muḥammad b. Tummar (*c.* 1078–*c.* 1130) in the Maghrib, and which established the famous al-Muwahid dynasty (*c.* 1133–1269); see P. Hitti, *History of the Arabs*, pp. 546–8. The works cited are found in many places, notably in Ọyọ, with al-hajj Parakoyi and the Imam.

144 Two copies of this were found with Afa Ara Ọyọ, in Ọyọ, 1963.

145 This deals with prayers and search for knowledge. There are many copies, but the one referred to here was found with al-hajj Jimọ Parakoyi in Ọyọ.

146 UIL, 82/490, 82/509. The latter work is listed as *Kitāb fī al-Ṣalāt*.

147 In this work, the pillars of prayers are accepted to be fifteen according to the belief of such scholars as Shaikh al-Imām, Aḥmad b. Ḥanbal, in contradistinction to Shaikh 'Alī who maintained they were eighteen.

148 El-Masri communicates that it was popular to have religious texts versified in order to facilitate memorisation.

149 UIL has copies of this: 82/468, 472, 476, and 493.

150 UIL 82/508/M29.

151 This work is now published in Adam 'Abdullāh al-Alūrī, *al-fawāk al-sāqita* (Cairo, n.d.), pp. 12–13.

152 UIL 82/42, 119; see also W. E. N. Kensdale, *op. cit.*, p. 3.

153 He is the author of *Tarīkh usul madīna al-k-s-n-ī usul Gubr*; UIL 82/467.

154 This has been found with various mallams in Yorubaland. A good copy can be found in NAK, catalogue KD.25,2. See also al-Alūrī, *op. cit.*, pp. 10–11.

155 C. Brockelmann, *op. cit.*, I, 301. See also UIL, 82/471, 82/480. See also al-Alūrī, *op. cit.*, p. 17. He is the author of *Kitāb al-Risāla*, in NAK, KD. 1, 40; C. Brockelmann, *op. cit.* I, 177.

156 Quite a number of these were found with al-hajj Kasimu in Iseyin, 1963, and al-hajj Abegunde in Ogbomọṣọ.

157 These works were found in Iseyin, through the efforts of the mallams. Some are available in CAD–248.

158 *Ibid.*

159 *Ibid.*; see also UIL.

160 UIL, 82/367.

161 C. Brockelmann, *op. cit.*, II, 435.

162 This is most probably a local work, citing as it does 'Uthmān b. Fūdī.

163 Iseyin Manuscripts. Seen with the mallams there.

164 Brockelmann, *op. cit.* II, 332. He is listed here as Muḥammad b. Muhammad al-Sinhājī b. Ajrum. al-Sinhājī is also well-known locally for his work on syntax, al-Ajurrumiyya mentioned in C. Brockelmann, II, 237. A. S. Arif and A. M. Abu-Hakima, *Descriptive Catalogue of Arabic manuscripts in Nigeria*, London, 1965, p 49 *et passim*.

165 UIL, 82/180, 181, 338. This may well be the same person as Muhammad b. Mu'tī b. Alī al-Kanawi who wrote the *Muqaddima fī a'l-I'rāb*.

166 Brockelmann, *op. cit.*, II, 925, 109.

167 Brockelmann, *op. cit.*, II, 282 refers to a certain Muḥammad b. Muḥammad b. Muḥammad Naqshabandī al-Bukhārī.

168 This author may be Wahb of Persian origin, who was 'one of the chief sources of information or misinformation about ibn Munbbih (*c.* 728), a Yemnite Jew of pre-Islamic Arabia and foreign land. See P. Hitti, *op. cit.*, p. 244. The full title of the book is *Masalat Hikayat al-Fara ina al-ladhina malakū Miṣr*.

169 al-Harīrī (1054–1122) modelled his work after that of al-Hammad-hani. See P. Hitti, *op. cit.*, p. 403.

170 This was a popular method in the Sudan. Compare the way

'Abdullāh b. Fūdī was educated, according to his own description in *Kitāb al-baraka* . . . translated by M. Hiskett, 'Material relating to the state of learning among the Fulani before the Jihad', BSOAS. See also M. Smith, *Baba of Karo*, pp. 131–4, about itinerant teachers.

171 Compare also the system in Hausaland. See J. B. Abuja, 'Koranic and moslem Law Teaching in Hausaland, *Nigeria*, 37, 1951; and P. Allison: 'Koranic Schools in Northern Nigeria', *West African Journal of Education*. See also M. Hiskett: 'Problems of Religious Education in Muslim Communities in Africa', *Overseas Education*.

172 Interview with the Chief Imam and Muslim community of Kishi.

173 He was the seventh Imam of Kishi. See Appendix I for the full list of Chief Imams of Kishi.

174 He was advanced in age when he performed his pilgrimage; but age is no barrier for this religious exercise, which is expected to be done at least once in a lifetime.

175 See p. 102 for a mention of a few of these.

176 For information as to how the Muslims accepted Western education, see Chapter 5.

177 *Lagos Standard*, 27 March 1895.

178 In a way, this move can be conceived as an attempt to solve a problem that Watt and others see as facing Islam in West Africa – the problem of Westernisation. See W. Watt, *Islamic Philosophy and Theology*; I. M. Lewis (ed.), *op. cit.*, pp. 86–91.

179 Interview in Lagos with some leading Muslims, particularly Afa Ekemode; see Chapter 6.

180 See Chapter 3.

181 NAI, CSO 1/2, Acting Governor to Secretary of State, 27 January 1899.

182 See the reports by H. Childs and E. J. Gibbons: *op. cit.* This Council was set up by Ordinance No. 15 of 1901; see *Lagos Government Gazette*, No. 55 of November 1901.

183 It should be appreciated that there were almost invariably Christian members on these Councils as counterparts. In Abẹokuta, to cite just one example, the presence of the Balogun of Ẹgba Muslims was matched by that of the Balogun of Ẹgba Christians.

184 NAI, CSO 1/1, Acting Governor to Secretary of State, 27 January 1899.

185 *Abass Papers*. These records bear out how much he exercised this influence. See Bibliography.

186 MacCallum to Blyden, 28 October 1897, in *Correspondence Relative to the Appointment of Blyden as Agent of Native Affairs*, UIL, hereinafter referred to as *Correspondence: Blyden*. Henry Carr was the Secretary of the Board.

187 MacCallum to Colonial Secretary, 28 October 1897, in *Correspondence: Blyden, loc. cit.* Out of its eleven members, six were Muslims, namely, Brimah Imam, Seidu Olowu, Yusaf Bey, Sunmanu Okere, Ali Olori Balogun and Kasumu Giwa.

188 Minutes of the Central Native Council in the Library of University of Ibadan. There were initially 24 members of the Council among

whom were about 14 Muslims, namely, Imam Buraimo, Kasumu Giwa, Sufianu Giwa, Asani Giwa, Sule Giwa, Yesufu Shitta Bey, Balogun Sumonu Okete, Seidu Ogbogun, Seidu Olowo, Ali Balogun, Aibu Lemomu, Yesufu Agoro, Braimah Edu of Epe and Seriki Abass of Badagry.

189 S. M. Tamuno, *The Rise and Development of British Administrative Control of Southern Nigeria, 1900–1912*, pp. 182–93. 1903 is the year which Tamuno describes as the 'golden year' of the council. The council had eight recorded sessions in that year.

190 CO 19091, Acting Governor to Lyttelton, 3 May 1904. The Imam and Noibi denied there was any such feelings towards them, but clearly there was no harmony or love. And the Awujale hinted that these members might have misused their position by receiving undue financial considerations from persons applying in the bush for permits to cut timber under provisions of the Forestry Ordinance. This, however, reveals the tension that can develop.

191 *Colony of Lagos Gazette*, 1901, pp. 648ff.

192 See, for example, the speech of Acting Governor Denton to an assembly of Awujale, Ijebu Chiefs and people on 27 February 1899. Reporting the occasion to his Home Government, he declared that he let it be distinctly understood not only that the Awujale and his chiefs were alone the persons to hear and dispose of all cases but also that the native laws of the country applied equally to Christians, Muslims and pagans alike: see NAI, CSO 1/2, Denton to Chamberlain, 3 April 1899. For further development of this point, see M. Crowder and O. Ikime (eds.), *West African Chiefs*, African Publishing Corporation, Ife, 1970, xix-xxii and J. A. Atanda, *The New Oyo Empire*, Longman, 1973, pp. 123–7

193 See Chapter 3.

194 It has been pointed out that even a straightforward enforcement of this principle was sometimes rendered difficult, for there was considerable dispute over not only what native law and custom were but even over which particular one to enforce in a council area that was composed of many nicely distinguished laws and custom. See S. M. Tamuno, *op. cit.*, pp. 99–100.

195 See Chapter 3, p. 69.

196 *The Lagos Weekly Record*, 21 July 1894. Blair, *Intelligence Reports, Abeokuta* (unpublished MS.), in UIL.

197 Ordinance No. 15 of 1901 in *Lagos Government Gazette*, No. 55 of November 1901.

198 NAI, H. Childs and E. J. Gibbons, *op. cit.*, para. 74.

199 *Ibid.* This report gives details of this council, the proceedings of which have not been traced.

200 See Chapter 3.

5 The challenge of Christianity, 1875-1908

The development of Islam in the nineteenth century was accompanied by the rise of Christianity and the establishment of British rule, two important new forces which were rapidly and effectively making their influence felt in Lagos and its hinterland. It is, therefore, essential to describe the relationship between Islam and these forces in Yorubaland, and the effects of this on the history of the Yoruba Muslim communities. These new forces in Yoruba society were inter-related at least in the minds of contemporary observers. But since each of them posed different problems for Islam, it would be more appropriate to treat separately the relationship between them and Islam.

Among the Yoruba, the relationship between Islam and Christianity was marked by the eternal competition for the souls of men. Islam, however, had an initial advantage. In the second half of the nineteenth century, as shown above,[1] the Muslim communities had grown both in size and in stature. In the society, the community was planted among the political, administrative and military classes, just as much as it had become popular with the rich and fashionable traders. In organisation, each community evolved a hierarchical and complex system which harnessed the resources of chiefs, merchants and mallams as well as the rising generation of local scholars and preachers. Nevertheless, the structure retained considerable flexibility. It admitted and promoted the services of non-indigenous mallams without rousing any racialist feelings. It also made allowance for differing local circumstances, without losing its essential Muslim character. Above all, it encouraged a great deal of individual enterprise, thereby giving room for the energetic men of talent. While there was some contact among the communities, each developed on its own; and within each one there was ample scope for everyone to teach, learn, preach or serve.

These features distinguished the Yoruba Muslim community from its rival religious community. Among the Yoruba Christians there was on the whole considerable dependence on foreign support for men and materials; and as a corollary, there was, to that extent, a comparative lack of the spirit of self-help. The leadership of the Christian community was essentially foreign in both personnel and ideas; and some, particularly in the Church Missionary Society, pursued a paternalistic policy which kept down the educated Africans. This repressive policy produced much bickering and racial animosity between the Europeans and the Africans in the Church.[2]

Thus the structure and social position of the Muslim community gave it a positive advantage over Christianity in Yorubaland. It enabled Islam to grow considerably in Yorubaland *vis à vis* Christianity. This growth often struck the Christian missionaries; and some of them, during their evangelistic campaigns, felt how powerful this Muslim influence could be in a number of towns. For example, Iṣẹyin was often visited by Baptist and CMS missionaries, such as Townsend and Bowen, who were zealous to establish their religion. But their travels were hardly successful, mainly because the town was a strong Muslim centre. When T. J. Bowen's messengers arrived at the court of Aṣẹyin in 1851, they found no fewer than one hundred Muslims in attendance.[3] The Aṣẹyin, like most Yoruba Ọbas, maintained the policy of open-mindedness and apparent support to all religions. When approached by Townsend in 1856, he had little hesitation in granting permission to the solicitous missionary to build a mission station; but when the Rev. G. F. Buhler, on the strength of this permission, came along in April to establish there, he met, in spite of the welcome of the king, stiff opposition from the Muslims, whom he described as 'very angry' when they heard of his arrival.[4] Indeed, before his arrival, they had endeavoured to prevent the Christians from settling down at Iṣẹyin;[5] and 'it was, therefore, spread everywhere that we should no more come to Iṣẹyin'.[6] This stiff opposition of the Muslims in a town like Iṣẹyin undermined the work of the missionary; and such was the situation that in 1858 a resolution was passed by the CMS in Abẹokuta to give up the station.[7] Consequently, missionary work in that area was abandoned until 1874.[8]

In Iwo the situation which confronted the Christian missionaries was different. There was the normal and initial evangelical
enthusiasm, followed by the preliminary tours. There were the
usual friendly welcome and good disposition to Christian missionary agents such as Meakin and Hinderer. The Oluwo[9] was
believed to have made a request for the provision of a Christian
teacher in Iwo. When, according to Meakin, the CMS agent, the
Oluwo reminded him of this request, he decided to go there with
the Christian teacher;[10] on arrival they were received very gladly.
He reported that he expressed his joy particularly 'at my keeping
word and presented me with a small elephant's tusk, a sheep and
some cows'.[11] But this did not in any way mean the immediate
housing and establishment of the Christian teacher in the town. A
council meeting of the elders and chiefs of the town had to be
summoned to discuss this issue, and after a rather long session
throughout the whole of the afternoon, it was reported to him
that the council had unanimously passed the motion that there
should be 'no Christian teacher in Iwo'.[12] He rightly attributed
this decision to the strong influence that the 'Mohammedan party'
had within the administrative hierarchy of the town. Indeed, such
was this influence that the Muslims could be regarded as the
'ruling power of that town'.[13] Thus at Iwo, again, prospective
missionary work was, for a while, effectively nipped in the bud
largely as a result of the decisive influence of the Muslim party
within the ruling hierarchy.

Such Muslim influence can be easily exaggerated and stretched
to explain Christian failure to establish in some areas. Indeed, it
was not always that the Muslims successfully exerted their
influence to block Christian missionary work. In Ibadan, for
example, the Muslims rallied round to exert their influence with
Atẹrẹ, the Muslim Sierra Leonian emigrant, with a view to
getting the newly arrived Rev. D. Hinderer ejected from Ibadan.[14]
In the town council meeting that was summoned to consider
whether or not the town should receive the Rev. Hinderer, Ọṣundina, a Muslim who was the third leading war chief, fulminated
against Christian evangelists, declaiming: 'awọn ọbaiyẹjẹ ni
iwọnyi' (these are the despoilers of the world).[15] In support of his
objection, he dilated upon the evil and baneful influence which
they brought on the society, and warned that 'there is no country
they enter but misfortune will follow for that place'.[16] This was
incidentally an opinion that would appear to have been encountered

in a few other places against the whites and the missionaries;[17] and this rather popular conception embarrassed, if not militated against, missionary work. For the time being the remonstrance of Balogun Oṣundina and that of his co-religionist brought the Council to an impasse.[18] The council saw its way out of this deadlock only by a resort to the traditional divination of Ifa, which allowed the admission of the Christian missionaries to the town.[19] They were left to nurture their grievance against the religious intruders and their converts, to whom they showed some abhorrence.[20]

In Ibadan, the results of Christian efforts at conversion were no less humble. By 1884 all the three CMS congregations, the only Christian missions in Ibadan – which were based at Kudẹti, Arẹmọ and Ogunpa – had only 133 communicants, and perhaps about that number again were 'connected' with the Church. The number of communicants at Ogunpa which in 1884 stood at seventy-four remained so till 1907, though the number of adherents increased a little.

As the Christian missionaries saw Muslim communities expand and grow in influence, they became very concerned, all the more so as their conversions in the field were, by their own estimates, not only in inverse proportion to their endeavours but also relatively insignificant, compared with those of their Muslim counterparts. This was particularly true of the CMS. The CMS was the oldest and easily the largest and most widely dispersed of the different Christian missionary agencies in the Yoruba country. It was the CMS that expressed most concern about the Muslim position. And it is essential to realise that the concern and challenge of the CMS was regarded by the Muslims as being keenly representative of the attitude of all Christians.

In 1875 Christian concern about the growth of Muslim influence came to a head.[21] In that year a Christian plan was, through the efforts of the Rev. James Johnson,[22] formulated to challenge the Muslim advance and position in Yorubaland. First, there was to be a shift of emphasis in the duties of the local ministers, whose role was now to be cast more in the form of missionaries than of pastors. This would step up evangelical work by Christian missions in a country dominated by non-Christians and especially by Muslims.[23]

In addition to increased evangelical work, there was a greater need, it was felt, for local clergy specially trained, particularly in Arabic, in order to be better equipped to combat, and discuss with, the Muslims. The Yoruba Muslims, it was admitted,[24] were not to be conceived as being 'altogether ignorant of the contents of their books', and consequently, it would be helpful to missionary work if some local missionaries were knowledgeable in Arabic, and could read the Qur'ān. This knowledge would give them access to intelligent Muslims. Proficiency in, and, indeed, accurate knowledge of, this language was vital, since the Muslims criticised the current erroneous English translations of the Qur'ān.[25] For the purpose of getting these trained men, some local clergy should be selected to proceed to Fourah Bay where, under a certain new Arabic professor, they could get themselves sufficiently versed in Arabic. It was expected that this measure would assist the local Christian evangelists and controversialists, if not to win more souls or to refute Muslim disputants, at least to earn for the Christian missionary the respect of Muslims.[26] As a corollary to the availability of local clergy versed in Arabic, there should be supplies of Arabic–Yoruba texts of Christian religious literature for the Muslim population.[27]

But the greatest reliance was placed on the literacy provided by the Mission. Literacy had been offered as an adjunct to missionary work among peoples not literate in English. Since literacy offered to the people possibilities of trade and employment with European firms and so on, converts and other people wanted to be literate in English. This popular desire for literacy, therefore, presented the Christian missions with what they would have called a divinely-provided opportunity for close contact and evangelisation among the people. In the urgent task of intensifying missionary work, this glorious opportunity was indeed to be fully utilised. Special attention seems to have been devoted to Muslims. As for the Muslims, James Johnson stressed 'our desire is to get as much as we can of our religion into the Mohammedan scholars before they leave school'.[28]

Thus, the four chief elements of the Christian challenge were: greater evangelism, trained clergy, literacy in English, and the production of Christian literature in Arabic-cum-Yoruba texts. The 1896 CMS Conference in Lagos agreed that 'Medical Missions which have already proved a successful auxiliary in mission work in the East be also employed in Yorubaland' among the Muslims. During this period nothing particularly significant came out of this resolution to employ 'charms'.[29] Consequently the four elements remained essentially the core of Christian challenge to counter Islamic propaganda and progress. Clearly articulated by the Rev. James Johnson, these ideas were widely held, and they persisted, with little modification, right down to the close of the period under study.[30] They constituted the substance of 'the spiritual sword' which the Christian Church must freely use against Islam.[31] It yet remains to be seen how the Yoruba Muslim community experienced the practice of this policy.

In offering this challenge to Islam, the Christian Church, particularly the CMS which was the most forward challenger, could rely on its potential resources. It could as a body meet to discuss, review and concert measures for the charge. It could also draw upon the experience and knowledge of its foreign sponsors who also had men working among Muslims in other lands. It also had within its fold many men interested in evangelism among Muslims: A. F. Foster, R. S. Oyebọde, I. A. Braithwaite, I. Oluwọle and A. W. Smith, to mention just a few. Above all, there was the favourable trend of prevailing circumstances – the advent and establishment of British power, and the growth of overseas trade which, *prima facie*, helped to enhance the position of Christianity.[32]

On the other hand, the Yoruba Muslims were at the time hardly aware of this planned Christian offensive against them. They had, however, long appreciated the rivalry between themselves and these 'people of the book'[33] whom they often locally called *Kiriyo*.[34] But they were not as organised as their challengers were; nor could they draw very much upon the heartlands of Islam for support.

The CMS in Yorubaland appeared to have left to private hands the issue of training native clergy in Arabic. Some clergymen who had an interest in Arabic exerted themselves to become passably conversant with it. James Johnson, for example, resumed his studies of the language.[35] Some others took advantage of the availability of local resources to study not only Arabic but also Islam under the direction of bilingual Muslim teachers. In Lagos, for instance, Idris O. A. Animasaun was, for some indefinite period in 1896, the teacher in Arabic to a group of some European and local clergymen.[36] Classes were held twice or thrice a week. Thus some people, such as the Rev. M. S. Cole, the Rev. James Johnson, the Rev. T. A. J. Ogunbiyi and the Rev. M. T. Euler-Ajayi, later emerged with some proficiency in Arabic.

It was this small number that formed the core of Christian lettered men who began and continued the tradition of translating and publishing a few Christian tracts specially meant for the Muslims. For instance, the Rev. T. A. J. Ogunbiyi produced *Aṣaro Kukuru*, its English version, *Tracts for Mohammedans*, and *Awọn Ọrọ Ọlọrun*, containing the Lord's Prayer, the Ten Commandments and a few scriptural texts both in Yoruba and Arabic.[37] Other works by him are *Awọn Imale*, which gives stories of some Muslim converts, and *Itan Mọmọdu*, which is a brief sketch of the life of the Holy Prophet. Certainly the most notable literary production was the Yoruba translation of the Qur'ān by the Rev. (later Canon) M. S. Cole, which was indeed a feat. These works, however, found little favour with those for whom they were meant.[38] Even the Yoruba Qur'ān moved, right down to 1908, 'very slowly' among the Muslims.[39]

It is well to note that the Muslim neglect of these works was to some extent in line with fairly general neglect, even among Yoruba Christians, of the Yoruba translations prepared by the Christian missions. The Bible in the vernacular was, for example, initially neglected just as other translated books and tracts were;[40] for although these translations into the vernacular were often made only by dint of hard, intelligent work, they nevertheless made little impression on people who set greater value on English and works in English. The neglect of the Muslim tracts, however, had this extra reason that the Muslims considered them as prejudiced[41] as they were ignorant. Indeed, the books necessarily tended to be so because of their religious rather than literary motivation. The Christian-translated Yoruba Qur'ān illustrates this point best. With the encouragement of members of his Church who felt that 'it will help the cause of Christianity', M. S. Cole chose to embark on this heavy assignment even though he was ready to 'disclaim any pretensions to depth in Arabic literature, or oriental research'.[42] His chosen aim was to combat what he conceived as 'error' of faith, and he went on to make a number of erroneous and prejudiced assertions.[43]

Ardent evangelical work among Muslims, however, involved more than the production of pamphlets. It necessarily meant persuading the Muslims to accept Christianity and attend the Church. It was in the course of this attempted persuasion that keen disputations arose with the Muslims on various aspects of theology. In the Ibadan of the 1880s, the Rev. J. S. Oyebọde took particular interest in these theological controversies, which were described as being occasionally 'warm', as was the case on 30 August 1882, on whether the Qur'ān or the Bible was the word of God.[44] Through-out the period of his stay in Iṣẹyin, the Rev. A. F. Foster regularly carried his evangelism to the Muslims; he used to visit Ijẹmba quarter, which was a preponderantly Muslim area.[45] There was hardly any Muslim communal gathering that he did not attend: prayer and religious meetings at the mosque and at the Court of the Aseyin; and even secular gatherings to arrange for the rebuild-ing of a burnt-down mosque.[46] On such occasions he sought and found an opportunity not only to bear his Christian witness to them[47] but also to counter Muslim preachers and solicit the Muslims to return from their 'false prophet' to the 'true saviour'.[48] One of such occasions was in the month of Ramaḍān when the Muslims of Iṣẹyin gathered early in the morning of 12 August at the central mosque in order to have their *Tafsīr*.[49] The reverend gentleman visited the Muslim community there early that morn-ing. He narrated this experience: 'I was kindly received by the priest[50] and also the others. A stool was offered to me.[51] I sat at the entrance of the mosque.[52] We have conversation in religious purposes for about half an hour, the mosque was crowded with people, about 100 souls'. The *Tafsīr* was, however, soon begun by the Muslim preacher, but still the missionary stayed back, patiently listening to the exposition of the forty-ninth *Sūra* of the Qur'ān.[53] He heard the preacher as he warned the Jamāʿa against the hard and improper use of their slaves; secondly, he (the preacher) encouraged them to be active in their profession; and thirdly, he warned them about maltreating their wives. At the end of this, he found little opportunity to utter any word and had to depart. But the following morning he was there again 'in earnest to talk with the Mohammedans on the forty-ninth sura'. When granted the opportunity, he tried to rebut the Muslim disquisition, not failing to impress on them that 'they are lost in their false religion'.

These disputations were often occasions which aroused much public interest. In 1882 when the Rev. James Okuseinde visited a convert in Ibadan, he was taken by the convert to a Muslim in a nearby house. On his arrival 'this Mohammedan saluted me in a most affectionate manner after I was seated'.[54] There was a preliminary talk about the current intra-Yoruba war, but this soon gave way, deliberately, to 'a spiritual one and in a few minutes, the piazza was crowded with people small and great and we discussed on several points about the Christian religion'.[55] Such was the keen interest and excitement of these open air Christian–

Muslim dialogues that the encounters were sometimes pre-arranged, each side with its own full support of men and books.[56] While he was in Lagos, Umar Savage, for example, had a number of these fixed open disputations with his Christian counterparts.

These disputations went on almost everywhere, in towns and villages, before churches, mosques, and private houses – everywhere that any interested Christian and Muslim met. In the course of his journeys to the areas within the jurisdiction of the Lagos Church, for example, Braithwaite often met Muslims even in such small villages as Orile Iganmu, Ise Village and Oso's Village.[57] There was almost invariably in such places 'warm argument with Mohammedan young men' on many issues, including 'ruhullahi'.[58] The range of these disputations sometimes extended beyond simple arguments on theology to include the history of the religion and its role in the world. Wherever Muslim influence was perceived and encountered, there was the place to direct the full charge of Christian missionary artillery. The mention or sight of fasting Muslims, their charms – anything bringing to the fore Muslim influence was a good occasion. There was the occasion in 1884 when the Christian evangelist Edward Burke visited the Olata of Otta and preached before him. The Oba was not a Muslim, but as he had known of Muslims around him, he referred in rather glowing tones to the fervour of a celebrated Muslim at Ilaro 'who used to fast for three months instead of one'.[59] Feeling rather piqued, the evangelist immediately 'replied and called the king, pointing to those charms which he hung up',[60] making it plain that by those 'expensive means they deceive you'.[61] The Oba nodded a flattering answer and allowed him to go.

It is doubtful if these theological disputations won over Muslims to Christianity. Failure was to be expected: winning an argument, if that ever happened, was quite a different issue from winning a soul. The experience of that tireless disputant, the Rev. R. S. Oyebode, proved this beyond any doubt.[62] In the course of his evangelisation tour to Ikirun in December 1887 he sought out some of his 'friends', one of them being a chief and a Muslim.[63] The latter soon picked up the scent and introduced some argument by asking the clergyman 'why do you hate Mohammed?' His long detailed answer only elicited from the chief and the crowd which had begun to gather 'a multitude of questions and assertions' which led to further argument and discussion ranging from polygamy to theology. After this seemingly interminable discussion, 'the chief rose up to accompany us out', said the clergyman; '[he] shook my hands and bade me good bye'.[64] The result: 'so I left him to his conviction'.[65] The typical reaction of the Muslims was a reaffirmation of their conviction in Islam; that 'Moham-medanism is the best religion'[66] was a reply which many a Muslim gave to pastors like Okuseinde.[67]

Sometimes, however, the reaction of the Muslims was one of withdrawal and studied rebuff. The Muslims were admonished by their elders and muallims to avoid all conversation with the *kiriyo*, who were portrayed as 'enemies of the truth'.[68] Even when, in some cases, some enthusiastic Christian preacher wanted to force such a dispute he was kept away at a pertinent distance either by an attitude of studied silence or by a reply, 'such as left him no room to doubt he was not with his company. . . .'[69]

The theological disputations were, however, only part of the general evangelical work of the Christian missionaries. Normal evangelism continued; and, in this regard, Christian endeavour was aided directly or otherwise by British rule.[70] Legally, the Christian missionaries were promised complete 'protection', 'assistance' and 'encouragement' in some treaties signed by the British and local chiefs,[71] as was the case in Lagos,[72] Abẹokuta,[73] and Ọyọ.[74] Occasionally a few top government officials would throw in their influence. In 1887 the Acting Administrator in Lagos, diplomatically enough, remonstrated with the Awujalẹ of Ijẹbu-Ode to allow and encourage the missionaries to work in Ijẹbu-Ode.[75] Besides, the Christian missions often tried to take advantage of the British 'pacification' of the country to extend their work of evangelism. Extra enthusiasm was exhibited by such interested missionaries as James Johnson, A. F. Foster, I. A. Braithwaite, James Okuseinde and A. W. Smith, in carrying on this Christian evangelical work among Muslims in the various Yoruba towns that came under British rule and protection.[76]

With or without the aid of the British Government, this ardent Christian evangelisation among the Muslims produced no appre-ciable immediate effect on the membership of the Muslim com-munity. In spite of the years of persistent Christian efforts and of the fact that the growing influence of the British was being felt all around,[77] Isẹyin, for instance, remained a predominantly Muslim town, yielding little ground to the Christian evangelists. The mission stations had been allowed to settle, but their gain and influence were evidently small. In 1893, after twenty years of proselytising, all the Christian missionaries appear to have won no more than twenty souls.[78] Iwo offered no better prospects; and by all accounts, Ọyọ, until 1908 and even beyond, remained what Melville Jones aptly described as 'a hard soil' to Christian evangelisation.[79] In the areas cited, the position of the Muslim community, as already noted,[80] improved as Islam expanded and gained favour with the people, chiefs and Ọbas.

Indeed, much of this activated missionary work would appear to have achieved little more than provoking an equally animated reaction on the part of the challenged Muslims. 'Our activity has provoked their own,' reported James Johnson. 'They were never warmer in the defence of their religion.'[81] On the ever-topical issue of the person of Christ, for instance, the Muslims, in spite of all Christian assertion to the contrary, insisted on the validity of Muslim teaching as 'they cease not to repeat the surat[82] of the Qur'ān that says, "God does not beget and is not begotten"'.[83]

The futility of ardent Christian endeavour among Muslims, as well as the latter's opposition and animated reaction were demonstrated best in Ẹpẹ. A strong Muslim centre, Ẹpẹ seemed to the Christian propagandists a promising area for invigorated Christian evangelism. Thus, in 1876, the Rev. D. Hinderer strove to plant the gospel there; but he was kept off by the plain categorical statements of the Ẹpẹ that 'we are already Muslims'.[84] These popular professions evidently made little impression on the Christian evangelists; for, the following year, two Christian gentlemen, the Rev. (later Bishop) Hill and I. A. Braithwaite,[85] ventured into the town and boldly commenced preaching. After they had had three successive days of open air preaching, they were, by their own reports, driven out of the town by the Muslims, who felt greatly affronted.[86] Missionary work thus had to be given up – but only for a while.

Subsequent to the Magbon War and the occupation of Ijẹbu-Ode by the British in 1892, the Christian missions breathed fresh air of hope about their hitherto futile efforts in Ẹpẹ. The enthusiastic CMS agent, Mr Braithwaite, undaunted by past futile experiences, had been taking an anxious note of the spread of Islam in Yorubaland; in 1893 he effected his transfer from Iganmu to Ẹpẹ Here he indeed exerted himself in Christian missionary work, and felt he had achieved a gathering of one hundred 'churchgoers', no doubt mainly from among the 'heathen' section. He was, however, met with the strong reaction and set opposition of the

Ẹpẹ Muslims. And it was not long before he noticed that 'the Mohammedans are using every effort to put difficulties in the way of Christianity taking root there'.[87] And throughout his long stay of thirteen years in Ẹpẹ this strong Muslim reaction was very evident, matching his own ardent militant evangelism. 'But Mohammedans are intolerant', he despaired. 'They have organised a house to house visit of the Church Attendants, and are endeavouring to win them away from Christianity.'[88] About three years later he had to confess to a wavering and a substantial dwindling of his group of 'Christian enquirers' to about forty.[89] Right down to 1906, when he quitted Ẹpẹ and was replaced by the Rev. Olubi, the Christian mission had only a tiny and ineffective following. This dwindling group tried to wage a regular but quite unequal battle with the established Ẹpẹ Muslim community.[90] More significant, however, was the fervour which Christian missionary work stimulated in the Ẹpẹ Muslims, who now embarked on a systematic campaign for their religion. Naturally, the Muslims would, as before and everywhere, have propagated their religion;[91] but the Christian challenge provided a stimulus that quickened the pace of the Muslim propagation in and outside Ẹpẹ. As the missionaries themselves testified, the Muslims went from 'village to village, building mosques, creating *alimanis*[92] and appointing sufficient teachers to assist them and this they do with great delight'.[93]

Discussion, preaching and baptism were no doubt essential elements of Christian propaganda. But, for a long time, the most potent instrument lay in the school. In the school the Christian missions had an enviable magnet to attract all, especially non-Christians, to the Christian way and outlook. At the start this educational charm of the Christians exercised no immediate influence among the Yoruba Muslims, for the latter were apathetic towards the Christian-sponsored Western education. It has already been noted how, in the early decades of the nineteenth century, the Muslims in a place like Iwo unanimously wanted no Christian teacher.[94] The reaction of the Muslims towards the Christian-sponsored education is buttressed by the observation of James Johnson. After a tour to the important Yoruba Mission stations and schools, he reported in 1878: 'the Mohammedans show no desire for the education that may be had at our schools'.[95]

Certainly, the material benefits of Western education were recounted to and urged upon the unwilling and unenthusiastic

Muslims. Many Christian evangelists, in their own veiled interest, solicited Muslim parents to send their children 'to our schools.'[96] Even in Ẹpẹ, the Commissioner, M. R. Menendez, and Dr O. Johnson, took time off in 1895 to speak to the leading and influential Muslims 'on the advantages of education and advised them to send their children to schools'.[97] There were many such pleas then as later.

The results of these pleadings and addresses were not altogether negative. This was particularly so in Lagos. Here Christianity was established and here were concentrated the Christian schools, where, indeed, some Muslim children were to be found. In 1893, for example, there were 412 Muslim pupils in the thirty-three government-assisted mission schools in Lagos Colony, representing about 12 per cent of the total number of children in these schools.[98] The following year, the number of Muslim pupils rose by thirty, still forming about 12 per cent of the pupils in the schools.[99] They, however, mostly wanted only the English language.[100] And the presence of this number of Muslim children in the Mission schools is significant only in that it indicates some Muslim willingness to try to receive some Western education at the hands of their Christian sponsors.

This is not, however, to be exaggerated, and should be properly seen in the context of the persistently reluctant and suspicious attitude of the entire Muslim population. In Iseyin, for all the ardour and long or permanent stay of the missionaries of both the CMS and the Wesleyan Missions, the Muslims seemed to have yielded little to Christian educational advances. In 1893 when the Governor, Sir G. Carter, visited the place, he was surprised to find that, in spite of the CMS and Wesleyan activities, there were only six schoolchildren.[101] And the Ẹpẹ Muslims still actively forbade their children to attend the Christian school almost as much as the Christian evangelist strove to persuade them to send their children to it.[102]

It cannot be argued that Muslim reluctance was to education *per se*. Most Muslim children went to Muslim Qur'anic schools. For example, among the Muslim children of school age in Lagos, a far greater percentage preferred the Qur'anic schools. In 1892 there were no fewer than fifty-five such Muslim schools, having 1,246 Muslim children in regular attendance;[103] and in 1893 there were about 1,400 Muslim pupils in the sixty Muslim schools.[104] But the remarkable point was that the percentage of Muslim pupils attending the mission schools was, up to the last decade of the nineteenth century, extremely small.[105]

At a time when the economic and political changes overtaking the country rendered the value of Western education obvious and important, the persistence of Muslim apathy and opposition to the increasingly valuable commodity requires some study and explanation. The activated zeal[106] on the part of some Christian evangelists may have accounted in some measure for the continuing Muslim attitude of opposition even to this intrinsically beneficial aspect of Christian endeavour. But the Muslim attitude evidently derived from more fundamental factors. Christian-sponsored Western education was evidently seen as a mirage designed to lure Muslim children from the straight path.[107] Muslim attendance of the Christian schools was conceived as dangerous and ominous. Muslim pupils attending such Christian schools would, to some extent, miss the basic education provided in the Qur'anic schools which was designed to orient them in a distinctly Muslim way of life. Such pupils, it can be argued, could still take advantage of these Muslim nursery schools since they could attend them in the evening on returning from the mission schools. Besides, they were always under the rectifying influence of the home, which was drawn upon to balance or even nullify whatever influence the mission school exerted. Indeed, the fact that the Muslim home could nullify Christian teaching dismayed the ardent ones among the Christian missionaries. 'The effect of our school gospel teaching', it was bemoaned, 'on some of our Mohammedan friends continues to be nullified at home.'[108]

However, it was by no means easy for the Muslim pupils to attend both the mission and the Muslim schools. Similarly, the combination of Christian teaching in the school and Muslim style of living at home was a difficulty entailing considerable embarrassment and confusion. Take the issue of Sunday rest, for example. A certain Muslim boy attending a Christian school had been taught 'to keep the day holy'; on getting home during the mid-year recess, he refused to go to the market to buy and sell on Sunday when his father sent him, because of the Christian reverence for Sunday already instilled into him.[109] The extent and degree of the confusion can be appreciated more when one considers the different festivals, rituals and religious observances of the two religions. Faced with this bewildering conflict and confusion, most pupils tended to choose the way of least resistance: take to one or the other, preferably the one whose neglect threatens them with a greater penalty.

Soon the Muslims realised that a great danger lurked in the systematic exposure of their children to Christian doctrine as a result of their association with the mission schools. Some Muslim pupils were put, to use the words of James Johnson, 'under Christian guardianship'.[110] Muslim pupils, like others, had to attend the mission church service, Sunday Schools and share in other essentially religious activities which the school planned in collaboration with the mission. Muslims today affirm that absence from these religious activities was hardly tolerated. At least, it was almost invariably visited by a not-so-mild flogging by the Christian teachers. To the Muslims, all this was plainly religious indoctrination about which they were, to say the least, unenthusiastic.

There was, indeed, some legal protection afforded to non-Christians against this religious indoctrination. Under the operation of the Education Ordinance of 1887, no child in a government-aided school could receive religious instruction to which the parent or guardian objected, or could be forced to be present when such instruction was given at such a school.[111] The indications as provided by people such as W. Howell, who were the Inspectors of the mission schools, are, however, that only few Muslims were aware of this legal right or took advantage of it to withdraw their pupils from the religious classes.[112] By far the greater majority either left the children for all classes in the schools or simply kept them back at home.

In any case, whatever legal protection might be given against compulsory attendance of classes for religious instruction in these schools, there was virtually none against the all-permeating religious atmosphere of the mission schools. The religious tone of the school might, to some extent, have been understandable in the light of the time; but it did not make the consequent religious exposure less resented by non-Christian parents and their wards. The Muslim parents and pupils who were caught in this position found the Christian education too much of a mixed grill, about which they felt sullen and resentful.

The religious indoctrination which the Muslim pupils underwent proved to be only a short step from outright conversion to Christianity. Today, many names of former Muslims who were converted at school can be cited, to the chagrin of the steadfast Muslims. There were, for example, Odutola, Rev. Joseph Suberu

Fanimokun, etc. The number of Muslim pupils and people who took this final step was certainly much less than that attending the mission school. Indeed, it was probably a small percentage of the total Muslin population. But this conversion of Muslim children and people generated among the Muslims considerable irritation. Cases are not wanting when conversion of a Muslim to Christianity strained normal social relationships even to breaking point. For example, when a certain Yoruba Muslim girl, Jemi, aged about ten, wanted to change to Christianity in November 1887, this caused a great stir within the Muslim family. With the girl's insistence on conversion, the issue was only 'resolved' by a mutual renunciation of filial connections.[113] Thus conversion of Muslims to Christianity often aroused passion, as Islam expressly denounces apostasy.[114] And it was this issue of conversion that made the Muslims react as much against Christianity as against the Western education which the Christian missionaries sponsored.

Essentially, it was this outraged feeling which at a time induced the Muslims to discipline those of their young ones who hob-nobbed with the Christians. It was soon noticed by the watchful Rev. James Johnson that 'the young Mohammedans were scolded, flogged and prevented by their elders and priests [*sic*] from attending Christian schools and Churches and even conversing with their Christian friends on religion'.[115] This Muslim irritation and reaction at the conversion, or prospect of conversion, of their children was crucial in stiffening the Muslim opposition.

Although Christian-sponsored education was thus shunned generally by the Muslims, it would be false not to realise that its acceptance in some places threatened the position of Muslims. This was particularly true of Ijẹbu, where Christian evangelisation once seemed uniquely successful but where Islam finally triumphed. It may, therefore, be worthwhile examining the situation there in the era between 1892 and 1908.

Before 1892, Islam had spread to Ijẹbu;[116] but Christianity had been largely kept at bay. The attempts made in the 1850s by the Rev. D. Hinderer and the Rev. C. A. Gollmer, and in 1888 by the Rev. James Johnson, in part a scion of Ijẹbu,[117] had not been quite successful in planting Christianity in Ijẹbu in the era before 1892.[118] But with the British conquest of Ijẹbu in 1893, Christian missionary work could be resumed afresh and with greater confidence. 'This event', narrated James Johnson, 'in a great measure helped us to get access to the country in a larger way than had been previously the case.'[119] There was some considerable drift from the pagan population to Christianity, much more than in Epe. Such was the growth of Christianity that the local agent joyfully complained: 'the work is now beyond my personal control and that of the fellow countrymen who worked with me'.[120] In 1899 Bishop Oluwole held confirmation services for about 266, baptised 296, and estimated the Christian adherents at about 1,000.[121] The Christian tide swelled; and the Rev. N. T. Hamlyn, on visiting Ijẹbu in October 1900, was amazed at the rapid spread of Christianity within a short space of time. 'I do not see that the work is one jot behind that in Uganda. . . . It is wonderful to see a whole country thus becoming christianised in a few years.'[122]

An appreciation of the basic reasons behind this rapid spread of Christianity is essential both for later developments in Ijẹbu and for the understanding of the relationship in this era between Islam on the one hand and Christianity on the other. Many reasons[123] have been adduced in explanation of this phenomenon. It has been said that the Ijẹbu shifted to Anglicanism because this was 'considered the true religion of the conquerors'.[124] This may be true; but since there was no similar rush to 'the religion of the conquerors' in other conquered and bombarded Yoruba towns, such as Ẹpẹ and Ọyọ, we may have to consider this explanation as unsatisfactory and inadequate. There is, perhaps, greater validity in the fact that much of the early success of Christianity was due to the exertions of the 'native clergy'[125] – James Johnson, Owen, etc. But this in itself provides no more than a clue to the rapid spread of Islam. As far as Christianity is concerned in Ijẹbu, the factor of the native clergy has its limitations, especially since in later years there was, so to say, a slump in the growth of Christianity, the exertions of the native clergy notwithstanding.

More valid explanations may be found in the wishes and desires of the people who accepted the new religion. Primary among their manifest wishes was literacy in English.[126] The number of intending scholars, the local missionary observed, was nearly the same as that of Sunday worshippers: 'for every one came to be taught . . . and everywhere the cry was for more teachers. Many congregations are very anxious that those who come to them as teachers should possess a knowledge of English. If the teacher can speak and teach English it goes a long way towards ensuring him a favourable reception.'[127] In other words, the desire for literacy, or as admirably put by the Rev. Oluwọle, 'the mystery of letters', was an effective lure toward Christianity in Ijẹbu.[128]

For Islam, this Christian lure of letters was significant; and the position in Ijẹbu only emphasised, and brought into clearer focus, the greatest challenge which Christianity offered it. The rush for literacy and Christianity gave to the Christian missions ready materials for systematic instruction in Christianity; and, in addition to the many pagans, many Muslims were affected. Instances are cited of how some Muslims thus became converted to Christianity. Even if such cases are relatively few, they roused no little excitement and irritation among the Muslims. In their response, the Muslims here exhibited no such counter-missionary work as that of the more Islamised Ẹpẹ; and it appeared as if Christianity would sweep the ground from under their feet.

But even here, the potency of the Christian charm of letters did not make Islam go down. The Muslim community was too strongly anchored in the society. It disputed every inch of the ground with Christianity.[129] And under circumstances which had been described elsewhere,[130] the position had undergone such a change that in 1907 the Rev. R. A. Coker, the Superintendent of Ijẹbu-Ode District of Lagos Church Mission, declared Ijẹbu-Ode 'as a Mohammedan nation';[131] and in 1908 Bishop Tugwell was constrained to declare that the opportunity of Christian evangelisation in Ijẹbu had gone.[132]

A general survey of the Christian challenge to Islam in the period up to 1908 shows, indeed, that, as James Johnson put it, the 'waters [were] troubled'.[133] But evidently Islam had, by and large, maintained its own in both the preponderant and the new centres of Islam in Yorubaland.[134] Islam, in its spread and growth among the Yoruba, had become solidly based and anchored in Yoruba social and organisational structure. It had been supported by people of substantial significance in the nineteenth-century Yoruba society – the well-to-do, the elders, the chiefs, and the Ọbas. Having this strong position in the society, Islam in Yorubaland did not yield ground or accept inducement to make it yield easily to another system.[135]

Largely because of this strong position of the Yoruba Muslim community, the Yoruba Muslims often displayed considerable pride and confidence in their professed faith. Compact and well-backed, they believed they had a religion, a system and culture that were self-sufficient and should not be abandoned. It was a

Christian missionary who bore an eloquent testimony to this: 'As elsewhere, so in Abẹokuta, he [i.e. the Muslim] claims to be in possession of the last, best and truest revelation of God's will given to man.'[136] The Muslims, consequently, tended not only to look down upon the heathens[137] but also to hold themselves 'as much superior to the Christian'.[138] On occasions, as the Rev. C. Gollmer found to his surprise, this Muslim sense of superiority induced them to seek his conversion and that of other European Christians to Islam.[139] This confident belief of the Yoruba Muslims made the situation in Yorubaland fall in line with what appears to have been a general experience that Islam was unyielding to another rival system,[140] although there were certain local factors which made this particularly so in Yorubaland.

The persistent growth of Islam in Yorubaland had various effects on the Christian challengers. Some felt that Christian evangelism would be more profitable if attention is shifted to areas such as Ekiti, which were relatively untouched by Islam.[141] Many more, however, were undaunted: people like M. T. E. Ajayi, A. W. Smith and Bishop Tugwell continued to advocate open confrontation with Islam.[142] Right down to 1908 and 1911, the Rev. A. W. Smith and S. M. Abiọdun easily succeeded in persuading the CMS Diocesan Conferences to pass the motion that 'the rapid growth of Mohammedanism in the Yoruba country calls for serious consideration and prompt action on the part of the Church'.[143]

Meanwhile, some clergy tried to explain away the futility of their work among the Muslims by recourse to certain theories which tried to discredit Islam. Indeed, in the attempt to project their religion and counter the advance of Islam, many of the Christian propagandists went out of their way to besmear the other religion, of which they had at best an imperfect knowledge. Thus we are told that the Yoruba Muslim priests maintained themselves by deceit and charm making;[144] their religion was the 'greatest obstacle to the progress of civilization and to all that is pure, holy and noble and Christian of which the world knows'.[145] Islam was stigmatised as being obstructive to progress.[146] 'It discourages free labour;[147] its concept of sin is as external parasite, for it is a sin for any Mohammedan to be a farmer.'[148] Much of this uninformed and misleading denunciation was of a piece with the age-old mutual recrimination between both religions in areas where they confronted each other.[149] Some of these ideas linger on in Yoruba society, an evidence – albeit a diminishing one – of inherited prejudice.

The bias and prejudice manifest in certain pronouncements and publications of the Christian clergy in Yorubaland did not, however, altogether prevent some Christians from appreciating the virtues of Islam especially as practised in African, particularly Yoruba, society. Some of the missionaries fervently admired the absence of racialism and clerical hierarchy among the Yoruba Muslims. These two factors, some felt, gave Islam what was sadly missing in Christianity of the late nineteenth century: prominence to the laity and freedom from any crippling racial wrangles. The religion of Islam in Yorubaland had been propagated by the Muslims themselves, young and old, paid and unpaid, and on their own initiative without demanding or receiving any foreign help or direction. The Muslim teachers had taught without formally receiving pay; the religious men preached about at their own expense. Each Muslim community by itself erected mosques everywhere out of its own local resources.[150] What the Rev. James Johnson candidly expressed in 1878 after his travels in Yorubaland only succinctly put what many others found and admired. On that occasion, he declared:[151] 'One thing impressed itself very forcibly on my mind during my travel and it is this that African and Yoruba Mohammedans manifest a superior capacity over African or Yoruba Christians to spread the religion they respectively believe . . . and this notwithstanding the disadvantages and ardour [sic] of learning to read in Arabic.'

This Muslim attitude of self-help and self-reliance deeply impressed some of the Christian men and agents. They bemoaned the absence of it among the Christian converts.[152] Their converts were heavily dependent on others, be it on their clergy or their home missions, for various forms of support and direction of their own local affairs. Thus the Christian clergy constantly tried to rouse their followers to emulate the Muslims in these regards. 'Their self-help', Johnson stressed in 1875, 'is a lesson for Christian emulation; and has been the subject of many addresses.'[153] In 1896 the CMS Conference in Lagos also noted the fascination exerted on Christians by the Yoruba Muslim 'system of priesthood, its method of maintaining it and its self propagating power'.[154]

But, perhaps, what impressed the Christians most about Islam in Yorubaland was its 'Africanness'. In a pertinent contrast to the Christianity in their midst, they appreciated that Islam was less intolerant of African customs. It accepted 'African' dress; allowed polygamy; and made use of local airs. Islam in Yorubaland made no root-and-branch assault on traditional African society; nor did it manifest any desire to establish, as the Christian converts were wont to do, an 'imperium in imperio'.[155] It lived more closely than Christianity with the pagans, whom it cleverly sought to convert.[156]

This tolerance or preservation of certain African practices had, indeed, persuaded some people to proclaim Islam as the religion of Africa. In 1893, the editor of *The Lagos Weekly Record* struck this point. He reported the speech which the Rev. I. Oluwọle made in English,[157] the essence of which has since been echoed by others in Yorubaland. The editor prefaced his statement with a profuse if unnecessary apology for being 'caught singing the praises of Islam' and pleaded that he was constrained to speak the truth. He agreed with the Rev. Oluwọle that with reference to Yorubaland 'Islam had become indigenous . . . it has allied itself to and become a part of and a power in Africa'.[158]

These three aspects of Islam in Yorubaland which impressed the Yoruba Christians – its organisation, spirit of self-help, and Africanness – were, up to a point, rosily conceived. For the Yoruba Muslims had received some nurture from outside Yorubaland, especially from Hausaland and Nupe. Besides, it was Arabic, a non-Yoruba language, that was the language of worship and scholarship. Neither is it sufficiently appreciated that Islam as a religion which provides a comprehensive scheme of social organisation cannot but seek to replace such indigenous values and institutions which are incompatible with Islamic ideology. However, these reservations could, and did, not vitiate the essential truth.

As the Christians admired these aspects of Islam, they began to formulate their ideas about how their Christian Church could be organised. They were assertive about African ability to propagate and direct the faith of his choice. Also, they affirmed the need for preservation of essentially African and non-religious customs within that faith; and also stressed the need to be rid of racism among the clergy. They strove to stimulate their co-religionists to an acceptance of these aspects of Islam.

These ideas were potentially catalytic within the Church in Yorubaland. Of course, it can be truly said that the events within the Christian Church, stretching from the last decades of the nineteenth to early twentieth century, were causative of the internal ferment which later produced the emergence of the African

Church movement.[159] But this is an essentially 'Church-centric' view, taking little account of the entire Yoruba and especially Lagos society, and of the interaction in that society of various groups and ideas. The contributory role of Islam, especially in Lagos, to the emergence and development of the African Church movement, through the vehicle of the keen and rosy Christian appreciation of certain aspects of Islam in Yorubaland, has yet to be fully studied. The catalytic agents, in this regard, were especially the Christian leaders such as Ajayi Crowther,[160] James Johnson,[161] Mọjọla Agbebi[162] and Edward Blyden.[163] These people had taken special interest in Islam, and were particularly impressed by its spread and growth in the country. In their various plans to combat this growth,[164] they had moved closely with the Muslims and came to cherish this 'Africanness' of Islam. Their ideas gained ground within the Church.[165] It was not without significance that the Yoruba African Church was developed to bear certain charactersistics observed within the Muslim community.[166]

The Christian challenge also had significant effects on the history of Islam in Yorubaland. By its offer and monopoly of Western education, the Christians possessed a potent instrument against the Muslims. Though Islam maintained its ground generally, yet this Christian lure of letters effected, in the course of time, a chink in the armour of the powerful religion.

The Muslims, however, benefited from the Christian challenge. It has already been noted that the Muslims were roused to a great defence and propagation of their faith. In the course of persistent Christian challenge, they began to gain a growing acquaintanceship with some Christian literature, particularly the Bible. This was particularly true of the mallams, who often searched the Christian scriptures for their dialectical value.[167] This eventually led to the rise of a class of mallams, called *Akewukewe*, who were fairly proficient in Arabic and Yoruba. This class later produced a number of works on Islam and Christianity.

Even Muslim attendance of Christian schools had its own salutary effects on the Muslim community. Those who were not converted to Christianity constituted an important group among the Yoruba Muslims. They had learnt about Christianity, at first hand, so to speak. Indeed, on the Christians' testimony, the Muslim pupils showed a remarkable knowledge of Christianity.[168] But their importance lay more in the fact that, as people who had received some measure of Western education, they were the torch-bearers of the new civilisation to their co-religionists. The influence of this group was in the 1900s gathering momentum, and was particularly apparent in the next two decades as pioneer founders of various Muslim literary societies and educational societies such as the Ansar Ud-Deen, Nawair Ud-Deen and the like. These were the societies principally concerned with bringing the leavening influence of Western education and modernity among the Yoruba Muslims.

Also, these educated Muslims were the new leaders of the Yoruba Muslim community in many ways. They soon had access to some English literature on Islam by which they came to know more about their religion than had previously been the case, when their knowledge of Islam was only gained by learning Arabic the hard and tortuous way. Edified by this knowledge, they were in a position, perhaps better than that of the age-old mallams, to enlighten their less privileged co-religionists on the tenets of their religion. Their leadership was based on literacy in English and on the grasp of Islam.

One other significant point must be made. It must be appreciated that in spite of the rivalry between both religious groups in Yoruba-land,[169] social relations remained, on the whole, courteous and cordial. There were incidents of intolerance, which can be attributed to some outbursts of ardour and passion on both sides. But these were rare. Normal courtesies were exchanged; and if the Muslims remained adamant and assertive about their religion and faith, the evidence reveals that they betrayed no general personal ill-will or fanaticism. The Christian men, clergy disputants, such as there were, often testified to their being well-received by the Muslims.[170] For instance, after a tour of the Yoruba Missions in 1887, W. Allen reported that 'the Mohammedans at Abẹokuta as at Lagos . . . appear to be friendly disposed and devoid of that fanatical spirit which characterise them in the Turkish dominions'.[171]

This general absence of rancour which, indeed, can be so easily generated by militant evangelism, was in part due to the courtesy and a sense of moderation displayed by both sides; but it was due, in greater measure, to the restraint imposed by Yoruba culture, which not only discountenances extremism but smugly allows what can be called religious co-fraternity.[172] It is essentially this cultural factor which explains the tolerant, kind attitude of the chiefs, Muslim[173] or not, and of the ordinary folk in their dealings with others.[174] It also explains some peculiar Yoruba religious traits: the religious co-existence of Muslims, Christians (and 'pagans') within the same family and lineage[175] and some spirit of co-operation observable not only between the Muslims and Christians[176] but even also between the Muslims and 'pagans'.[177]

Notes

1 See Chapters 3 and 4.
2 See, for example, the contrary views and policies personified in Townsend and Venn about the place of the educated African clergy within the set-up of the CMS about the middle of the nineteenth century. This wrangle led to the removal of Bishop Ajayi Crowther as Bishop of the Niger Mission in 1890, an event that generated considerable racial acrimony within the Christian Church. It, however, marked the beginning of the 'purge' of Africans from the Niger, and the triumph of the policy of European control and dominance. For further information see J. F. Ade Ajayi, *Christian Missions in Nigeria*, pp. 174–89, 241–69; E. A. Ayandele, *The Missionary Impact on Modern Nigeria*, pp. 175–85, 210–32; J. B. Webster, *The African Churches Among the Yoruba, 1888–1922*, pp. 15–17. Also, see J. F. Ade Ajayi 'Henry Venn and the Policy of Development', *JHSN*.
3 T. J. Bowen to Bro. Taylor, December 1851, in *Correspondence of the Missionaries of the Southern Baptist Convention: Yoruba Mission, 1850–1890*. This correspondence is hereafter cited as *Bowen's Correspondence*.
4 CMS, CA2/024, G. F. Buhler's Journal for the quarter ending 25 June 1856.
5 CMS CA2/068, Maser's Journal for the quarter ending 25 June 1856. Curiously it alleged the Muslims, for example, to have cleared away the trees which were used to demarcate the plot given to the Christians, and to have 'buried a powerful charm, to kill us when we passed over it'.
6 CMS CA2/068, Maser's Journal for the quarter ending 25 June 1856.
7 CMS CA2/051, Holinhead to Sec., CMS, 28 June 1858. One dissentient voice to this resolution seemed to have been Holinhead's, who tried to plead against it, saying that he knew the Iseyin and the people knew him, and that 'even the ignorant Mohammedans desire it'. The basis of his supplication that the Muslims, even his so-called 'ignorant' ones, want Christian evangelisation is hardly acceptable, if not for its illogicality at least in the face of the practical experience of the Christian evangelist at Iseyin.

8 The Rev. A. F. Foster took up residence in Iṣẹyin as a Native Catechist in 1874. CMS CA2/069, Meakin to Sec., CMS, 29 November 1859.

9 This must have been Oluwo Anide. He died in 1859 or 1860.

10 CMS CA2/069, Meakin to Sec., CMS, 29 November 1859. The agent was not presumably particularly enthusiastic, for he claimed to have forgotten Oluwo and his request. His forgetfulness may have been due to a sense of the doomed futility of his cause in a place such as Iwo.

11 *Ibid.*

12 *Ibid.*

13 *Ibid.* See also CMS CA2/069 Meakin to Sec., CMS, 29 November, 1859. Hinderer also described Iwo in similar terms: 'a sort of stronghold of Islam' – for which see CMS CA2/049b, D. Hinderer's Half-Yearly Report ending September 1859.

14 *Church Missionary Gleaner*, March 1859, pp. 34–5, quoting Hinderer's Report. See also Miss Tucker, *Abeokuta or Sunrise within the Tropics*, p. 235. See also Bowen to Bro. Taylor, 1 October 1850, in *Bowen's Correspondence*. Bowen compares this with his experience at Ketu, where the Muslims persuaded the Alaketu to keep him out of the country.

15 S. Johnson, *The History of the Yorubas*, p. 316.

16 *Ibid.*

17 Bowen notes: '[There is] a popular notion abroad that war and disease follow us wherever we go and that if a white man comes into a town, it will be destroyed by war as some places were not long after the visit of Landers'; Bowen to Bro. Taylor, 1 October 1850, in *Bowen's Correspondence*.

18 S. Johnson, *op. cit.*

19 There is no evidence of any objections to the Ifa arbitration.

20 *Church Missionary Gleaner*, March 1859, pp. 34–5, quoting Hinderer's Report. See also Miss Tucker, *op. cit.*, p. 235. See also Bowen to Bro. Taylor, 1 October 1850, in *Bowen's Correspondence*.

21 The Christian concern at poor evangelical yield, especially among Muslims, was clearly a universal one, affecting areas outside Yoruba-land, such as other parts of Africa, India, China and Turkey. This general concern was the driving force behind the summoning, in 1875, of the Edinburgh Conference which discussed the general issue of Christian Missionary work in Muslim and progressively-Muslim areas. A résumé of the proceedings and resolutions of this Conference was published in *The Muslim World*, 1, 1911, pp. 59–66. See also E. Stock, *History of the Church Missionary Society*, vol. 3, p. 133.

22 The Rev. James Johnson attended the 1875 Edinburgh Conference where it was resolved to have 'a special mission of Mohammedans', and he was appointed Superintendent, subject to the supervision of the local Finance Committee (see CMS CA2/056, James Johnson to Sec., CMS, 18 January 1877). Thus the chief agent of the new deal was to be the Rev. James Johnson. E. A. Ayandele, who has written a full-length biography of Rev. (later Bishop) James Johnson,

Holy Johnson, Pioneer of African Nationalism, 1836–1917 (Frank Cass, 1970) informs me that Johnson was, however, not formally appointed, largely as a result of some politics in the Yoruba Church Mission. Indeed nobody was. But, this notwithstanding, he evidently showed very keen interest in missionary work among Muslims in Yorubaland. He soon detailed to the Secretary of the CMS what the Yoruba Mission could do, and in fact did, about the situation.

23 CMS CA2/056, James Johnson to Sec., CMS, 29 April 1875.
24 CMS CA2/056, James Johnson to Sec., CMS, 29 April 1875.
25 *Ibid.*
26 *Ibid.*
27 CMS CA2/056, James Johnson to Sec., CMS, 6 March 1876.
28 *Ibid.*
29 A résumé of this conference was published in *Lagos Standard*, 4 March 1896. This report quotes the resolution cited here.
30 In 1896, 1902, 1908, the various CMS major meetings upheld these ideas. See CMS 1896 Conference already cited; *Niger and Yoruba Notes*, No. 25, vol. III, July 1896; *Western Equatorial Africa Diocesan Conference, 1902*, London, 1903; and *Report of the First and Second Synods of the Diocese of Western Equatorial Africa, 1906–1911.*
31 CMS CA2/056, James Johnson to Sec., CMS, 6 March 1876.
32 See below, particularly Chapter 6.
33 *Ahl al-Kitāb* – This was the Qur'anic description of Jews and Christians, since they possessed certain divine books of revelation such as *Injīl* (Gospel), *Tawrāt* (Torah), *Zabūr* (Psalms). Although these books were, according to Muslim belief, transmitted in a falsified form, their possessors were in a more privileged position than the 'pagans'. For more information, see particularly Qur'ān 2, 75; 3, 71; See also *EI*, article on 'Ahl al-Kitāb'.
34 *Kiriyo* is the rather opprobrious term by which the Yoruba describe 'Christians'. Many of the early Christians in Yorubaland were called 'creoles', which is also the name for the returned emigrants from Brazil; see R. C. Abraham, *Dictionary of Modern Yoruba*.
35 CMS CA2/056, James Johnson to Sec., CMS, 29 April 1875.
36 Idris Animasaun to Blyden, 1896, in *Correspondence Relative to the Appointment of Blyden as Agent of Native Affairs*, UIL.
37 The address of Bishop Oluwọle to the Third Session of the Second Synod of the Diocese of Western Equatorial Africa, May 1911, in *Proceedings of the Third Session of the Second Synod of the Diocese of Western Equatorial Africa.*
38 CMS CA2/056, James Johnson to Sec., CMS, 29 April 1875.
39 See the 1906 Synod Report cited in Note 30.
40 CMS CA2/056, James Johnson to Sec., CMS, 30 January 1878.
41 Compare similar works prepared elsewhere under similar circumstances; for example, *Life* W. Muir, *of Muhammad*, London, 1912; T. Hughes, *Dictionary of Islam*, London, 1885; and other works cited in Stock, *op. cit.*, vol. 3.
42 M. S. Cole, *al-Quran in Yoruba*, Lagos, Native Literature Publishing

Society, 1906. The Preface, written in both English and Yoruba, is of some historical value.

43 *Ibid.* He wrongly asserted for example that the Holy Prophet, Muhammad, does not realise the guilt of sin and the existence of an eternal moral law.

44 CMS G3 A2/03, J. Johnson, Journal Extracts for the half-year ending December 1882.

45 CMS G3 A2/01, A. F. Foster, Journal Extract for the half-year ending December 1880.

46 CMS G3 A2/01, A. F. Foster, Journal Extract for the half-year ending December 1880.

47 CMS G3 A2/01, A. F. Foster, Journal Extract for the half-year ending June 1880, entry for 15 August 1879.

48 CMS G3 A2/01, A. F. Foster, Journal for the half-year ending 1881.

49 It is customary to have this early morning address, which is often based on select portions of the Qur'ān.

50 This must have been the Imām. He is often but erroneously regarded by others as 'priest'. The Yoruba Muslim regards every *mu'allim* as an *afaa* and the Christian priest is generally called *alufaa*. This may have been a cause of the confusion in non-Muslim language of regarding as a priest the *mu'allim* who is made the leader of the Muslim community, Imām (known in Yoruba as *Lemomu*).

51 His obvious inability to sit on the floor in the Muslim style must have been responsible for this.

52 This must have been the central mosque which was and still is at Ijẹmba Quarter, Isẹyin. He would have had to remove his shoes if he would sit inside the mosque.

53 The Qur'ān is generally the basis of this Ramadan religious exercise. The interpretation is, of course, done with the aid of the popular commentary by Jalalain. For further details about this, see Chapter 4.

The 49th *Sūra* of the Qur'ān is Sūrat al-Hujurāt, a Medina chapter which deals with the manners and social relationship of members of the community – among themselves and with their leader. It is in this chapter that we have the famous verse that God has created man from a single stock, and that there is no basis for superiority or distinction save that of piety and righteous conduct. The Muslim preacher might well have been elaborating this theme. See A. Y. Ali, *The Holy Quran – Text, Translation and Commentary* (Dar al-Arabia, 1968).

54 CMS G3 A2/03, James Okuseinde, Journal Extract for the year ending December 1882.

55 *Ibid.*

56 Interview with Mr S. A. Dawodu (about 50), Lagos, June 1967. He relates how in his childhood days he and others used to carry the their Muslim master to such theological arena.

57 *The Fourth Report of the Lagos Church Mission for the year 1885*, p. 24; *The Fifth Report of the Lagos Church Mission for the year 1886*,

pp. 29–32; *The Sixth Report of the Lagos Church Mission for the year 1887*, p. 20.

58 *Ibid.* This is the classic question as to to whom the prophecy by Christ (John 14, verse 16) regarding the 'Comforter', 'Spirit of God' (*rūh Allah* or *rūh al-quds*) refers, whether to the Holy Ghost, as the Christians maintain, or to Muhammad as the Muslims do. This is still a live, hot issue today.

59 CMS G3 A2/03, Edward Burke to Sec., CMS, 30 April 1884. It was, of course, the one-month fast at Ramaḍān that is obligatory for able Muslims. (Qur'ān 2, 185.) But there is a supererogatory fast which is well known among the Yoruba Muslims as 'awe Arugbo' (lit. 'fast for the old people'). This fast takes place a month before the Ramaḍān fast and is generally observed by the devout. It may well be the junction of these two fasts which makes it appear as a three-month fast to non-Muslim observers.

60 *Ibid.*

61 *Ibid.*

62 CMS G3 A2/05, R. S. Oyebọde's Journal Extract for the half-year ending December 1887, various entries.

63 *Ibid.*

64 *Ibid.*

65 *Ibid.*

66 *Ibid.*

67 CMS G3 A2/03, James Okuseinde's Journal Extract for the year ending December 1882.

68 CMS CA2/056, Annual Letter of James Johnson, 1875.

69 *Ibid.*

70 E. A. Ayandele, 'The Mode of British Expansion in Yorubaland in the second half of the nineteenth century: the Ọyọ Episode', *Odu*. He illustrates here his thesis that in Yorubaland the missionaries were 'pathfinders of British influence', the people who 'prepared the way for the governor, exploiter and teacher'. See his *Missionary Impact on Modern Nigeria*, Chapter 2). This is true, no less than the fact that the Government, to non-Christians, appeared pro-Christian.

71 Some treaties, e.g. the 1892 Anglo-Ijẹbu Agreement, did not contain this 'missionary' clause; see O. Ayantuga, *The Ijebu and its Neighbours*, pp. 275–6 *et passim*.

72 Article 8 of the Treaty signed with Commodore H. W. Bruce in 1852 spells out how 'complete protection . . . and encouragement' shall be given to the Christian missionaries or ministers. The Lagos authorities were even 'to set apart a piece of land . . . to be used as burial ground' for the Christians. See *PP*, *Papers Relating to the Occupation of Lagos*, C.2982 for a copy of this Treaty.

73 Article 4 of the Treaty of Friendship and Commerce made at Abẹokuta on 18 January 1893. By this the Ẹgba authorities were to 'afford complete protection and every assistance and encouragement to all Ministers of the Christian religion'. See Appendix 1 of Carter to Ripon, 11 October 1893 in *PP*, C.7227, for a copy of this Treaty.

74 Article 5 of the Treaty with Ọyọ, 3 February 1893. This article has

identical wording with the Abẹokuta Treaty cited above. See also *PP*, C.7227, for a copy of this Treaty.

75 Fred Evans to Stanhope, 6 January 1887, in *PP*, C. 5144. Note also that the influence of Captain Goldsworthy went some way to help the introduction and establishment of the CMS in Ondo in 1873. See Bishop Oluwọle's address to second Synod in 1925, and article by Rev. A. B. Akinyẹle in *Leisure Hours*, 1922.

76 CMS CA2/056, James Johnson's Annual Letter 1875.

77 It was only in 1893 that Ọyọ, the 1830 transplant of the citadel of Ọyọ Empire, was bombarded by the British. For details of this see A. B. Aderibigbe, *Expansion of the Lagos Protectorate, 1863–1900*. See also E. A. Ayandele, *op. cit.*, for a treatment of how the British conquest of Ọyọ in 1893 illustrates the role of the Christian missionaries as 'secular imperial agents'.

78 *PP*, C.7227. See also Note 21.

79 NAI, CMS (Y) 3/1 No. 10. In a detailed report on Ọyọ District submitted to the Executive Council, Lagos, Melville-Jones deplored the fate of the Church in Ọyọ: it 'shows no signs, or very few signs of growth, if it is growing at all. . . . This Yoruba country is a hard soil.'

80 See Chapters 3 and 4.

81 CMS CA2/056, Annual Letter of James Johnson, 1875.

82 This is *Sūrat al-Ikhlās*. Qur'ān 112, 3. makes this clear statement. The absolute unity of Allah is, of course, a fundamental principle in Islam.

83 CMS CA2/056, Annual Letter of James Johnson, 1875.

84 *The Annual Reports of Lagos Church Missions for 1895–6*, pp. 40–1.

85 I. A. Braithwaite served the CMS and the Lagos Church in its missionary work first as a schoolmaster, later as a catechist for twenty-seven years and, finally, from 1895, as an ordained clergyman.

86 *The Annual Reports of the Lagos Church Missions for 1897–8*, p. 47.

87 *The Annual Report of Lagos Church Missions 1895–6*, p. 41.

88 *Ibid.*

89 *Ibid.* The number came down first to about sixty, but the indifference of yet another sixteen made it necessary to strike their names from the list of Christian enquirers or churchgoers.

90 *The Annual Report of Lagos Church Missions, 1897–1898*, p. 49.

91 See Chapter 3.

92 The reference here is evidently to *Imām*, the head of the Muslim community. The word 'alimani' (pl. alimanis) is a variant of *al-Imām*.

93 *The Annual Reports of the Lagos Church Missions, 1898*, p. 49.

94 See pp. 126ff.

95 CMS CA2/056, James Johnson to Sec., CMS, 30 January 1878.

96 CMS CA2/056, James Johnson to Sec., 29 July 1875. See also his Annual Letter of 1874, entry for 26 August.

97 *The Annual Reports of Lagos Church Missions, 1895–6*, pp. 12–13.

98 H. Carr, 'Report on Assisted Schools of the Colony for the year 1893', in *Blue Book*, 1893. See also Carter to Ripon, 18 December 1894, in *Colonial Report Annual*, No. 132, Lagos.

99 H. Carr, 'Report on Assisted School of the Colony for the year 1893',

in *Blue Book*, 1894. The number of assisted schools still stood at 33. See also Denton to Chamberlain, 1–27 August 1895, in *Colonial Report Annual*, No. 150, Lagos.

100 CMS CA2/o56. James Johnson's Annual Letter of 1875. See also his letter to Sec., CMS, 30 January 1878. In their desire for only the English language, the Muslims were one with many others who wanted the Christian bait but were unwilling to get hooked. For both, however, instruction in English and Christianisation were found to be inextricably intertwined in that age. There is this difference in the situation – the Muslims were being particularly sought after as part of the general plan to combat the Muslim advance.

101 *PP*, C.7227, p. 11.

102 *The Annual Reports of the Lagos Church Missions, 1895–96*, p. 12.

103 H. Carr, 'Report on Assisted Schools of the Colony for the year 1892', in *Blue Book*, 1893. See also Denton to Ripon, 29 September 1893, in *Colonial Report Annual*, 1892, No. 31, Lagos.

104 H. Carr, 'Report on Assisted Schools of the Colony for the year 1893', in *Blue Book*, 1894. See also Denton to Chamberlain, 27 August 1893, in *Colonial Report Annual*, No. 150, Lagos. The figures for 1894 are not available.

105 The unpopularity of the mission schools with the Lagos Muslims was very obvious to the Christian Missions as well as to the government. It became an object of concern for the latter. For an explanation about how the Muslims eventually came to embrace Western education, see Chapter 6.

106 There were instances when Christian Ministers pressurised Imams to encourage fellow Muslims to send their children to 'our schools'; see CMS CA2/o56, Annual Letter of James Johnson, 1874.

107 The Muslims believe they follow *sirāt al-mustaqīm* (the straight path); see *Sūrat al-Fātiha*.

108 CMS CA2/o56, James Johnson to Sec., CMS, 29 July 1875.

109 *Ibid.*

110 CMS CA2/o56, James Johnson to Sec., CMS, 30 January 1878.

111 This was Ordinance no. 3, passed by the local Legislature on 30 May 1887. It was particularly referred to in *Colonial Report Annual*, 1887, Lagos, p. 32.

112 *Proceedings of the C.M.S., 1900–1910*, London, 1901, p. 72.

113 *The Sixth Report of the Lagos Church Missions*, 1887, p. 22.

114 *al-Qur'ān* – various verses. See particularly Chapter 2, verse 217.

115 CMS CA2/o56, James Johnson to Sec., CMS, 24 September 1875.

116 See Chapter 4.

117 His mother was from Ijebu-Ode and his father from Ijesha. See E. A. Ayandele, *Holy Johnson* (Frank Cass, 1970), p. 16.

118 Report on Rev. J. S. Owen, *Proceedings of the C.M.S., 1904–5* (London, 1905), pp. 48–9. See also Rev. James Johnson, 'Planting of Christianity in Ijẹbu', in *Proceedings of the C.M.S. 1900–1* (London, 1901), pp. 74–5. See also Anna Hinderer, *Seventeen years in the Yoruba Country*, p. 109.

119 Rev. James Johnson, 'Planting of Christianity in Ijẹbu', *Proceedings*

of the C.M.S., *1900–1* p. 74. See also his article in the *Church Missionary Gleaner*, 1900, p. 44.

120 *Ibid.*

121 *Ibid.*

122 *Proceedings of the C.M.S., 1889–1900*, London, 1900, pp. 65–6.

123 *Church Missionary Gleaner*, 1898, pp. 188–9. Here Bishop Oluwọle adduces three principal reasons – reaction against oppression and exactions of the Chiefs, curiosity, and mercenary motives. See also E. A. Ayandele, *op. cit.*, pp. 155ff.

124 See particularly Webster, *op. cit.*, p. 101. See also *Niger and Yoruba Notes*, No. 75, vol. 7, September 1900, p. 21 *et seq.*

125 Webster, *ibid.* See also E. A. Ayandele: *The Missionary Impact on Modern Nigeria*, p. 156. Ayandele also brings out the fact that liberated Ijẹbu Christians in Lagos exerted themselves financially in this regard.

126 This fact has been rather under-emphasised in comparison to other factors. It is very significant in the context of Christian–Muslim relationship in Ijẹbu.

127 R. Owen, 'Report of a Tour to Ijebu', in *Proceedings of the C.M.S., 1903–4*, London, 1904, pp. 48–9. See also *Church Missionary Gleaner*, 1898.

128 In the course of his tour to Ijẹbu-Ode and Ijẹbu-Igbo from June to July 1896, Bishop Oluwole was often presented by the Christian converts with requests for resident pastors and teachers. See *Niger and Yoruba Notes*, iii, 28, October 1896, pp. 30–1.

129 *The Annual Reports of the Lagos Church Missions for 1897–1898*, p. 17.

130 See Chapter 4.

131 *The Twenty-sixth Report of the Lagos Church Missions for the year 1907*, pp. 14–15.

132 CMS G3 A2/013, Herbert Tugwell's Report of 1908, p. 46.

133 CMS CA2/056, Annual Letter of James Johnson, 1875. He possibly meant that the Muslims were roused or shaken out of all complacency.

134 Compare also the futility of Christian endeavour among Muslims elsewhere. Right up to 1914, Groves notes that for all the exertions of various Christian bodies in North Africa, 'sound conversions' to Christianity were few; see C. P. Groves, *The Planting of Christianity in Africa*, vol. I, pp. 118ff.; vol. 3, pp. 161–2. See also E. Stock, *op. cit.*, vol. 2, pp. 454ff.; vol. 3, pp. 512–36; and vol. 4, pp. 115–24. Stock, in these works, reviews the invigorated challenge of the CMS among Muslims in North Africa and the Sudan.

135 There were, indeed, few examples of Christians such as Gbadamosi Olosu who became Muslims under special circumstances. See B. F. A. Adinlewa, *Akure District Church Council: Diamond Jubilee* Akurẹ, n.d., p. 7.

136 *Niger and Yoruba Notes*, 1, 1894, pp. 30–2.

137 Compare the memorable words of Afa Kokewukobere, who dismissed the pagans as 'egbin' (filth).

138 *Ibid.*

139 *Report of the Select Committee on Africa of 1865* (PP, 412, 412–1),

pp. 241, 248. To the Christian missionary Gollmer, 'Mussulmans [*sic*] are our decided enemies' – as he declared to the same Parliamentary Committee.

140 *Ibid.*
141 *Niger and Yoruba Notes*, iii, 25, July 1896, p. 6, carries a report of the meeting of the Anglican clergy in Ibadan in 1896.
142 The 1902 Conference of the Diocese of Western Equatorial Africa was, to a large extent, dominated by the concern about the growth of Islam in Yorubaland. In a powerful episcopal address, Bishop Tugwell focused attention on this issue which, to him, was 'a matter of great anxiety, of profound regret, sorrow and humiliation'. This same tone was taken by M. T. E. Ajayi and others in their speeches. For all this, see *Report of the Western Equatorial Africa Diocesan Conference, Lagos, 1902*, London, 1903.
143 *Report of the Proceedings of the Third Session of the First Synod of the Diocese of Western Equatorial Africa 1908*, Exeter, 1908. See also *C.M.S. Proceedings, 1909*, London, 1910, pp. 29–30. See Appendix V for the text of the remarkable speech by the Rev. A. W. Smith.
144 CMS CA2/08, Annual Letter of D. Coker, 4 December 1877.
145 Report of the Lagos Diocesan Conference, 1902, p. 20. This was part of the Episcopal charge delivered by Bishop Tugwell. Compare the view of the 1896 Ibadan clergy meeting that Christianity was 'confronted everywhere by the obstinate and sullen force of *retrograde* Islam' (italics mine).
146 A certain Rev. M. J. Luke delivered a fatuous sermon at Breadfruit Church, Lagos, on 7 December 1886, in which he declared: 'Isin Imale ko se ire kan ni ilẹ wa, ko kọ awon enia lati ṣe ara wọn li ohunkohun.' ('Islam has done no good in our country, and has not taught the people anything whatsoever'). This is reported in *The Fifth Annual Report of Lagos Church Missions for the year 1886*, p. 14.
147 Rev. M. T. E. Ajayi, 'Christian Missions to Mohammedans', in the *Report of Western Equatorial Africa Diocesan Conference, 1902* London, 1903.
148 *Ibid.*
149 Religious clash or open controversy sparked off this recrimination.
150 *The Lagos Weekly Record*, 26 August 1893. The Christian editor, quite aptly, describes the African Muslim in these words: 'A Muslim African develops into a mosque-erecting, self-reliant propagandist,' and Christians as 'house-builders and apron-string saints'.
151 CMS CA2/056, James Johnson, Annual Letter of 1878.
152 CMS CA2/056, Annual Report, 1880 of James Johnson. He, for instance, bemoaned the fact that the Christian population of Abẹokuta was once dead set against the increase of class fees from $2\frac{1}{2}$ to $7\frac{1}{2}$ strings of cowries. In contrast, the Muslims freely supported their teachers and religious leaders, albeit in no organised form.
153 CMS CA2/056, James Johnson to Sec., CMS, 6 March 1876.
154 Résumé of the CMS Conference, 1896, in *Lagos Standard*, 4 March 1896. By 'its system of priesthood' the Conference probably meant simply the 'afaas', i.e. the Muslim teachers and devout men.

155 See also *Church Missionary Gleaner*, 1898. People looking for protection against established authority, according to Bishop Oluwọle, sought out the mission and offered themselves for conversion.

156 CMS CA2/056, James Johnson to Sec., CMS, 6 March 1876.

157 Rev. I. Oluwọle, the Assistant Bishop of Western Equatorial Africa, made the speech at Exeter Hall which he ended with an impassioned appeal for foreign missionaries 'to occupy the Yoruba country where a considerable number of the people are Moslems [*sic*] and several of the crowned heads and princes of royal blood are devotees of Islam'; see 'Our Islamic Prospects', in *The Lagos Weekly Record*, 26 August 1893.

158 *The Lagos Weekly Record*, 26 August 1893. The indigenisation of Islam in Africa is also well appreciated by many others. See particularly J. S. Trimingham, *A History of Islam in West Africa*, p. 232 *et passim*; E. D. Morel, *Nigeria, Its Peoples and Its Problems*, London, 1912, pp. 214ff.; E. W. Blyden, *Christianity, Islam and the Negro Race*, p. 354.

159 Christian historians such as Ajayi, Ayandele and Webster have, for example, stressed the importance of the Crowther episode in this regard. For an analysis of these events within the Christian churches, see particularly J. B. Webster, *op. cit.*, pp. 42–91; H. W. Turner, *African Independent Church*, vol. 1, p. 5.

160 E. A. Ayandele, *op. cit.*, p. 118, has drawn attention to 'the impetuous and relentless . . . effort' of Ajayi Crowther to push the missionary frontier even northwards to the Muslims on the Niger. But even in Yorubaland, particularly in Badagry, and Abẹokuta, Crowther took special interest in evangelism among the Muslims with whom he often engaged in disputes, after giving them copies of the Arabic Bible (see Chapter 2). Stock speaks of Crowther's plea for shrewd and tactful approach towards non-Christians; see E. Stock, *op. cit.*, vol. 2, pp. 458–9.

161 For further information about him, see the two articles on him by E. A. Ayandele, 'An assessment of James Johnson and his Place in Nigerian History, 1874–1917'; Parts I and II, in *JHSN*; and his autobiograpy, *Holy Johnson: Pioneer of African Nationalism, 1836-1917*, Frank Cass 1970

162 J. B. Webster, *op. cit.*, p. 99; E. A. Ayandele, *The Missionary Impact on Modern Nigeria*, pp. 254–6. This rather fiery 'nationalist' was the leader of the Native Baptist Church.

163 The influence of Blyden within the Yoruba Christian community has been analysed. See particularly Ayandele, *op. cit.*, pp. 217–19. He places his influence within the perspective of that of James Johnson. See also J. B. Webster, *op. cit.*, pp. 65–6, 99ff. For his influence within the Muslim community, see Chapter 6.

164 The Christian gentlemen obviously all believed that Christianity was the best form of religion for Africa. Even people like Blyden felt that Islam was only a stage in the religious evolution of Africans towards this ideal. See Blyden to Wilkinson, 17 November 1891, published in *Lagos Weekly Record*, 3 December 1892. See also H. R.

Lynch, *Black Spokesman: Select Published Writings of E. W. Blyden*, Frank Cass, 1971, pp. 271–311.

165 Webster, for example, showed how 'the Niger purge [i.e. Crowther's displacement], African leadership, Blyden and foreign forms loomed large in United Native African Church thinking'. J. B. Webster, *op. cit.*, pp. 69–89.

166 J. B. Webster, *op. cit.*, pp. 47, 99–100, 110–11. In spite of some prevalent Christian scorn of Islam, the African Churches tried 'to replace Islam as the preserver of the traditional structure'. They adopted local airs, individual effort, polygamy and even what they took to be the Islamic pattern of evangelisation: preach, baptise and teach. See also J. S. Coleman, *Nigeria: Background to Nationalism*, pp. 174–8. J. B. Webster, 'The African Churches', *Nigeria Magazine*.

167 One remarkable feature of the counter-arguments mounted by many a Muslim disputant was the facile reference to Biblical texts. See, for example, CMS G3 A2/01, Journal of Charles Phillips for June to August 1887, where a Muslim teacher in Ondo quoted the Old Testament text to support a point.

168 See CMS CA2/056, James Johnson to Sec., CMS, 29 July 1875. See also Reports by Rev. (later Bishop) A. W. Howell, the Diocesan Inspector of Lagos District Schools.

169 The Yoruba Muslims look upon the whites as *kiriyo*.

170 CMS CA2/062, Meakin's half yearly Report ending March, 1860. See also CMS G3 A2/02, Report on the Yoruba Mission by W. Allen, 1887.

171 *Ibid.* He relates how he was offered kolanuts and other gifts by the Muslim leaders and influential men.

172 See Chapter 7. Cragg correctly writes that among the Yoruba there is 'inter-religious fraternity'; K. Cragg: 'West African Catechism' *The Muslim World*. See also J. S. Trimingham, *Islam in West Africa*, pp. 129 and 222.

173 Daniel Olubi was obliged to comment on 'the kindness of the Mohammedan head chief [the Are] to us and our religion'; CMS CA2/075, Daniel Olubi, Journal Extract for the half year ending Dec. 1879.

174 Sir W. MacGregor once wrote that the Yoruba 'might serve as a model of Politeness to any people in Europe'; MacGregor, 'Lagos, Abeokuta and the Alake', *JAS*.

175 K. Cragg, *op. cit.*, ably speaks of 'a surprising degree of Muslim–Christian interpretation' among the Yoruba. Truly as he says, 'different individuals in one family belong to different faith with . . . mutual respect and tolerance'. See, for example, how the al-hajj A. B. I. Kukoyi describes how Muslims and Christians are together in his family; see *The Truth*, 4–10 August 1961. This religious co-existence is true of other places in the Western Sudan. See J. S. Trimingham, *op. cit.*; V. Monteil, 'L'Islam Noir', pp. 198ff.

176 *Lagos Times*, 12 October 1881. This records Muslim–Christian co-operation at bazaar sales.

177 See Ch. 7, especially for how the Muslims dealt with 'pagan' rulers.

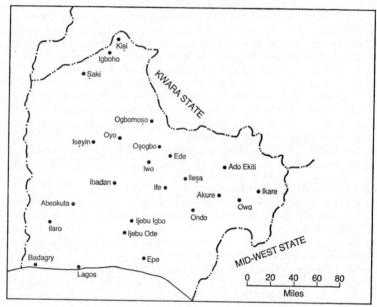

Islamic expansion in Yorubaland by 1908

6 Relations with the Colonial Government, 1875-1908

Before British rule was established among the Yoruba, the Muslims had been living under pagan rule. They were of course, trying to acquire political power and influence.[1] But, in the meantime, they tolerated pagan rule since it granted them freedom of worship.[2] This experience might have predisposed the Yoruba Muslims to accept British rule, which to them was essentially another non-Muslim government. Events later showed that the Yoruba Muslims not only perforce accepted British rule, but were also ready to co-operate with it to settle some problems of the country. Eventually, the relationship that was established between the Muslims and the British Government was essentially friendly and cordial. On the one hand, the British treated the Muslims with considerable respect, deference and understanding. On the other hand, the Muslims saw in the government a sympathetic if not impartial administration which they respected and with which they were ready to work. This attitude of mutual respect and help was built up over the years between 1875 and 1908.

At the start, the contacts between the Muslims and the new rulers were rather rough, if not definitely unpleasant. It will be recalled that ever since the return of Muslims to Lagos in 1840, the position of Islam had been growing strong, reaching a peak in 1845 when Kosoko, a royal patron of the Muslims, came to the throne.[3] But in 1850 the British, largely for reasons of trade, forced Kosoko to go into exile.[4] A direct consequence of this was that many leading Muslims in Lagos who were Kosoko's supporters were seriously embittered.

Events of the next decade only worsened Muslim feelings of bitterness and resentment. For some time after 1851, Kosoko's Muslim followers and sympathisers, such as Iposu, Ajeniya and

Afa Salu who was the Chief Imam of Lagos, continued to leave Lagos to join Kosọkọ at Ẹpẹ.[5] In August 1853 Kosọkọ and his people tried to take Lagos by storm; but they were repulsed with heavy losses.[6] Even the fact that Kosọkọ was made King of Palma and Lekki in 1854 did not improve relations.[7] By the counter-attacks which were launched on Ẹpẹ by the government in 1863,[8] Kosọkọ's power might have been reduced, but it was certainly not broken. Ẹpẹ, under Kosọkọ, continued to dominate the Eastern waters, constituting a thorn in the side of the government, or, to use the apt phrase of Burton, its 'horror and *bête noire*'.[9] The futility of a policy of force was apparent.

As the events of 1850 to 1862 must have overawed the Lagos Muslims and disposed them against the government, they there-fore conceived of the government as being anti-Islam. And this impression must have been reinforced by the fact that this govern-ment was understandably also pro-Christian. The government personnel was largely Christian; and the Governor was often given instructions which have a pro-Christian ring. From 1862 to 1886 he had instructions 'to take such measures in the country as he might consider necessary for the conversion of the people to the Christian faith and their advancement in civilisation'.[10]

This initial feeling of resentment was in the course of time assuaged considerably. Relations between the Muslims and the new rulers began to improve with the change of British policy in 1862 towards those in exile. In that year, it will be recalled,[11] the famous Glover Resettlement Scheme was concluded, whereby Kosọkọ and his followers were allowed to return to Lagos, and large plots of land were generously granted them for resettlement. The government evidently had come to appreciate the political force of the Muslims in Lagos and Ẹpẹ, and would seem to prefer to conciliate rather than alienate them.

It was not until 1875 that the government came face to face with the Muslims again, and had occasion again to play its hand. In that year, there was, it will be recalled, a split among the Lagos Muslims about the all-sufficiency of the Qur'ān.[12] This split created considerable commotion in the town, and rocked the Muslim community to its very foundations. The point of interest here was the government's attitude to this issue. Strictly speaking, the government need not have bothered about what was obviously an internal affair of a religious group. But here was an opportune moment for the government to demonstrate its concern about

Muslim welfare, and to show its spirit of tolerance towards all shades of religious opinion. The Governor called the two Muslim factions together on 13 October 1875 with the ostensible aim of settling their differences.[13] Present also were officials of the government, and, remarkably enough, dignitaries of the church, such as James Johnson and Charles Phillips. The Governor listened to both sides patiently, and then stressed that the government was concerned about Muslim welfare, and that its policy was fairness and freedom of worship.[14] The theological dispute remained insoluble; but the impression was left in the minds of the Muslims that the government was not interested in Muslim affairs.

Henceforth, the government tried to build up its good impression. It invited leading Muslims to Government House to meet distinguished Muslim sympathisers, such as Sir Richard Burton and Dr Edward Blyden who had come from abroad.[15] The Muslim lawyer from Britain, 'Abdallah Quillam, was given an honourable and official treatment on his arrival in Lagos.[16] The Governor himself once visited the Shitta-Bey Mosque when it was under construction, and together with the Chief Imam and other Muslim leaders[17] held a conducted tour round the mosque. And to mark the opening of this mosque, a government dinner was held on 4 July 1894 which was attended by government officials, Muslims and notable traders.[18] All these gestures were fairly successful in establishing a decent and friendly relationship between both sides in Lagos.

Important incidents soon occurred elsewhere, enabling both sides to come in closer contact and gain better understanding of each other. Early in 1898 there developed another major dispute among the Muslims, this time in Ẹpẹ.[19] The precise origins of this dispute are now obscure; but it might well have grown out of a certain dowry case, as affirmed later by Hornby-Porter, the Commissioner of Ẹpẹ.[20] The dispute, however, dragged on and led to the formation of two rival factions. Each was led by a notable Ẹpẹ Muslim: one by Muhammad Abu, a respected scholar; and the other by Braimah Edu, an influential Muslim trader.

On 10 April 1898 the Governor, who was on tour to Ẹpẹ, was confronted with this dispute. Although he was in the thick of perplexing political problems in the Lagos hinterland, the Governor, remarkably enough, took some time off to attend to this Ẹpẹ Muslim dispute.[21] He summoned the principal leaders of the two factions and endeavoured to 'settle their differences'.[22] The task was no doubt well-intentioned; but it was certainly not an easy one. All effort was directed to persuading both groups to worship together with the Balẹ, obviously because he was the 'sole authority' for the area.[23]

The government effort at reconciling both parties was only partially successful. Only one leader, apparently together with his followers, agreed to go to the mosque with the Balẹ so as to let the people see that 'they were friends again'.[24] The mediation only papered over the cracks, bringing into the town some uneasy peace; but it did not remove the basic cause of rancour between the two groups.

The lingering discontent within the Muslim group occasionally flared up, as in April of the following year, when 'an organised street fight'[25] broke out. Whenever Muslim disputes took such a violent turn, the government was again roused to swift action, particularly in the interests of public peace. The 'ringleaders' were arrested, and bound over in substantial sums to keep the peace.[26]

The longer this dispute dragged on, the deeper was its effect on the life of the Ẹpẹ Muslim community. Mutual antagonism intensified; and, soon, issue was joined on the ownership of the central mosque, which as elsewhere, was built by the communal effort of all the Muslims in the town, and was, therefore, normally open for all Muslims there to worship in. But as one group tried to prevent the other from using the mosque, it soon became obvious that the struggle would lead to violence. In January 1903 the Government therefore ordered the closure of the mosque to both parties.[27] The action certainly forestalled any possible breach of the peace; but as might be expected, it did not by any means bridge the division between the groups. One of the parties, that led by Braimah Edu, looked round for an alternative place of worship and found one in an old half-neglected mosque belonging to their fathers. This they repaired, renovated and used as their own mosque.[28] The other party, in the meantime, continued to urge the Governor to open the closed central mosque for their own use,[29] arguing that it was 'their own fathers who built it'.[30]

Meanwhile, the Governor, who had been evidently interested in the peaceful development of the Muslim community, had followed with growing concern the sad course of events in the Ẹpẹ Muslim community. Sensing that it was time again to intervene in the festering Muslim dispute, he sent for the prominent leaders of Lagos Muslims, such as the Chief Imam Ibrahim, his deputy, and

Shitta Bey. The Governor addressed them strongly on the advisability of the two factions in Ẹpẹ composing their quarrel and praying together in unity in the same mosque.[31] Could the Lagos Muslims not use their influence with their Ẹpẹ co-religionists to unite the two parties there? There had been since 1862 a very close connection between the Muslim communities in Lagos and Ẹpẹ. Thus apart from the appeals of religion and unity, there were extra reasons of blood and trade affinity to induce the Lagos Muslim community to serve as peacemakers between the two Ẹpẹ Muslim factions. The meeting felt inspired by the sympathetic attitude of the Governor, and went swiftly into action. And the Governor kept himself constantly informed of their progress and development.[32]

The relevant point of interest that emerges from this is not so much the intractable nature of the Muslim dispute in this Muslim town, but that in the history of government and Muslim relationship in Yorubaland, it serves as an example of what the government did. It was more evident here than in the case of Lagos in 1875, that the government attitude and role was a paradox of interest and detachment. The government showed concern about Muslim welfare: it called on both parties to reconcile, maintained interest in attempts to compose the quarrels and now encouraged neighbouring Muslims to mediate between the two factions. But it gave no overt support to any side, leaving it to the Muslims to sort out the intricate issues by themselves. Any threat to the peace of the town was, however, to be averted, if possible, by the presence of government policemen or soldiers, or even by the closure of the mosque.

The effect of the government's reaction was not lost upon the Muslims, if one considered the attitude of the Lagos Muslims who sought or obtained government help in settling the Ẹpẹ Muslim dispute, the co-operation of the Ẹpẹ Muslims themselves during the reconciliation meetings; and the prolonged nature of the Ẹpẹ dispute by itself. The result was that the Muslims came round to see the government as interested in their affairs, and capable of being impartial in intra-Muslim affairs. The relationship between the government and the Muslims both in Lagos and Ẹpẹ had now become more friendly and respectable.

More momentous events were yet to take place which drew the Muslims and the government more closely together. First, there was the issue of the establishment of Western education among

Yoruba Muslims. On this issue the government was, more than ever before, very helpful to the Muslims, while the Muslims were fully appreciative of government concern and action. Because this issue was of great importance not only in the history of the growth of Islam generally, it will be necessary to deal with it in some detail.

It has already been shown how Muslim apathy and opposition to the Christian-sponsored Western education persisted for a considerable period.[33] This Muslim attitude caught the attention of the government in a rather indirect way.

By 1867 the government was already showing its concern about educational development when it began to make available certain sums for the maintenance and education of the children of liberated African slaves. In 1872 the government widened the scope of its educational commitment by making some token grants of ten pounds each to the three Missionary Societies by way of assisting them in their educational programme. Government interest in, and financial assistance towards, education continued and increased as the government became more firmly established. But it was soon noticed that attendance at these schools was not increasing as steadily as could be expected; it was, indeed, far short of the number of children of school age. On the instigation of the Secretary of State for the Colonies, a Committee of the Board of Education was set up in July 1889 to look into the problem of poor attendance in schools in Lagos.[34] The committee found that the attendance was low largely because the Muslims stayed away from the mission schools. It thereupon made some recommendations to the government as to how Muslims could be made to share in the educational enterprise. Thus from 1889, the government's attention was engaged by the problem of Muslim abstention from mission schools and Western education in Lagos.

It was recommended[35] that the Governor should, in a meeting with the mallams and elders, impress on the Muslims the advantages of Western education. Secondly, the Christian schools were to be induced by an offer of fifty pounds to include Arabic in their curriculum with a view to making their schools more attractive and useful to the Muslim pupils. Thirdly, the Muslims should be asked to incorporate into their own (Qur'anic) schools' curriculum the teaching in English of the 3 Rs, the basis of Western education.

These recommendations signified government readiness to tackle the problem of Muslim non-attendance but in a rather superficial fashion. Some of the prescriptions were by themselves impracticable, based as they were on scanty knowledge of the local situation. For there were but very few people who knew Arabic and English enough to be useful and acceptable as teachers in either the mission or the Muslim schools respectively. There was the larger issue as to whether or not both sides, in spite of government financial inducement, would not regard the introduction of new subjects into their school curriculum as devices that would eventually hamper their own religious and educational programmes.

For the time being, however, these recommendations were accepted and formed the basis of government policy on Muslim education in Nigeria: government persuasion of the Muslims to accept Western education; extension of the curriculum of the Muslim schools to include the 3 Rs; and the inclusion of Arabic in the curriculum of the mission schools.

The first Governor to implement this policy was Sir C. A. Moloney. He was undoubtedly much interested in educational work and particularly in the Muslim aspect of the problem. On the strength of these recommendations and in the same hope of obtaining a larger attendance in the schools from among the Muslim population, he offered to the Christian schools special financial inducements for proficiency in Arabic.[36] He also held discussions with the Muslim leaders and encouraged them to extend the scope of the curriculum of their schools.[37] As could be expected, his efforts met with little success. No Christian school offered or could teach Arabic; and the influential Muslims were wary of modifying their traditional school system along the novel lines suggested by the government.[38]

As there had yet been no solution to the problem of making the Muslims accept Western education, government concern continued. The next Governor, Sir G. T. Carter, showed particular interest in the Muslim community; and on this issue he intensified government efforts though, at first, only along the lines laid down by his predecessor. Shortly after his arrival in the Colony as Governor, the Lagos Muslims called on him to pay their respects and welcome him to Lagos. The Governor seized this first opportune meeting to broach afresh the issue of Muslims accepting Western education, and extending their curriculum. 'I impressed upon them', he reported to the Secretary of State, 'the advantages of being able to secure a government grant for their schools and the obvious benefits which must accrue to the rising generation from a knowledge of English and the elementary subjects usually taught in English Schools.'[39] This meeting was only the first in a series of public meetings which were held with the Muslim community in Lagos[40] – to encourage the Muslims to send their children to Christian schools, or, with the offer of government financial help, to induce them to reconstruct the educational programme in their own schools along lines similar to those on which the Christian schools were operated.[41] But, as usual, the suggestions only excited 'suspicion and resistance in the minds of the Mohammedan priests'.[42]

Nevertheless, a noticeable rise was evident in the number of Muslims attending Christian schools. To take Lagos as an example: the 1892 figure[43] of 408 Muslim pupils in the Mission schools meant an increase of 61 over the previous year. In 1893, the total number of Muslims in Christian schools was 412, which represented an increase of 0.3 per cent of the total number of registered pupils.[44] By 1894, the number had risen to 442, 13 per cent of the total pupil enrolment. This was the highest figure and percentage so far of Muslim attendance,[45] an improvement which can be attributed to the government's persistent admonitions to the Muslims, though other factors, such as normal development, and pressure of circumstances, may also be presumed to have played a part.

More significant was the gradual awakening of the government to the real objections of the Muslim community to Western education. Sadly enough, these objections had not been properly investigated before, and there had been a too facile tendency to blame Muslim apprehensions on 'the conservatism of their elders'.[46] Consequently, government policy had not been very successful. But in the course of the series of government–Muslim meetings, the government came to appreciate the Muslim stand more clearly. It was on the Governor, Sir Gilbert Carter, that it first dawned that the core of Muslim opposition was religious. All government offer of money, he came to realise and admit, 'could not banish their prejudices against the religious question which in their minds a knowledge of English involved'.[47] It was clear that it still seemed to the Muslims that to encourage them to go to Christian schools was to ask them to apostacise; and to advise them to initiate the reconstruction of the traditional system of Muslim schools was to arouse their fears of bringing their schools under the influence of Christian teaching.[48]

Government realisation of the Muslim position and fears

predisposed Governor Carter to modify government policy. In a despatch[49] to London, he stressed his conviction that 'the initiative would have to come from the government. A proper school must be established with competent teachers who should be Mohammedans.' In other words, the government must take the bold step of establishing a school with Muslim teachers for the Muslims.

The Governor went ahead with the implementation of this major modification of policy. He initiated several discussions with influential Muslim officials and elders and, particularly, Muhammad Shitta, with a view to persuading them to support the placing of at least one Muslim school under the Board of Education.[50] Details of this scheme were not spelt out; but it was plain that by being under the Board of Education such a Muslim school would have to conform to the 1887 Code, receive grants, and introduce new subjects. If this was done, Sir Gilbert was convinced, such a school would serve as a pioneer which eventually would practically induce many of the fifty-odd Muslim schools to receive government aid and extend their curriculum in the direction desired.[51]

While the government was exploring new avenues as regards Muslim education, the Lagos Muslim community was itself experiencing some internal ferment and stir. On 20 April 1894 al-hajj Harūn al-Rashīd arrived in Lagos from Sierra Leone, his native country.[52] He was a young man in his early thirties, and a distinguished Arabic scholar trained in the University of Fez, who had served as an Arabic tutor at Fourah Bay College.[53] On his arrival in Lagos, he inevitably became involved in the stir which the issue of Western education had caused within the Muslim community. He held a series of meetings with the Muslims and did 'a great deal to stir up his co-religionists to the necessity of enlarged education for their youth'.[54]

Also, as this stir increased, and as the government exerted further pressure to induce the Muslims to accept Western education, the Lagos Muslim community decided to contact the Sultan of Turkey who, in July 1894, addressed them a letter urging them to provide instruction in Western learning for the rising Muslim generation.[55] The Turkish plea was reinforced by the pleadings of Mr 'Abdallah Quillam, the personal representative in Nigeria of 'Abd al-Hamid II, the Sultan of Turkey. A lawyer by profession, Mr Quillam was a solicitor of the Supreme Court of Judicature, Liverpool. Ever since his conversion to Islam, he had been actively engaged in the propagation of that faith.[56] At the time of his visit to Lagos as the personal representative of the Sultan, he was currently the President of the Liverpool Muslim Association. On the occasion of the opening of the famous Shitta Bey Mosque in July 1894, he publicly urged the Lagos Muslims to accept Western education.[57]

With all this internal ferment, the opposition of the Lagos Muslims began to diminish, and only a few dissentients still held out. The major persuasive force was not so much the advertised material advantages of Western education as the demonstration that Western education was not necessarily a concomitant of Christianity but a desirable entity by itself which did not have to involve christianisation. It was clear that it was being acquired by Muslims elsewhere who did not thereby lose the fervour of their religious conviction.

As the initial standpoints of both the government and the Muslims gradually shifted, the gap between them narrowed. It narrowed further and was eventually closed through the efforts of Dr E. W. Blyden[58] who, for both political and educational reasons, was appointed by Governor Carter in October 1895 as Agent of Native Affairs. It was a major part of his assignment to treat with the Muslim community especially on the issue of education.[59] He was to execute government policy in this regard; to remove the known Muslim prejudices against Christian teaching and methods; to induce the Muslims to take advantage of the provisions of the Education Ordinance; and to encourage the Muslims to place themselves in a position to share in the government grant provided for educational purposes. Blyden was well qualified for this task. He himself had had four years' experience in organising Western education for the Muslims in Sierra Leone.[60] His reputation for learning as well as his sympathy for Islam[61] had preceded him to Lagos, as much with the government as with the Muslims.[62] After holding a series of consultations with the Muslims, who developed increasing confidence in him, he succeeded in devising an agreement acceptable to both the government and the Muslims.[63] The plan was to place one of the best Muslim schools in Lagos, the one at Bankole Street, under some government control.[64] The 3 Rs and English would be introduced, and the government was to pay all the teachers' salaries. The teachers and the pupils were to be all Muslims; and the school was to retain its essentially Muslim character, due place being given to Islam and Arabic studies. The Muslim community, at its own insistence, was to keep the control of the buildings, paying the rent of the school house. Above all, it was to be an experiment for one year, after which the situation was to be reviewed.[65] Wisely, the agreement was left flexible, and sufficient concessions were made to Muslim susceptibilities.

The school generated considerable interest and confidence among the Muslims. The headmaster, Idris Animasaun,[66] was thrilled by the idea; and in the interest of the Muslims, he pledged his full support for the scheme. 'I took it as my duty', he wrote to Dr E. W. Blyden, 'to encourage what you and the Government want to establish and especially for the interest of Muslims.'[67] He, accordingly, volunteered to work in the school for one year without pay.[68] Among the Muslim parents, there was some enthusiasm also. Some withdrew their students from the Christian schools and put them in the new school. Of the forty boys in the new school, more than half had been formerly in Christian schools.[69]

The school was officially opened on 15 June 1896 as the Government Muslim School. It opened with forty boys and forty-six young men[70] under the direction of the Principal, Idris Animasaun, assisted by two teachers recruited from Sierra Leone on a salary of £2 10s. a month each.[71] The boys were divided into five graded classes, twelve in class I, eight in II and the 'rest of the children are divided into three classes'.[72] English, Yoruba, reading and arithmetic were taught in each class, the depth depending on the level of intelligence of the class concerned. In the leading class, the pupils read the Standard Primer in English, Books I to III; studied some grammar, pronouns, etc.; did arithmetic, simple addition and subtraction, compound addition, long division, avoirdupois weight, and so on. As for the young men, they concentrated on the Sunday School Primer, the first Standard Reading Book, and did some arithmetic.

Due prominence was given to Arabic and Islamic studies in the Government Muslim School. According to the reports of the school which were compiled by the headmaster, Arabic was taught and translated into Yoruba. Islam was also taught. The pupils, the reports often added, made progress in these subjects. Classes were held only five days in the week, Saturday to Wednesday, from 9.00 a.m. to 1.30 p.m. for the boys, and, for the young men, 11.00 a.m. to 12.30 p.m. There were no classes on Thursday and Friday in order to prepare for and attend Jumat Service on Friday.

The opening of this school in June 1896 was quite properly hailed by the Government as marking 'indeed a new era in the history of Lagos when the most conservative element of the Muslim population have concluded to enter into competition with the Christians in their effort to acquire western learning'.[73] The happy experiment of 1896 proved successful, thanks to the co-operation of both the government and the Muslims.

Thus in 1897 when the issue was re-examined, both sides were ready to discuss and settle certain outstanding issues. There was the case of the headmaster's pay. The headmaster, who had rendered free services for one year, indicated that as he had not enough income from other sources, he would want to work else-where 'though [he was] still prepared to attend [the school] two or three times a week if no better arrangement' could be made.[74] On account of his commendable services and influence, he was urged to stay on in his post, and put on a salary of £60 p.a., on the recommendation of Dr E. W. Blyden.[75] Two more assistant teachers were employed, each on a salary of £30 p.a., making the total number of teachers four. The school rent of £3 a month, which the Muslims had paid for one year, was henceforth to be paid by the government, on the understanding that the Muslims would 'consent to the inspection and report on the school by the Government Inspector of Schools'.[76] In the meantime, arrangements were made for the erection by the government of a more commodious school building with a capacity for about 250 pupils and costing between £400 and £500. At the instance of the Governor, who was anxious that they should have some responsibility in the matter, the Muslims were to be responsible for the maintenance of the building. At the instance of Blyden, efforts were made to ensure that the school retained the simplicity and atmosphere of the traditional Muslim schools[77] by the use, for example, of mats in place of chairs.

The key to the success of this experiment lay essentially in the anxiety of both sides to continue with the scheme. On the government side, it involved greater expenditure than ever before; but as the Governor strongly pleaded when seeking approval for the estimates, this was inevitable in order to keep the achievement of 1896. He said:

It was not until April 1896 that Mohammedans gave way and allowed one of their schools to be conducted on western principles. We fought for this point for years and now that we have gained it, we must, in my opinion, give substantial encouragement to the teachers if the scheme is to be successfully developed.[78]

On the Muslims' side, the combination of English and Islamic studies proved exhilarating. 'The parents', reported Blyden, '[were] as a rule very much pleased with what [was] to them, the astonishing progress made by their children in the English language.'[79] And well may Blyden assert in 1897, that 'the enterprise [might] now be considered as established in the minds of the Mohammedans'.[80]

The successful establishment of the Government Muslim School in Lagos had immediate beneficial effects among the Muslim community as a whole. The Muslim town of Ẹpẹ, which had for long remained practically closed to Christian evangelisation and their Greek gifts,[81] drew up a petition which it presented to the Acting Governor, Captain G. C. Denton, on the occasion of the tour of the latter to Ẹpẹ in June 1898.[82] In that petition, the Ẹpẹ Muslims, at the inspiration of the influential Braimah Edu, and under the leadership of their Chief Imam, Uthman Audu, and Kujeniya, the Muslim Balẹ, requested the government to establish at Ẹpẹ a Muslim school 'conducted on similar lines to the one which was established in Lagos in 1896'.[83] Denton was much fascinated by this idea, coming as it did from Ẹpẹ, a Muslim stronghold; and in view of the government's earnest desire to introduce a system of European education among the Muslims, he thoroughly discussed the issue with the Ẹpẹ Muslims.[84] The latter made clear their eagerness about it: they had about 200 Muslim pupils ready to attend the school, and were prepared to erect the necessary buildings at their own expense. The government, they felt, could help by paying the teachers, as in Lagos. The Governor found the proposals attractive, and lost no time in seeking to implement them. The matter was discussed with the Inspector of Schools, Mr H. Carr, who welcomed the idea and agreed with the Governor that a staff of two was adequate for the time being. It was then brought before the Legislative Council which unanimously agreed that every support should be given to the undertaking. It voted £45 for half-year salaries of the principal teacher on a salary of £60 *per annum* and his assistant on a salary of £30 *per annum*.

Work began in earnest on the Ẹpẹ Muslim School although

there was some delay in completing it because of the rains.[85] Meanwhile the Muslims raised additional funds to the tune of £40 to purchase the necessary books, appliances and furniture.[86] When all was ready, the school was officially opened on 16 November 1898, by the Governor in the presence of all Ẹpẹ Muslims and at least six leading Muslims from Lagos.[87] In view of the local enthusiasm for this school, the Governor reposed much confidence in its future development.

Events were to justify his expectations. About a year later, the school was visited by Sir William MacGregor.[88] He found it to be a rough mud building with a sloping mud floor, a grass roof, and not well provided with doors. The children sat on wooden forms and had books, slates and so on. The attendance was eighty-seven, and the school was conducted strictly in accordance with the education code. The conduct of the school was essentially the work of the staff, mostly Sierra Leonians, under the leadership of the headmaster, al-hajj Harūn al-Rashīd, also from Sierra Leone.[89] The pupils could count in English up to one hundred, sing a little in English and were beginning to write in English. Several of them read their Qur'ān correctly. 'The impression left on [one's] mind after assisting at all their work was that if encouraged they [would] forge ahead. . . .'[90] Another visit to the school later that year elicited from the Governor the positive report that the school was 'already producing good results'.[91]

News about the establishment and progress of these Government Muslim Schools at Lagos and Ẹpẹ spread far and wide among the Muslims. There was hardly any surprise, therefore, when Badagry Muslims, on 4 April 1899, followed the Ẹpẹ precedent and forwarded a petition[92] to the government for the establishment of a school similar to those at Ẹpẹ and Lagos. And having ascertained the ready and enthusiastic support of the Badagry Muslims,[93] the government went ahead to meet their demands under the same conditions as at Ẹpẹ and Lagos. The school was opened in 1899.

Indeed, the last years of the nineteenth century provided an atmosphere so favourable for Muslim education that in April 1899 Blyden formulated for the government a scheme[94] of higher education in Lagos. His idea was that the government should establish a higher institution for the training of Muslim youths. This institution would serve the immediate purpose of producing the educated Muslim teachers so much in demand. He also argued that it would have the far reaching effect of acting as a counterpoise to French influence, and strengthening British influence among Muslims in the West African interior. The scheme was carefully planned and advocated in terms calculated to win the support of the British Government. 'The enterprise', Blyden explained,

> was in close harmony with the comprehensive and philanthropic schemes for the development of the Estates of the Empire which Mr. Chamberlain has so much at heart and in the carrying out of which I beg most respectfully to offer my humble co-operation.'[95]

The Governor was so persuaded of the value of the scheme and so encouraged by the experience of Blyden that he recommended it to the Colonial Office for the most careful consideration.[96] But the advanced age of Blyden, then sixty-seven, and the opposition of certain members of the Legislative Council, who objected to the religious implications of the scheme, nipped the proposition in the bud.[97]

Given, however, the enthusiasm displayed by both the government and the local Muslim population at the close of the nineteenth century, it was to be expected that more Muslim elementary schools would be built in the Muslim towns in Yorubaland which had by 1896 come under the British Government. In September 1897, there arose the issue of establishing in Ibadan a similar Government Muslim School. Blyden, after consultation with the leading Lagos Muslims, pointed out that welcome as the idea was, no suitable teachers were available. In the circumstances, it was suggested that Ibadan pupils be encouraged to send their children to Lagos;[98] or alternatively, more teachers could be recruited from Sierra Leone.[99] The Governor preferred children to be taught in their own towns where their parents resided,[100] in spite of the observation of Blyden that there were four children from Ilọrin in the Lagos Muslim School.[101] As for recruitment, which might have solved the problem, the Governor was silent. Consequently, the whole issue of having a similar school in Ibadan lapsed. There is also evidence of a verbal request from Ijẹbu-Ode which Blyden forwarded in writing to the government in April 1899.[102] But there were in Yorubaland no more than the three Government Muslim Schools which, however, continued to expand.

A pertinent question here is why no more such schools were established after 1899. An obvious explanation was the drying up of government enthusiasm. The Acting Governor, Denton, was superseded in 1899 by the new Governor, Sir W. MacGregor. On settling down to his post, he was principally preoccupied with the problem of local administration. Besides, the limited objective of the government had been achieved. If, indeed, the whole purpose of government effort was to induce the Muslims to embrace Western education, it can be argued that the way had already been clearly shown by the joint establishment of three schools. In any case, there were practical problems of obtaining an adequate number of suitable and qualified personnel to execute the scheme. Blyden, the live wire of Muslim educational activity, resigned from his post of Agent of Native Affairs in 1899; and the office, which had given considerable direction and sympathy to Muslim issues, was replaced by a Council of Native Affairs, whose administrative duties were as wide as its composition. In other words then, by the beginning of the twentieth century, government concern about Muslim education, if not Muslim welfare, in Yorubaland declined, at least for a while. But the obligations already incurred in respect of the three Government Muslim Schools continued to be discharged until 1926, when they summarily ceased to be government concern.[103]

The question can now be raised as to the significance of these Government Muslim Schools in the context of the government's endeavour to promote Western education among the Muslims in Yorubaland. These schools had come into being partly as a result of petitions by the Muslims but largely as a result of the growing concern of the government at the Muslims' apathy towards Christian-sponsored Western education. Even if some credulity is, for the sake of argument, given to the possibility of these petitions being inspired, it is still remarkable and historically significant that the Muslims accepted the ideas contained in the petitions. It is particularly noteworthy that apart from contributing substantially to the establishment of these schools, the Muslims jealously guarded the schools and continued to patronise and support them. In the case of Badagry, for example, the Muslims had occasion in 1900 to complain of the conduct of the teacher in the Government Muslim School. The objectionable behaviour of this teacher displeased the Muslim parents, and to a great extent accounted for the drop in the attendance of Muslim pupils at the school.[104] As soon as the Governor satisfied himself about the complaints of the teacher, he replaced him with a more agreeable one;[105] and the confidence of the Badagry Muslim population in the school was restored.[106] Thus the school, together with the other schools at Lagos and Ẹpẹ, continued to enjoy the unalloyed support and confidence of the Muslim communities whose interests they were meant to serve. The schools were continually expanded as the demand for them mounted; and on more than one occasion, larger and more commodious buildings had to be built, and more teachers employed in order to keep up with their increasing expansion. In Lagos, for example, even the new and larger school building which was erected at Lafiaji in 1898 at a cost of about £500, had to give way seven years later to another one at Isalegangan, costing no less than £1,500,[107] with an immense increase in the number of pupils.[108] Within a fortnight of the opening of the new Isalegangan school, about 505 applications were received for admission; and the question of fresh accommodation and increased staff immediately arose. Thus it can be maintained that these schools in a sense represented a joint endeavour entered into and sustained by the Government and the Muslims.

The enterprise was, to all intents and purposes, successful. The reports[109] compiled on these Government Muslim Schools were often brief; but they all generally show an increase in the number of pupils. There was in Lagos in 1899 the outstanding fact that the number of pupils dropped, largely because, as the Muslim parents complained, of the great distance of the school.[110] Also there was the peculiar fact that in Badagry, the school tended to decline with the general decline of the town at the turn of the century.[111] Nevertheless, the reports speak of general satisfactory progress. The 1908 reports[112] compiled by W. Henley-Bickel, the Acting Inspector of Schools, were the most detailed, and commended the three schools. Singled out for particular praise was the Ẹpẹ Government Muslim School which was described as 'a good school throughout . . . the tone and discipline of the School are very satisfactory. A word of praise is due to Mr. Seriki for his intelligent work.'[113]

Although the Government Muslim Schools were only three in number, with only a total Muslim attendance of a few hundreds, they had a significance which outstripped their number. They signified that the Yoruba Muslims, or at least those in the colony, had come to accept Western education. Their acceptance had been the result of their practical realisation that Western education could both be disengaged from Christian evangelisation and successfully allied with Islam. For this Muslim realisation, much credit should go to the government, particularly to the individual Governors, and to Blyden, who as from 1895 exerted themselves in this direction. It was they who eventually found and applied the formula which helped to dislodge the Muslims from their former attitude of unqualified opposition to Western education, and made them favourably disposed towards it. The significant role of non-officials, such as al-Rashīd and Quillam, and the gently persuasive force of changing circumstances must also be taken into account. There can hardly be any doubt that the conversion of Muslims at the close of the nineteenth century to acceptance of Western education represented a major government achievement in the history of the relations between the government and the Muslims in Yorubaland. The fact that the government could not extend this imaginative experiment to Ibadan, Iseyin, Oyo and other Muslim centres in the interior could, in part, explain the limited response of these areas to Western education.

The attempted synthesis of Western and Islamic education provided the Muslims in the colony with their first practical experience in the management of schools along Western lines. For these schools were only government schools largely in the sense that they were financed and inspected by the government; the administration and day-to-day management of the schools were the responsibilities of the local Muslim community. The Muslims provided land and labour; they tackled the problems of organisation, staff, equipment and the like. They even sometimes provided the necessary finances. All these inspired confidence; and the experience gained here was to prove beneficial later when these schools ceased to be government schools in 1926. Some of the teachers, such as I. A. Animasaun and Tiamiyu, later established their own schools in Lagos, managing them in a way similar to that of the previous decades.[114] In spite of the withdrawal of government help, all the former Government Muslim Schools continued to function well under the full management of the local Muslim communities, the Ẹpẹ School being later taken over by the Ansar Ud-Deen Society.[115] Above all, the success of the endeavour also encouraged some of the dynamic Muslims to introduce, though on a modest scale, this synthesis into their own Muslim schools.[116]

While the government's role in promoting the cause of Western education among Muslims in the era before 1900 can hardly be gainsaid, it has been pointed out that within the Muslim community in the 1890s there were stirrings and ferment which facilitated government efforts in the educational field. These internal stirrings were assisted by the actual demonstrated success of the Government Muslim Schools. Thus, even though government help eventually stopped, the impulse towards the acquisition of Western education remained; and it was further strengthened by the increasing number of educated Muslims who remained Muslims, their attendance of Christian schools notwithstanding.[117]

However, it would be naïve to imagine that all the Yoruba Muslim community had been completely dislodged from their former apathy towards Western education. The educated Muslims themselves were to experience an uphill task persuading their fellow Muslims to establish their own schools, where Islam and secular subjects could be taught. A few British junior officers occasionally remonstrated with the Muslim elders to reform their piazza schools. To such remonstrations, as F. C. Fuller, the Resident at Ibadan reported,[118] 'the invariable answer was "Allah will teach us the right way"' – an answer on which he sarcastically commented: 'I regret to say that so far their prayer has not been answered.' Evidently, the tradition of the past was still very strong; and evidence abounds attesting to the popularity of the traditional Muslim schools down even to our own times.[119]

As there were practical difficulties in the way of these new efforts, availability of adequate numbers of Muslim teachers, for instance, the old system of education persisted more easily. The case of Ibadan in 1897 comes to mind in this context. But difficulties and tradition notwithstanding, a remarkable breakthrough had been achieved, thanks to the government's initiative and the subsequent collaboration between the government and the Muslims.

Besides the issue of Western education, the other momentous issue in the second half of the nineteenth century which drew both sides together was the problem of establishing peace in the immediate interior of Lagos. If it was the government that helped Muslims on the issue of providing Western education, it was the Muslims who, as friends of the government, now rallied round to assist it in solving a problem confronting the country as a whole.

The government in Lagos had been very anxious, especially in the interests of trade, to end these wars and re-open the trade routes which brought valuable produce to Lagos. Motivated by this desire, the Governor, Sir G. T. Carter, went to the interior on his famous 1892–3 expedition which took him to Ijẹbu, Abẹokuta, Ọyọ, Ilọrin and finally to the war camps at Kiriji. During this tour he tried where he could to establish some basis for friendly relationship with the various Yoruba rulers. He no doubt clearly appreciated that the hardest nut to crack was the Ilọrin–Ibadan hostility. The Ibadan side of the war was dealt with quickly and effectively enough. But Ilọrin posed problems: the problem of uninterrupted trade and peace with the productive hinterland; and the problem of the northern boundary of the Lagos Protectorate. It was in tackling these Ilọrin problems that the government made appeal to some Yoruba Muslim communities.

Governor Carter had visited Ilọrin, spending almost a full week there from 21 to 27 February 1893. During this stay he had the opportunity to observe the quality of the religion of the people and had witnessed the colour and stir of the Friday *ṣalāt*, when the whole town seemed 'en fête'.[120] He discussed with the Emir, Moma, whom he found plain and sensible, the issues of peace in the interior. As regards the immediate question of breaking up the last pitched camps of war in Yorubaland, the Emir agreed to the Governor's suggestion that the Ilọrin and Ibadan war camps at Otun should break up at the same time.[121] The foundations of future co-operation between Ilọrin and Lagos would appear well laid. The Emir made 'many protestations of friendship and assurance that no further aggressive action against Ibadan would be taken without reference to Lagos'.[122] Under so auspicious conditions, Governor Carter went back to the battlefield, and effected the simultaneous breaking-up of the war camps. He returned to Lagos, joyful at having brought to an end the crippling wars which had continued for so long in the Lagos hinterland. The point of interest here is not so much that it was Ilọrin which made the end of war possible; too many factors and personalities have strong claims to that credit.[123] Rather it was that friendly relationship had been secured by the government with this Muslim emirate which played such a key part in the Yoruba wars and politics of the nineteenth century. And this had assisted in the final processes of re-establishing peace. It was the desire of the Lagos Government to preserve this fair relationship with a view to finding solutions to the outstanding problems of trade and boundaries which were important for the entire Yoruba country.

The Governor turned to the Lagos Muslim community in order

to maintain this friendly contact with the Muslim emirate, Ilọrin.[124] Indeed, it can be presumed that this formed an interesting part of the 'interior' questions for which Dr E. W. Blyden was appointed as the Agent of Native Affairs in 1895.[125] There was considerable contact over the fixing of the boundary in 1894 by the representatives of Ilorin itself; this Lagos–Ilorin contact did not bring the Emir any credit but was greatly resented, largely because the 1894 boundary, fixed at River Awere, had deprived Ilọrin of Ikirun and some valuable areas in Ekiti over which it felt it had some claims largely by right of conquest.[126] This resentment grew particularly among the warrior classes led by the two Baloguns, the Yoruba Balogun Alanamu, and Balogun Gambari.[127] This, together with the planned intrigue of his brother, Alege, resulted in a bloody *coup d'état*[128] about the middle of September 1895.[129]

The death of the conciliatory Emir, Moma, in 1895 cleared the way for the rise in Ilọrin of radical and uncompromising men. Leaders such as Balogun Alanamu and Balogun Ajikobi, otherwise called Biala, arose and asserted the claims of Ilọrin.[130] They were not prepared to accept the 1894 boundary arrangements; and they were white-hot in their denunciation of all white men, with whom they swore they would have nothing to do at all.[131] Thus under the militant leadership of Balogun Alanamu and Sulaiman, the new Emir, Ilọrin renounced the boundary settlement and resumed in 1896 its belligerent activities in Ekiti and Ọffa districts. Quite patently, it also aimed to 'get rid of European influence in the country'.[132]

The significance of the new intransigent mood of Ilọrin, consequent on the rise of the new Herod there, was not lost on the Lagos Government.[133] More than ever before, it urged on the Governor the necessity of re-establishing contact with this Muslim emirate. As before, the line of communication was the Lagos Muslim community. The Governor's plan was to proceed to the interior as far as Ogbomọṣọ, the nearest important Yoruba town to Ilọrin, to meet Ilọrin delegates.[134] To bring this about, he arranged with the Chief Imam of Lagos to send trustworthy messengers to Ilọrin with a letter from him to the new Emir intimating the desire of the Governor to meet Ilọrin representatives at Ogbomọṣọ.[135] This meeting, it was hoped, would settle the boundary question in an amicable way. The Chief Imam also wrote a long covering letter[136] to Sulaiman, the Emir of Ilọrin.

The letter attempted to clear the confusion then prevalent in

Ilọrin, as elsewhere, about the 'white man', distinguishing the evangelists, Christian missionaries, from the impartial British Government. The latter, it was explained, protected both Muslims and Christians and, as such, Muslims could make friends with the British Government on the basis of the argument of 'Fakh Razi-yu'.[137] After all, the Queen had Muslim subjects in India. Besides, the Governor had, in practical terms, shown that he had the love of Muslims at heart: he had opened the Shitta Bey Mosque, spoken favourably of Islam to the disappointment of Christians who subsequently criticised him; and he had allowed Muslims to worship publicly in Ijebu and to erect mosques. Because of this demonstrated love of the Governor towards the Muslims, the Chief Imam urged the Emir to be friendly, 'peaceful and quiet' and, above all, to send his representatives to meet Carter.

Evidently by employing the good offices of the Muslims, the Governor had hoped to restore good relationship between Ilọrin and the government. This was simply following the idea of approaching people through their favourites. And in this move, he had received the co-operation of the Lagos Muslims who, in the light of their experience, believed in the friendly disposition of the Governor towards them. For it was the British Government that had shown signs of interest on the issue of Muslims' acceptance of Western education. In spite of his friendly approach through the Muslims, Governor Carter had his own clear political intention towards Ilọrin. He wanted Ilọrin to desist from its attacks on Yoruba country, accept the former boundary line and take its eyes off Odo-Otin. Insisting on these, the Governor admonished Ilọrin to keep these terms, 'otherwise trouble which they will not be able to avert will fall upon them'. The warning went on: 'But the Governor . . . does not wish to deal harshly with any Native Tribe excepting under compulsion. . . . He does not desire to take your country. . . .'[138]

Obviously, the essence of this diplomatic move by the government consisted in the use of blandishments and veiled threats. But these were no empty threats, for early in the year, great military preparations were being made to destroy Ilọrin if need be; and to this effect, no less than five hundred men with modern artillery had been obtained in readiness for any eventuality.[139]

After these diplomatic and military arrangements had been made, the Governor proceeded to the interior, and arrived at Ogbomọșọ which, he noted, was a sizable town of about 70–

80,000 inhabitants, 'able to hold its own against the Ilọrin'.[140] He waited in vain for the expected messengers from Ilọrin. He soon realised that his own messengers had been sent back at Idi Emi, a station between Ogbomọṣọ and Ilọrin. What was more, he realised that this station was heavily guarded by a large body of Ilọrin cavalry forces under the direction of the Sarumi. This officer had sent back the messengers of the Governor at Idi Emi, and later he sent two delegates from there to ascertain from Carter personally his 'true intentions'. The Governor reiterated his desire to have peace and settle boundary questions with Ilọrin; and thereupon he sent letters and presents to the Emir. Whether to give battle or not must have been an issue which agitated his mind for a while. However, he bided his time and after waiting a little further at Ogbomọṣọ, the Governor went to Oṣogbo, Odo-Otin and Ibadan. At Ibadan, he met his Ogbomọṣọ messengers, who confirmed that they had not been allowed to go to Ilọrin and had been sent back to him with his letters unopened.

The diplomacy and threats of 1896 had failed to make Ilọrin agreeable. The failure was certainly not due to any lack of co-operation from the Lagos Muslims, who did what they could in the circumstances. The failure was essentially due to the fact that the anti-white feelings which had become dominant in Ilọrin were so strong that it would have been suicidal for any Ilọrin leader at that time to countenance any friendly relationship with any foreigner, particularly a Christian one. For Ilọrin, the issue was larger than the redrawing of the boundaries. The bombardment of Ọyọ and the 1896 threat were clear writings on the wall, warning the Muslim emirate of Ilọrin about its own survival as an independent political entity.[141] This would explain the solid military preparations made at Idi Emi for the defence of Ilọrin. It induced the Ilọrin to boast that unlike the Ọyọ, neither the Royal Niger Company nor the Lagos Government could interfere with them.[142] Thus the Ilọrin officer Idi Emi affirmed that he would be risking his life to forward any letters to the political authorities in Ilọrin, knowing full well that they would have nothing to do with the Governor of Lagos or any white man for that matter.[143]

The government in Lagos was not willing to give battle until the issue had been sorted out with both the Colonial Office and the ambitious Royal Niger Company, which was keenly interested in this large market town.[144] For the time being therefore, Lagos, after the failure of its diplomacy, could take no more decisive action than that of imposing an economic blockade that same month against Ilọrin. The two roads from Yorubaland to Ilrọin, one passing through Odo Otin and the other through Ogbomọṣọ, were blocked by Captain Bower on the instruction of the Lagos Government.[145] The blockade was kept tight against Ilọrin traders, and those of them who tried to break it were ill-treated and deprived of their goods.[146] Besides, friendly local people were, in greater numbers, armed with guns to scout in the bush against the incursion of Ilọrin into Yoruba territory.[147]

In the light of this, it was no surprise that the relationship between Ilọrin and the Lagos Government deteriorated fast. In those hard and sore circumstances, it was the Lagos Muslim community, which had so far served as the line of communication between the two parties, that now took the initiative of attempting to bring both sides together again. The elders of the Lagos Muslim community sought an interview with Governor Carter in Lagos, during which they obtained his permission 'to endeavour to make peace between our Muslim brethren at Ilorin and the Government here'.[148] They indicated their desire to write a letter and send messengers to Ilọrin for this purpose. Carter assured them that these messengers would be allowed to go and return – that is, pass the blockade unmolested. With this assurance, they despatched their envoys to Ilọrin.

In Ilọrin itself, the effects of the blockade which had been on for a number of months had begun to be felt. For Ilọrin, a large town teeming with Hausa and Yoruba traders who came and went about in Yoruba country, the blockade created disaffection and disposed the political authorities to negotiate with the white men through Muslim emissaries.

Thus when the emissaries from the Lagos Muslims arrived, they were warmly received. The Emir declared himself pleased with the message from Lagos and sent word back that he would like to send his own messengers to the government there but for the fear of ill-treatment on the road.[149] If only there would be assurance that they would not be molested, he would, 'if God please', send good and trustworthy men.[150] This signified a thaw in the cold relations. Not much could be done to further this improvement in relations because Carter was then about to proceed on leave. Thus, when the Muslim elders approached him as to what next they could do in view of his impending departure, they had to content themselves with his assurance that his successor, a good and faithful man, would soon come and would adjust matters properly. The issue hung on until the Governor arrived in July.

Meanwhile, between March and May 1896, Ilọrin now and again harassed the military outpost at Odo Otin.[151] And at the other end, the Lagos Government was building up before the Colonial Office the argument that an early opportunity should be taken to destroy Ilọrin and hand over the place to Ibadan under the general supervision of the Resident there.[152] In other words, it was this government rather than the R.N.C. which was better equipped to subdue Ilọrin – and quickly too. The point was that Lagos Government had begun to believe reports reaching it through the jingoistic Captain Bower of Ọyọ bombardment fame that Ilọrin was intriguing with 'a certain section of the Yoruba' to rid the country of European influence.[153] It itched to bring Ilọrin, a prosperous trading centre, under its control and influence.

These events and plans were hardly known to the mediating Muslims for, on the arrival of the new Governor in Lagos, the Imam and the leading Muslims met the Governor, and briefed him about the Lagos–Ilọrin transactions in which they had been involved since 1893. They again requested permission to send messengers to the Emir of Ilọrin, which the Governor readily granted. As to the issue of protection and safety of Ilọrin emissaries, the Governor gave a Delphic reply which the Muslims embodied as part of their letter to Ilọrin. In this letter to Sulaiman of Ilọrin, a copy of which was sent to the Governor,[154] they greatly entreated the Emir to do all in his power to bring the present war to an end in the interests of peace and trade between them and Ilọrin. So far as the Governor in Lagos, 'the Christian ruler here', was concerned, he, like the Queen whose minister he was, hated war, liked Muslims and above all, wanted peace.[155] As regards the blockade, the letter conveyed the Governor's word that if their people would come with white flags and cause no trouble whatsoever, they would be allowed to pass. The letter was an obvious attempt to urge the Ilọrin Muslims sufficiently on the path of peace.

Judging from the contents of this letter, the Lagos case had been clearly impressed upon the writers. For example, they strove to make it clear to Ilọrin that the Christian rule under which they lived was a peaceful one (a controversial matter if the events of 1861, 1892 and 1895 are considered[156]). Their advice that a white flag be used might also appear as a government request to the

Ilọrin to surrender. But in spite of whatever views they really had of the intentions of the Lagos Government, there was no doubt that by their initiative in this issue, and by the tone of their letter, the Lagos Muslims were earnest and sincere in their effort to bring about amicable relations between their Ilọrin co-religionists and the Lagos Government.

The emissaries from the Lagos Muslims departed, passed through Ibadan and the Ogbomọṣọ blockade to Ilọrin. Within a month, they returned to Lagos, bringing back the awaited news from Ilọrin.[157] The delegates had been well received by the Emir; but in spite of the pressure of the envoys, the Emir would not send envoys down to Lagos for fear of their being molested on the way. In his reply to the Chief Imam of Lagos, the Emir urged him to entreat the Governor to remove the blockade, which was affecting Ilọrin adversely. As regards the present war, he argued that it was the previous Governor[158] who had provoked it. Though it was this same officer who had settled a previous war, he it was who 'made plans which the Ilorins did not like' and, as he still pursued these, war inevitably followed. In the circumstances, the Emir appealed to the Chief Imam 'to do his very best to bring matters to a favourable conclusion'.[159]

The Emir was silent on the issue of boundaries and the cessation of hostilities. In spite of entreaties, he would not negotiate; and without giving any concrete proposals, he wanted the Chief Imam to settle 'matters' favourably in Lagos. The attitude of Ilọrin, to judge by the latest reply, had hardly changed: it was still belligerent and sore,[160] all the more so, perhaps, because of the blockade. It was this biting blockade that he would urgently want to be lifted.

The Ilọrin reply was communicated without delay to the Governor. The new Governor confessed his difficulty in understanding the allusions of the Emir to the provocative plans of the officer mentioned. And after thanking them, the Governor only promised to review the whole issue when on leave in England and do what he could. In the meantime, the blockade continued.

The ball was now in the court of the Governor, and there it was to remain for a while. The government obviously did not want to capitulate to Ilọrin and, had it not been for the tussle with the Royal Niger Company as to which of them should take the decisive action against Ilọrin, the Lagos Government would have acted. In the meantime, this tussle continued in the secret citadels of power, unknown to the mediating Lagos Muslims. Both Ilọrin and the Lagos Government remained firm in their menacing and uncompromising stance. The government troops remained at Odo Otin while Ilọrin forces were at Ọffa, Ọtun and Erinmope.

But the odds were increasing against Ilọrin. In January, Ilọrin made a rash attack on Erinmope and this was repulsed with very heavy losses by Sgt-Major Dangana.[161] The Ilọrin were reported to have lost a powerful war chief, Adamu, the son of the redoubtable warrior, Karara, and 150 people in the rout.

Flushed with victory, Acting Governor Denton hoped that the defeated Ilọrin might now be more favourably disposed towards entering into friendly relationship with the Lagos Government. To bring this about he, from Otin, cast about for fresh mediators. Lagos was too far away, but he still adhered to the principle of communicating with the Ilọrin Muslim political authorities through their respectable co-religionists. In this regard, therefore, he approached the Muslim ruler of Iwo, who was an elderly and strict Muslim with considerable influence.[162] He demurred over this affair, frankly diffident about the success of his mediation in the conflicts.[163] On the insistence of the Acting Governor, however, he agreed to send a letter to Ilọrin to inform the authorities there that if they would send an influential delegation down to Odo Otin, the Governor would be ready to discuss the present situation with them.[164] As the Oluwo had expected, nothing came out of this communication.

Soon Ilọrin was in considerably troubled waters with the advancing R.N.C. The latter had had as much interest as the Lagos Government in extending its influence over Ilọrin, and had kept up a keen observation of the turn of events. Since April 1896, the company had declared itself ready to attack Ilọrin, though it pleaded for time partly for financial reasons and partly for reasons of convenience. But after dealing with Nupe, the company was fully ready to face Ilọrin forces which were already weakened by the Erinmope disaster. On 22 February 1897 it inflicted a heavy defeat on Ilọrin, and thereby firmly brought Ilọrin under the company's 'sphere of influence'.[165]

It is clear from the above that in its dealings with the intractable interior problem of peace and trade, the Lagos Government had inevitably run up against the Muslim emirate of Ilọrin. In its endeavours to settle trade and boundary questions with this preponderantly Muslim town, the government had utilised to a large extent the services of the Lagos Muslim community. This community progressively became involved in the problems of Lagos–Ilọrin relations. It served as the line of communications, and tried to compose matters between both sides. In this regard, the action of the Lagos Muslim community was a constructive and disinterested one, being largely that of putting amicably together their Muslim counterparts and the government whom they had come to find helpful and friendly. If their efforts failed to reconcile both, this did not reflect on their sincerity of purpose, or still less on the strength of their peaceful exertions. The failure was in essence due, first, to the fact that both sides were too intransigent for the limited mediatory forces of the Lagos Muslims to control; secondly, the Ilọrin problem of the 1890s raised wider political issues which were unknown to the mediators and were beyond their capacity.

The mediation of Iwo and particularly of Lagos signified Muslim desire to assist in the solution of the political problem facing Lagos – to establish friendly relationships with all neighbours and local people, including Muslims. Their role as intermediaries was made possible partly by the normal religious bonds and sympathy existing between Muslim communities, and particularly by the acknowledged obligation which every Yoruba Muslim community owed to Ilọrin as the local Mecca. This bond was now reinforced further by the action of Lagos.

The relationship between both sides was so cordial and helpful that Muslims in the first decade of the twentieth century had no hesitation in approaching the government on a fairly wide number of issues. To the 'impartial' government,[166] they freely brought various requests, and complaints even of a minor character. In 1903 the Lagos Muslims through their leaders, such as Chief Imam Ibrahim Yesufu Shitta Bey[167] and al-hajj Ishau, complained to the Governor about the proximity of an incinerator to their mosque at Oko Awo.[168] Similarly, the ban on drumming in Lagos[169] was objected to by the Muslims. Through their members of the Central Native Council, they complained[170] to the government that the ban deprived them of the services of the drummers who normally woke them up for their early meals at the time of the Ramaḍān.[171] And above all, there was even a complaint to the government in 1903 that a certain Muslim infant had been seized and detained for three months in Ijẹbu-Ode.[172] Two years later, Ijẹbu-Ode Muslims requested the government to help resolve their Imamate dispute by sending someone down to arbitrate and examine the two candidates to the Imamate.[173]

Yet it was remarkable that the government often took prompt action on these matters, however minor some may have seemed. To Ijẹbu-Ode a government official was sent, and for a long while he battled with the issue.[174] In Lagos, the public incinerator was soon removed;[175] the ban on drumming was lifted;[176] and investigations were made to help restore the detained child to his parents in Lagos.[177]

This attitude of mutual respect and help was of considerable significance. It enabled the Muslims to establish themselves further,[178] and to adjust to the changing circumstances of the late nineteenth-century Yoruba society. It also meant that the Muslims were far from resisting British occupation, as the events of 1850 to 1862 seemed to have presaged. Rather, the Muslims not only helped the British in the pacification of the country but also co-operated with that government. The loyalty and co-operation of the Muslims can be explained to a great extent by the fact that they enjoyed under this government freedom of worship, respect and considerable assistance.

The government's attitude of deference and help was no doubt in line with the generally cautious and courteous attitude of the British Government towards Muslims in Lagos, Nigeria and elsewhere.[179] But certain factors in the local situation also conditioned this attitude. First, some of the Lagos top officials, such as Moloney, Denton and Carter, were people who sympathised with the local Muslims or admired them for their strong moral fibre and dignity. Maloney was not alone in his declaration of 'the greatest respect' for Lagos Muslims.[180] Besides, the Muslims themselves were fast becoming an important social and political force in the country,[181] and in the interests of peace and development, the government could not but endeavour to show a benign attitude towards them.

Notes

1 See Chapters 3 and 4.
2 See Chapter 1.
3 See Chapter 2.
4 For a full treatment of how Lagos was bombarded, see *PP Papers*

Relating to the Occupation of Lagos, C.2982. See also A. B. Aderibigbe, *Expansion of the Lagos Protectorate,* 1861–1900.

5 *Lagos Official Handbook, 1897–1898* (London, 1898), p. 6. See also R. F. Burton, *Wanderings in West Africa,* pp. 233–4; *Epe Confidential Report,* 1934. Posu and Ajeniya (spelt 'Pellu', 'Iposu' and 'Aginia' by these records) left Lagos around July 1853. The 1934 Report stated that Posu was expelled from Lagos, but I prefer to go by the report of the 1897 Official Handbook, which confirms Burton's on-the-spot report of 1863.

6 *Ibid.* This is the famous 'Ija Afasegbojo' (the Futile Combat). See also *Lagos Official Handbook, 1897–8,* London, 1898, p. 6.

7 *Epe Confidential Report, 1934.* This was in return for renouncing all claim to Lagos and a government subsidy of 2,000 head of cowries or 500 dollars.

8 *Ibid.* It was Governor Freeman who carried out these counter-attacks.

9 R. F. Burton, *op. cit.,* p. 234. It is a bit surprising that Newbury made little or no mention of this Ẹpẹ influence at this time; see C. W. Newbury, *The Western Slave Coast and Its Rulers.*

10 NAI, CSO 5/8 No. 1. In subsequent years he was required 'to do his utmost to promote religion and education', the religion in this context being presumably Christianity; *see* NAI, CSO 5/8 No. 2.

11 See Chapter 1.

12 See Chapter 3.

13 CMS CA2/056, James Johnson to Secretary, CMS, 6 March 1876. As James Johnson was present at this meeting, he gave a first-hand report of its proceedings.

14 *Ibid.*

15 See R. F. Burton, *op. cit.,* pp. 8–10. He held a long and informal meeting with them, too.

16 *The Lagos Weekly Record,* 30 June 1894.

17 *The Lagos Weekly Record,* 13 December 1893.

18 *The Lagos Weekly Record,* 4 July 1894.

19 NAI, CSO 1/1, MacCallum to Chamberlain, 5 May 1898.

20 NAI, CSO 1/1, Acting Governor to Chamberlain, 25 February 1899. Enclosure 1, Hornby-Porter to Acting Governor. Hornby-Porter took over the supervision of the districts from F. Manning, who had been the Acting Commissioner.

21 NAI, CSO 1/1, MacCallum to Chamberlain, 5 May 1898.

22 *Ibid.*

23 Unity was made an issue of reconciliation largely in deference to a popular Yoruba Muslim belief that all Muslims in a town must worship together under one Imam who is acknowledged by all, and that it was evil and inconceivable that differing Muslim groups should worship and pray apart in the same town.

24 NAI, CSO 1/1, MacCallum to Chamberlain, 5 May 1898.

25 NAI, CSO 1/1, MacGregor to Chamberlain, 6 October 1899.

26 *Ibid.*

27 *Lagos Government Gazette*, 17 January 1903.
28 *Ibid.*
29 *Ibid.* See also *Lagos Government Gazette*, 24 January 1903 and 28 March 1903.
30 *Lagos Government Gazette*, 24 January 1903.
31 *Ibid.*
32 *Lagos Government Gazette*, 30 January 1903; also that of 28 March 1903.
33 See Chapter 5.
34 NAI, CSO 1/1, Lord Knutsford to Moloney, 19 April 1889. See also M. W. Walsh, *The Catholic Contribution to Education in Western Nigeria, 1861–1926*, pp. 166–8.
35 NAI, CSO 1/1, Moloney to Lord Knutsford, 9 September 1889. See also Acting Governor Denton to Lord Knutsford, 26 November 1889, in *Blue Book*, 1888; M. W. Walsh, *op. cit.*
36 *Colonial Report, Annual, 1892*, No. 31, Lagos, p. 7.
37 NAI, CSO 1/1, Carter to Knutsford, 30 April 1892.
38 *Ibid.*
39 *Ibid.*
40 *Colonial Report, Annual, 1892*, p. 25.
41 Acting Governor Denton to Marquess of Ripon, 29 September 1893, in *Colonial Report, Annual, 1892*.
42 *Ibid.*
43 *Colonial Report, Annual, 1892*. Enclosure in Acting Governor Denton to Ripon, 29 September 1893. See also Encl. 1 in Denton to Ripon, 1 May 1893.
44 *Colonial Report, Annual, 1893*. Enclosure in G. T. Carter to Ripon, 18 December 1894.
45 *Colonial Report, Annual, 1894*, No. 150, Lagos.
46 NAI, CSO, 1/1, Denton to Ripon, 1 May 1893, encl. the Report of H. Carr, the Inspector of Schools.
47 NAI, CSO 1/1, Carter to Knutsford, 30 April 1892.
48 The Report of Mr Sunter, the Inspector of Schools. Enc. 1 in Carter to Knutsford, 30 April 1892, see NAI, CSO 1/1.
49 NAI, CSO 1/1, Carter to Knutsford, 30 April 1892.
50 NAI, CSO 1/1, Carter to Denton, 1 June 1893.
51 *Ibid.*
52 *The Lagos Weekly Record*, 28 April 1894.
53 *Ibid.*
54 *The Lagos Weekly Record*, 5 May 1894.
55 *Colonial Report, Annual, 1894*. The government was informed of the purport of this letter. Turkey was contacted no doubt because it was regarded as the head of the Muslim Community, and promoter of Pan-Islamic ideals. It had, as 1892 showed, been taking interest in the growth of Islam in this area; see Chapter 4.
56 *The Lagos Weekly Record*, 3 October 1891. He was reported to have been the author of a certain *The Faith of Islam*; see, *The Lagos Weekly Record*, October 1891.
57 He evidently urged this point as well in private discussions. *The Lagos*

Weekly Record, 23 February 1895. See also the *Annual School Report*, 1895 by H. Carr, which this issue of the paper carried.

58 For a full-length biography of Blyden, see H. R. Lynch, *Edward Wilmot Blyden, 1832–1912, and Negro Nationalism.* He sees Blyden more as a Pan-Negro patriot than as a sympathiser of Muslims.

59 Governor's Speech to Legislative Council on the appointment of Dr Blyden in December 1895. See also Minute Paper, 'Establishment of Mohammedan Schools in the Colony', in NAI, CSO 1/1 vol. 26.

60 *Ibid.* See also *Macaulay Papers*, II, 2; *Correspondence Relative to the Appointment of Blyden as Agent of Native Affairs.* These records are available at the UIL.

61 Blyden was not a Muslim; and to the end, his religious preferences were for Christianity. But alive as he was to the salutary effects of Islam on West Africa, he worked happily with the Muslims. He believed that Islam fostered scholarship, unity, egalitarianism, industry and abstinence in West Africa.

Notable works by Blyden himself reflecting his Islamic bias include 'Mohammedanism in West Africa', *Methodist Quarterly Review*; 'Mohammedanism and the Negro Race', *Fraser's Magazine*; *Christianity, Islam and the Negro Race*; 'Islam in the Western Sudan', in *JAS*, V, October 1902; 'West Africa Before Europe', *JAS*, viii, July 1903; 'The Koran in Africa', *ibid.* See also H. R. Lynch, *Black Spokesman.*

62 On the invitation of Moloney, he had been to Lagos in 1890. He was warmly received by the Muslims, and he made a considerable impression on them. See *The Lagos Weekly Times*, 31 December 1890; *The Lagos Times*, 14 February 1891.

63 *African Messenger*, 6 March 1924. Report of the text of welcome address presented to Mr A. B. Augusto on his return from United Kingdom, where he studied Law.

64 Blyden to Colonial Secretary, Minute Paper, 11 May 1896 in *Correspondence: Blyden.* The School has been consistently well reported on. It consisted of two buildings in a large compound, with a well-paved yard or court separating the buildings, and a wall surrounding the whole compound.

65 NAI, CSO 26, File No. 17611, Hewson to Grier, 6 October 1926. He reviews the history of the School up to year 1926.

66 He died on 21 July 1968; see *Daily Times of Nigeria*, 22 July 1968.

67 I. O. A. Animasaun to E. Blyden, in *Correspondence: Blyden*, pp. 14–15.

68 I. O. A. Animasaun to E. Blyden, 2 May 1896, *Macaulay Papers*, II, 2, p. 14; see E. Blyden to Carter, 8 May 1896, *Correspondence: Blyden.*

69 I. O. A. Animasaun, No. 1 Report of the Muslim School, 31 August 1896. This Report is contained in the *Correspondence: Blyden.* See also Appendix.

70 These were slightly older people.

71 E. Blyden to Colonial Secretary, Minute paper, 11 May 1896,

Correspondence: Blyden. See also *Lagos Standard*, 10 June 1896, reporting proceedings of the Legislative Council.

72 See Note 69.
73 MacCallum to Chamberlain, 22 September 1897 encl. Report by the Colonial Secretary, Denton, *Colonial Report, Annual*, 1896. The Report went further to describe the opening of the School as 'the most important event connected with education . . .'
74 Blyden to MacCallum, 12 June 1897, *Correspondence: Blyden*.
75 *Ibid*.
76 Governor to Denton, 30 July 1897, *Correspondence: Blyden*.
77 E. Blyden to Colonial Secretary, 8 June 1897, *Correspondence: Blyden*.
78 NAI, CSO 1/1, Denton to Secretary of State, 15 April 1897.
79 Blyden to MacCallum, 12 June 1897, *Correspondence: Blyden*.
80 *Ibid*. See also Blyden to the Colonial Secretary, 25 September 1897, *Correspondence: Blyden*.
81 See Chapter 5.
82 NAI, CSO 1/1, enclosure in Denton to Chamberlain, 11 June 1898.
83 *Ibid*.
84 NAI, CSO 1/1, Denton to Chamberlain, 11 June 1898.
85 Interview with the Ẹpẹ Muslim Community, June 1963. See Bibliography: Oral Evidence.
86 NAI, CSO 1/1, Acting Governor Denton to Chamberlain, 27 August 1898.
87 NAI, CSO 1/1, Acting Governor Denton to Chamberlain, 19 November 1898.
88 NAI, CSO 1/1, MacGregor to Chamberlain, 9 August 1899.
89 T. Ola Avoseh, *A Short History of Epe* (Ms.), pp. 28–9. I am grateful to him for allowing me to use his personal copy. This work is reported published, with little modification; but no copy has come to hand.
90 NAI, CSO 1/1, MacGregor to Chamberlain, 9 August 1899.
91 NAI, CSO 1/1, same to same, 6 October 1899.
92 NAI, CSO 1/1, Denton to Secretary of State, 12 April 1899, Enclosure I. The petition was written by J. I. Hotonu, the clerk to Chief Abasi.
93 NAI, CSO 1/1, MacGregor to Chamberlain, 10 October 1899.
94 NAI, CSO 1/1, Blyden to Denton, Enclosure in Denton to Chamberlain, 14 April 1899.
95 *Ibid*.
96 NAI, CSO 1/1, Denton to Chamberlain, 14 April 1899.
97 Walsh reported 'that certain members of the legislative Assembly would not vote money for any Institution placed under Dr. Blyden', because they felt that he had no strong moral character; see M. W. Walsh, *op. cit.*, p. 174. The Governor, however, certainly made a note of the advanced age of Blyden, see NAI, CSO 1/1, Denton to Chamberlain, 14 April 1899. See also MacGregor to Chamberlain, 7 August 1899.
98 Blyden to Colonial Secretary, 25 September 1897, in *Correspondence: Blyden*.
99 Blyden to Colonial Secretary, 1 October 1897; *Correspondence: Blyden*.

100 MacCallum to Colonial Secretary, 28 September 1897, *Correspondence: Blyden.*

101 Blyden to Colonial Secretary, 5 October 1897, *Correspondence: Blyden.*

102 NAI, CSO 1/1, Denton to Chamberlain, 14 April 1899. See also Minute Paper 1926 in NAI, CSO 26.

103 For more information about these schools in the period before 1926, see G. O. Gbadamọṣi, 'The Establishment of Western Education among Muslims in Nigeria', *JHSN.*

104 NAI, CSO 26, R. J. B. Ross, *Western District Report, 1900–1901.*

105 *Ibid.* See also NAI, CSO 1/1, Denton to Chamberlain, 3 September 1900.

106 NAI, CSO 26, R. J. B. Ross, *op. cit.* It took some time for the parents to respond. The new teacher often had to go round the houses of the Muslims in an obvious effort to win their confidence.

107 NAI, CSO 26 File 17611, Newson to Grier, 16 October 1926. The Superintendent of Education gave here a concise and accurate account of the history of the Lagos Government Muslim School.

108 Papers before Legislative Council, 1907; Report by Henry Carr, 1907. See also Annual Report of Western Provinces 1906 by W. E. B. Copland-Crawford, in NAI, CSO 26.

109 *Blue Books, 1897–1906.*

110 NAI, CSO 1/1, Denton to Chamberlain, 18 August 1900 encl. Report with the *Blue Book* of 1899.

111 For further information about this, see B. W. Hodder, 'Badagry: one hundred years of change', *The Nigerian Geographical Journal.*

112 Annual Education Report, 1908, in *Blue Book*, 1908.

113 *Ibid.* Mr Seriki was the headmaster of the school.

114 *The Times of Nigeria*, 26 April 1920. Tiamiyu had been a teacher in the Government Muslim School, Ẹpẹ. He established his school at Ebute Awo in Lagos; and Idris Animasaun called his school Animasaun Memorial School, Lagos.

115 The Badagry School was taken over by the Ansar Ud-Deen Society in 1941. The Ẹpẹ School continued as an undenominational Government School till 1938, when it became the Ẹpẹ Native Authority School.

116 *Annual Report of Education Department*, 1907, p. 16.

117 See Chapter 5.

118 NAI, CSO 26, *Report for the Year 1900 on that portion of the Lagos Hinterland under the control of the Resident of Ibadan*, p. 27.

119 *Colonial Report, Annual, 1907*, No. 583, Southern Nigeria, p. 17. The pupils in regular attendance at the Muslim Schools in the Western Provinces were estimated to have been about 2,500 in 1907. But in view of the various difficulties of counting at the time, the accuracy of this number is open to dispute. More appropriately, the number can be taken as reflecting the popular patronage which the Muslim schools still have from among the Muslims. See also S. Hakim, *Report, The Teaching of Arabic in Schools and Colleges in Nigeria*, Ibadan, 1961.

120 It was an impressive occasion, for the Governor witnessed the Emir proceed in state to the mosque, amid a grand display of horsemen; *qq.v.*, Carter to Ripon, 14 March 1893, in NAI, CSO 1/3.

121 This was on 14 March; see B. Awe, *The Rise of Ibadan as a Yoruba Power*, pp. 321ff. See also S. Johnson, *The History of the Yoruba*, pp. 628–9. The simultaneous breaking up of the war camps was the suggestion that met the objections of the two camps who were anxious that the mistake of 1886 should not be repeated. On that occasion, retiring troops were attacked from behind. See works just cited above.

122 NAI, CSO 1/1, Carter to Ripon, 14 March 1893.

123 See A. B. Aderibigbe, *op. cit.*, and B. Awe, *op. cit.*, Chapter 8, for a full treatment of these factors.

124 Carter may also well have been persuaded to use the Lagos Muslims since the peace Mission of Phillips and Johnson had failed in Ilọrin largely because, on the evidence of the Commissioners, they were Christians. See Phillips's Report, 4 May 1886; Enclosure 9 in *PP*, C.4957.

125 *Macaulay Papers*, II, 2. See also *Correspondence: Blyden*, p. 6.

126 CO 147/96, Carter to Ripon, 19 January 1894; 24 November 1894; 29 December 1894; 31 December 1894.

127 Ilọrin had different Baloguns for the three main sections of the town: Fulani, Gambari and Yoruba (Imale) Quarters; see G. J. Lethem, Acting Resident, Ilorin, to Chief Secretary, Zungeru, 18 May 1912, in NAK, 702/1912. The resentment of these people to the whites persisted for a long while and culminated in the expulsion from Ilọrin of P. M. Dwyer, the Ilọrin Resident and the symbol of British rule, in 1900; see P. M. Dwyer to the Governor, Northern Provinces, 7 September 1900, in NAK. For their influence, see also Chief S. O. Ojo, *A Short History of Ilorin*, pp. 33–4; H. B. Hermon-Hodge; *Gazetteer of Ilorin Province*, London, 1921, pp. 78–81.

128 *Ibid.* The officials of the Company found out that the Emir was murdered, together with five of his sons and a number of his principal followers; see CO 21160, F.O. to C.O., 27 November 1895 encl. R.N.C.'s letter.

129 The exact date of this is uncertain; but it must have been in mid September 1895. The despatch of Denton to the Secretary of State on 5 November 1895, just reported his death; see NAI, CSO 1/1, Denton to Chamberlain. This despatch said the Emir was killed by his people 'sometime about the second week in September'.

130 NAK, E. C. Duffy, Quarterly Report on Ilọrin, March 1915. He described Alanamu as being virtually the king of the country. See also Dwyer to Lugard, 18 July 1900.

131 NAI, CSO 1/3, Carter to Chamberlain, 9 January 1896. See also CSO 1/1, Denton to Chamberlain, 5 November 1896.

Anti-white feeling had been building up many months before Captain Bower related his personal experience when he visited Ilọrin in October 1894. The house where he was to be lodged was reportedly burnt down the night before his arrival; one of his men who went

out by himself contrary to orders was seized, robbed and beaten;
and himself – 'on my way to and from the Emir's palace, I
passed through crowds of very excited people who cursed me
by name and told me to go away'. Bower to Colonial Secretary,
30 October 1894, enc. I in CO 22148, Carter to Ripon, 24 November
1894.

132 NAI, CSO 1/1, Denton to Chamberlain, Confidential despatch 14 of
20 April 1896.

133 *Ibid*. The Governor believed that the Ilọrin were intriguing 'to get
rid of European influence in the country'. See also NAI, CSO 1/1,
Carter to Chamberlain, 9 January 1896. He traced this desire to the
influence of 'the foreign ones [among the Ilọrin] that is, the descendants
of the Foulanis and Gambaris who were imported into the place by
the rebel Afọnja. . . .'. See NAI, CSO 1/1, Carter to Chamberlain,
Confidential II of 6 April 1896.

134 NAI, CSO 1/3, Carter to Secretary of State, 9 January 1896.

135 *Ibid*.

136 Ibrahim, the Chief Imam of Lagos, to Sulaiman Muḥammad, the
Emir of Ilọrin, 12 December 1895, encl. in Carter to Secretary of
State, 9 January 1896.

137 Presumably this is Fakhr al-Dīn Abū 'Abd Allāh Muḥammad b.
'Umar b. al-Husain al-Razī (1149–1209). He was a highly distinguished Muslim scholar, whose major contribution to Islam was the
reconciliation of philosophy with religious traditions. For more
information about him, see *EI*, article on 'al-Rāzī'. See also M. M.
Sharif, *A History of Muslim Philosophy*, vi, pp. 642–56.

He is here referred to, however, largely because of his voluminous
Qur'ān commentary, *Mafatih al-Ghaib*, popularly known as *Tafsir
al-Kabir*, which is famous the world over. It is his view on the attitude
of not making friends with the Christians that is herein quoted in
order to gain the ear of the Muslims (i.e. that Muslims could be
friends with them, if it is to their advantage).

138 Chief Imam Ibrahim to Sulaiman Muhammad, the Emir of Ilọrin,
12 December 1895. Here the Chief Imam was transmitting the
message of the Governor.

139 NAI, CSO 1/3, Denton to Chamberlain, 4 January 1896.

140 NAI, CSO 1/3, Carter to Chamberlain, 9 January 1896.

141 NAI, CSO 1/3, Carter to Chamberlain, 9 January 1896.

142 *Ibid*. Ọyọ fell to the British in 1895 after its bombardment.

143 *Ibid*.

144 *Ibid*. See also J. E. Flint, *Sir George Goldie and the Making of
Nigeria*, pp. 237 *et seq*., for the R.N.C. moves against Ilọrin. Flint
seems unaware of the local efforts being made by the Lagos Government to placate Ilọrin.

145 NAI, CSO 1/3, Carter to Chamberlain, 9 January 1896.

146 NAI, CSO 1/1, Griffith to Chamberlain, 25 August 1896.

147 NAI, CSO 1/1, Carter to Chamberlain, 25 April 1896.

148 Chief Imam Ibrahim and other leaders of the Lagos Muslim community to the Acting Governor, 19 July 1896. Enclosure in Griffith

to Secretary of State, 25 August 1896 in NAI, CSO 1/1. A review is made here of the progress so far.

149 *Ibid.*
150 *Ibid.*
151 NAI, CSO 1/3, Carter to Chamberlain, 6 April 1896. See also another despatch from same to same on 10 April 1896; MacCallum to Chamberlain, 22 September 1897, enclosing report by the Colonial Secretary, G. C. Denton in *Colonial Report, Annual*, 1896.
152 *Ibid.*
153 NAI, CSO 1/3, Carter to Chamberlain, 20 April 1896. See also NAI, CSO 1/3, Carter to Chamberlain, 9 January 1896. This dwells on the inquiry conducted at Ọyọ on 21 December 1895 about the circumstances that induced the Alafin to attack Captain Bower, the representative of the Lagos Government. The Governor learnt that Ọyọ had been taunted by Ilọrin for its subservience to the white man who was progressively acquiring Yorubaland. In contrast, 'the Ilọrin flaunted their independence and announced with triumph that neither the Niger Company on one side nor the Lagos Government on the other are able seriously to interfere with them'.
154 Imam Ibrahim of Lagos to Emir Sulaiman of Ilọrin, 19 July 1896.
155 Effort is made here to stress 'peace' and 'Islam', both words having the same root in Arabic (S-L-M).
156 The annexation of Lagos in 1861, the conquest of Ijẹbu in 1892 and of Ọyọ in 1895 throw some doubt on this idea of 'peaceful' penetration and rule.
157 Ilorin reply is reported in NAI, CSO 1/1, Griffith to Chamberlain, 25 August 1896. Enclosure 1, Ibrahim to Acting Governor, 19 July 1896.
158 This 'European' was named 'Malika' in the document. It must have been Carter or MacCallum that was meant.
159 This was obviously clear to the government, for the Colonial Secretary, G. C. Denton, in his Report, affirmed that in 1896 'Ilọrin still held an aggressive attitude against this Government'. But it went further to say that so firm was Ilọrin determination not to have any communication with the government that 'they informed Lagos Mohammedans that they would kill any messenger sent by them with Government letters or messages'. This is evidently a bit of an overstatement: *cf.* MacCallum to Chamberlain, 22 September 1897, enclosing report by the Colonial Secretary, G. C. Denton, in *Colonial Report*, 1896.
160 *Ibid.*
161 CO 6330, Denton to Chamberlain, 8 February 1897.
162 NAI, CSO 1/1, Denton to Secretary of State, 9 February 1897.
163 *Ibid.* See also NAI, CSO 1/1, Denton to Secretary of State, 8 February 1897.
164 *Ibid.*
165 See J. E. Flint, *op. cit.*, Chapter 11. See also R. A. Adeleye, *The Overthrow of the Sokoto Caliphate, 1879–1903*, Chapter 4, for a

treatment of how the R.N.C. eventually attacked Ilọrin. While Flint sees Ilọrin only in conjunction with Nupe, he views the attack on Ilọrin in the general context of the European assault on the Sokoto Caliphate.

166 In 1901, for instance, the government had to intervene in Muslim internal controversy over the office of the *Mufassir*; see *Tukuru Papers*, vol. 1; *The Lagos Weekly Record*, 2 February 1901. This was in a great measure similar to the Ẹpẹ dispute of 1899.

167 This is the successor of Muhammad Shitta Bey to the title of Bey. He was a relation of the first Bey. See *Macaulay Papers*, 2, II.

168 *Lagos Government Gazette*, 30 January 1903.

169 The ban was supposed to bring some much needed quiet to the town. Drumming was only allowed by special permit which was sparingly given. For further detail, see *Lagos Government Gazette*, 1903.

170 *Minute Book of the Central Native Council*, UIL, pp. 137–40. See also *Lagos Government Gazette*, 24 December 1903.

171 This early meal is called *sare* by the Yoruba Muslims (Arabic: *Sahūr*). It is supposed to be taken as *late* as possible after midnight but before day-break; see *EI*, article on 'Sawm'.

It is a common practice for young boys and men to go round the town at night beating drums, tins, etc., in order to wake up the Muslims for the early meal and prayers.

172 *Lagos Government Gazette*, 30 January 1903.

173 NAI, CSO 26, Butterworth's Letter Book, 1904–8. See also *Ijebu Province: Diary, 1905*, in NAI. Details are not given as to the merits of the two candidates, but one was believed to have been more knowledgeable in Arabic than the other.

174 NAI, Ijẹbu Prof. Ijẹbu Letter Book, 1904–8. The dispute proved a bit intractable and a few leading Muslims such as Ashiru who proved difficult had to be arrested.

175 *Lagos Government Gazette*, 30 January 1903. The Governor explained, however, that public health utilities were 'necessary evils' which had to be sited somewhere.

176 *Ibid.*

177 *Ibid.*

178 Many believe that 'the total effect of "pax colonica" as much voluntary as intended was to promote an unprecedented expansion of Islam'. See I. M. Lewis (ed.), *Islam in Tropical Africa*, pp. 82, 168–71.

179 At the 1910 Edinburgh Conference many voices were raised in indignant expostulation at the 'excessive deference' of the British Government to Muslims in Egypt, Sudan and Nigeria; see 'Government and Islam in Africa', *The Muslim World*, v., II, 1921, pp. 8–9.

180 CO 876/29 Moloney to Macdonald, 2 April 1889.

181 See Chapter 3.

7 Islam and Yoruba Society

The general progress of Islam in Yorubaland has been discussed; an attempt can now be made to describe not only the nature of the relationship between the growing Muslim community and traditional society, but also the effect of Islam on Yoruba society.

Right from the start, the establishment of Islam in Yorubaland had necessarily been attended by conflicts with the larger society. As has been shown, attacks were made on the Muslims as they tried to make the public calls to prayer, to erect mosques and conduct worship openly. The Muslims, however, weathered these crises and established their community, practising their faith according to their own lights. As the Muslim communities began to grow in size and stature they witnessed a greater amount of conflict with traditional society, conflicts which are better described as the 'conflicts of growth'.

The numerical expansion of the Muslim community caused great anxiety, for very often this involved the conversion of certain influential persons within the 'pagan' traditional society. Some of these were key people such as Balogun Kuku of Ijẹbu-Ode, and Asade, the Oba of Ado-Odo.[1] In Ẹpẹ, Balogun Alausa, finding succour only from the Muslims at his hour of sorest need, decided to embrace the faith when his trials had passed.[2] In Iwo, diehard 'pagan' leaders became Muslims.[3] The elevated social position of the converts sometimes insured them and their colleagues against the possible hostile reaction of their erstwhile pagan associates. Such protests as were made were overwhelmed by the acclamations of the larger number of people who flocked to Islam with such prominent people. But this was not always the case. The conversion to Islam of the more or less eminently placed, and particularly the conversion of those who had been more deeply engaged in the pagan customs, occasioned serious conflict with traditional society. The stronger the attachment of such people to

197

Islam, the more furious was the reaction of their former associates. It was related in Fiditi, for example, how the conversion to Islam of a certain heathen dignitary sparked off a long-drawn-out row that greatly disturbed the peace of the town.[4]

To the extent that the expansion and growth of Islam meant the undermining of the position of traditional worship, it proved in many places to be a constant source of tension between the votaries of the new and the traditional religions, most acute during periods of high incidence of conversion. In various towns in Ijẹbu, Abẹokuta and Ogbomọsọ, many former Ogboni, Osugbo and others were converted to Islam by the hundred.

Particularly illustrative here was the experience of Afa Koke-wukobere, the veteran Muslim preacher.[5] In Abẹokuta,[6] for instance, Kokewukobere preached both in the mornings and evenings in the course of his stay in that town, especially in the time of Ramadan. He proved to be an eclectic preacher, fearlessly denouncing the pagans and the Ogboni[7] as vermin – 'ẹgbin lẹ jẹ' – and encouraging all to convert to Islam, the way of salvation. He composed ditties embodying his message and these made his fame spread far and wide. In a short while, scores of people trooped to him for the ritual ablution of conversion,[8] and short songs were composed to commemorate the conversion of die-hard 'pagans' to Islam, and their acceptance of Muslim names in place of their former ones.[9] His success gave the non-Muslims no comfort. On several occasions, the Ogboni came down in formal formation to challenge him, his group of assistant preachers, audience and Muslim catechumen. There was no physical conflict; but there were threats and profuse incantations.[10] Nevertheless, the Muslim group remained steadfast, always chanting their *shahāda* in their most popular tune. The Ogboni soon gave up the unequal struggle, leaving the Muslim group undaunted and apparently invigorated. The preacher continued, preaching and converting more people.

This was not an isolated experience for this singular propagator of Islam in Yorubaland. In Ijẹbu-Ode he was openly confronted by the Osugbo; and in Ekiti, he was assailed by the *Egungun* – as they all saw how he literally depleted their ranks. Also, it is clear from the experiences of other propagators of Islam, such as Afa Kuranga of Isẹyin and Afa Arannibanidebẹ, that these open confrontations were not peculiar to Afa Kokewukobere or any single Yoruba Muslim community.

These conflicts, consequent on the initiation into Islam of large numbers of pagans from the pagan ranks, did not necessarily resolve the issue between the two sides but were followed by more confrontations, as the Muslims grew in confidence. For instance, in Abẹokuta, there were such conflicts notably on the festival outings of the Ogboni.[11] In Iwo, the Muslims were sadly troubled by the *aborișa*.[12] Above all, in Ado-Ekiti[13] the *Elegungun*, particularly the Esa, enjoyed harassing the Muslims – especially their erstwhile colleagues – flogging them, stripping them of their turbans, and sometimes even of their dresses. These harassments and confrontations were sometimes tolerated, but sometimes were intolerable. In Iwo, the Muslim Ọba had to make a firm stand; and ordered that Muslims were no longer to be persecuted.[14] In Ado-Ekiti,[15] when the Muslims found the situation impossible, they had to go in a body to the Ewi to lodge a protest about their insecurity in the town. When they failed to obtain any satisfactory assurance or protection, they offered to emigrate; and many did emigrate out of the town under the leadership of their Imam. They were begged to come back, with fair assurances of religious toleration.

The conversion of many 'pagans,' especially notable ones, no doubt represented a considerable threat to the position of non-Muslims. But a greater threat to traditional society lay in the new set of values which Islam was introducing into the society through its adherents. The introduction of new Islamic values was gradual, for they were only known piecemeal thanks to the discreet Mallam and the long if not arduous process of Islamic education. But such new concepts as had been accepted by the Muslim community soon influenced the relationship between the society and the community. For example, Muslims could not accept the custom by which women were confined indoors during festivals involving certain rituals that women were forbidden to see. The Muslims would recognise no curfew imposed for reasons of traditional worship;[16] nor did they place any premium on other traditional social taboos. But, perhaps, the strongest of the new ideas was the setting at nought of all gods and their appurtenances and regarding Allah as the one and only God. This was strongly evident as much in the general attitude of the Muslims as in their songs. Many and popular were the short ditties[17] which mocked and derided the dummies to which the pagans prayed for help. To the Muslims, they were no more than helpless effigies,[18] which, it used to be said, 'could not even raise their arms or feet in their own defence' even when involved in a fire disaster.

In a society like the Yoruba, which was religious and had a panoply of oriṣa (gods), this new uncompromising doctrine about God set the Muslim community and the Yoruba society at logger-heads. The clash of values was well dramatised in the 'Ewe Akoko Incident' in Badagry.[19] The leaves of the tree *Newboldia laevis* were generally held sacred in traditional Yoruba society, and sometimes used to mark pagan groves.[20] In Badagry the Muslims had rejected such ideas; and some Muslims, particularly Yanda, son of Habibu, in Badagry once invaded a pagan grove to pick these leaves in order to thatch the roofs of their houses. This brought them into a serious conflict with the infuriated pagan custodians of the grove. They, in retaliation, wanted to use these sacred Akoko leaves to cordon off their mosque. The Muslims would not allow this. The matter was taken to Ọba Iposu Aporogan and the chiefs of the town for arbitration, the Muslims firmly asserting that a leaf was a leaf.

More memorable was the attitude of Muslims towards the social concepts of Ṣango, a Yoruba deity. Any house that was struck down by lightning or consumed by fire in a thunderstorm was expected, according to Yoruba belief and practice, to be purified by the expiatory rites of the votaries of Ṣango. The Yoruba Muslims no longer entertained this belief; and a difficult problem arose when the building concerned was a mosque. Social values and tradition firmly stood for the normal measures to be taken in the interests of all; but Islam and the Muslims could not allow this. Several were the conflicts arising from this, particularly in the towns of the open savannah such as Isẹyin, Kishi, Ọyọ and Igboho.[21]

These confrontations did not retard the growth of Islam; it is very doubtful whether any substantial number of Muslims relapsed into paganism. The number of open-air Muslim preachers increased; for after Kokewukobere, there were scores of others such as Afa Agbagi and Arannibanidebẹ, both of Isẹyin, and Afa Odọla,[22] Afa Kulahun[23] and others from Ilọrin who stuck unyield-ingly to the propagation of the faith as if there were no conflict. Moreover, a certain aura of awe came to surround the Muslims, particularly such of their notable mallams as had courageously faced the pagan onslaught. And the belief of the pagans in the potency of the Muslim 'charm' in defence or in aggression was a substantial force which emboldened the Muslims and kept their enemies at bay.[24]

Indeed, these confrontations served to consolidate and strengthen further the position of the growing community. Islam was on the upsurge, and the pagan society on the defensive; and every conflict marked the progress of the first and the gradual decline of the other. Like the Ewe Akoko Incident of Badagry, or the conflict over Ṣango purification of a mosque, each conflict was almost invariably resolved in favour of the Muslims. This made Islam wax stronger still. It was not without significance that in the very towns affected – Abẹokuta, Ijẹbu-Ode, Iwo, Ogbomọṣọ and Ado-Ekiti – there were substantial increases in the position of Islam, as already shown.[25]

It would be erroneous, however, to picture the relationship between the expanding community of Muslims and the larger traditional society as one of a series of conflicts. Arresting as these conflicts were, they would be more truly conceived as ripples in the otherwise generally calm and peaceful atmosphere in which both Islam and the traditional system of religion co-existed. This religious co-existence can be perceived not only in the same town or village but, indeed, in the same Yoruba families. An essential factor aiding this was the degree of congruency of values between both religions. A good range of moral values was extolled by both – honesty, charity, respect to elders, etc.; they both allowed polygamy and Islam accepted the Yoruba enlarged family system and was ready to adjust its local organisation according to local ideas and demands.

It is in this context of peaceful religious co-existence that one can consider what Islam did in Yoruba society. A remarkable feature of the history of the Yoruba Muslim community was its relationship with the political authorities. An important element in this regard was the attitude of the Yoruba Muslim community to such Muslims as took up political titles within the traditional set-up. The community neither forbade nor encouraged any Muslim to take up such titles, and those Muslims who became Ọbas or Chiefs in the Yoruba towns did so with little or no reference to the Muslim community. To such title-holders, the attitude of the Muslim community as a whole was generally ambivalent. On the one hand, the community tended to demur at such of them as, in varying degrees, inevitably performed the 'pagan' acts of their offices. On the other hand, the Muslim community approved of whatever support such Muslim titled men rendered to Islam – support against persecutors, support in cash or in kind for the re-building of mosques and the encouragement of others in the royal families or in the town to become Muslims.

In spite of their support of Islam, and, perhaps, because of the tepid nature of their faith, Muslims holding titles within the 'pagan' society were not generally made officers of the Muslim community. One of the exceptional cases was that of Abudu Rahman Adewumi, who was both the Imam and the Onaṣokun of Ilaro.[26] He had been the Imam before he became the Onaṣokun, a title bestowed on him by the Olu of Ilaro, Ọba Tella Agbenuaran, in appreciation of his services in ensuring the resettlement of Ilaro after the Ẹiyẹ War.[27] By this title he became one of the Ilaro Kingmakers – an office that did not entail the performance of pagan rites.

The Muslim community recognised and were loyal to the traditional political authorities, irrespective of their religion. This Muslim attitude can be explained in various ways. It is permissible under Muslim law to recognise non-Muslim authorities so long as the latter do not forbid or threaten the practice of Islam. Besides, the general growth of the Muslim community was accompanied also by the growth of its political influence; consequently, it was neither prudent nor possible for the growing Muslim community not to recognise or be loyal to the traditional political set-up. Indeed in some areas, the political hierarchy was headed by Muslims and in Ikarẹ and a few other places in Akoko, the title of the political ruler had become Islamised. With these political authorities the Yoruba Muslim community fostered some relationship on this basis of loyalty and mutual recognition.

The most obvious relationship has been connected with the Muslim festival of *'Id al-Kabīr*. The practice became established in most Yoruba towns that the political head provided the sacrificial ram for the use of the Muslim community at this festival. Precisely how this practice came to be established is difficult to determine – it may have been originally a paternalistic gesture by the political head, or a symbol of the social recognition of the Muslim community. Once the practice became established and customary, it tended to strengthen further the connection between the Muslim community and the rest of society.

The Yoruba Muslim community also established, over the years, the custom of making a courtesy call on the political head during this all-important festival.[28] This call took place on a fixed day when the Muslims were formally received at the palace. They prayed for the Ọba and the Chiefs, the welfare of the town, and exchanged gifts with the political head. The result today is that in some towns like Ijẹbu-Ode this is an established tradition called 'Iwajude-Ọba'. On the appointed day, the Awujalẹ sat outside his palace in full regalia, flanked by his eminent court and town officials. The entire Ijẹbu-Ode Muslim community resolved itself into various groups, which in turn, came before the royal presence gaily dressed, and with some on horseback; each group then danced forward to pay their obeisance, pray for the Awujalẹ, and exchange gifts. This 'Iwajude-Ọba' has become one of the most popular and colourful days in the Ijẹbu-Ode calendar.

At the time of the *ashūrā* festival on 10 Muharram, some mallams normally did what can be called the annual divination and sacrifice. On this occasion the community, on the basis of an antiquated but religiously revered text,[29] predicted through a leading mallam[30] the events, dangers and blessings of the new year.[31] In some towns, such as Oṣogbo, this ceremony took place at the Ọba's courtyard, and the ruler himself was in attendance though all his Chiefs need not be present. In most other towns such as Abẹokuta and Ijẹbu-Ode, this ceremony was done at the central mosque. What concerned the entire society and the political head in particular was that this prediction was for the town as a whole, and the necessary sacrifices were the responsibility of the Ọba or Chief. Almost invariably, these sacrifices were performed, indicating further the nature of this close relationship.

These are 'festival relationships', so to say; and except in the singular case of the annual prediction festival, which was of generally diminishing interest, they became well eetablished. Any departure from them could signal the displeasure of the one and arouse the protest of the other party.[32] When in later years, for example, the Muslims of Ilamuren in Ijẹbu refused to accept the offer of the sacrificial lamb from the Alamuren, the latter protested to the Awujalẹ against this violation of tradition and custom.[33]

Similarly established and general among the Yoruba Muslim communities was the role given to chief officers of the Muslim community. Whenever a candidate was agreed upon by the community, it used to be customary to present him to the ruler. In many towns, if not all, such an important officer was turbanned and installed in the court and in the presence of the ruler himself. This ceremonial practice grew with the times. Probably begun as a matter of courtesy, or astute policy, it became a strong link binding the political head with the Muslim community in a working relationship. This practice gave rise to the common statement among many Yoruba Muslims that 'Ọba lo nfi enia nje' (it is the Ọba who makes one a chief). The Ọba's role was largely ceremonial, involving no religious rights; in a way, it was analogous to his role in the conferment of titles in traditional society.

Although this function of the Ọba in the affairs of the Muslim community was actually honorary and bereft of power, it had in certain circumstances developed into an active participation and meddling in the whole process of appointment of Muslim officers. Where the Ọba himself had a forceful character, such as in Ijẹbu-Ode, or where he was a Muslim, as in Iwo and other places, situations arose when the Ọba tried to exercise a doubtful right of approval of candidature[34] or the equally doubtful right of direct nomination.[35] The result of this was not often a happy one; for, with the involvement of the Ọba, the dispute about succession to the Imamate in many Yoruba towns acquired new dimensions and intricacies. This was particularly evident not only in long-drawn-out disputes at Ijẹbu-Ode, Ijẹbu-Igbo and Isẹyin but also in Lagos.[36]

In between the festivals and installation ceremonies, the Muslim communities tried to maintain good relations with the local political authorities. To the latter they turned in times of conflict with the irreconcilable non-Muslims, as pointed out above, and also in periods of internal unrest and disputes, for arbitration.[37] On such occasions, the fact that the political authorities were not Muslims does not appear to have been very significant. In Ijẹbu and Abẹokuta there were occasions when the Ọba together with the Oṣugbo or Ogboni did, strangely enough, arbitrate for the Muslim communities.[38] That the Muslim accepted their arbitration and rulings were fair enough; but the striking point here was this working relationship, and the implicit confidence that existed between Islam and traditional society.

This Yoruba Muslim attitude and relationship towards the traditional political authority whether Muslim or not, is significant for a number of reasons. First, this was proof enough that Islam in Yorubaland had not erected an *imperium in imperio*.[39] Established and waxing strong among the Yoruba, Islam could not but seek to change the old values it inevitably criticised or had already conflicted with. But the desired transformation of society was to be gradual and non-violent; it was to be achieved not through withdrawal from that society, but by the processes of association and the introduction of change from within. In short, if the ultimate aim of Islam in Yorubaland was a radical change of society, its approach, as indicated by the relationship with the political authorities, was an evolutionary and friendly one.

This attitude bore beneficial results for the cause of Islam. Only in exceptional cases did any of the rulers exhibit a hostile attitude towards the Muslims;[40] indeed, many of them became converts by various means.[41] The net result was that, given the Yoruba basic cultural tendency to respect the authority of rulers and elders, the cause of Islam received no inconsiderable boost from this association.[42] Indeed, it was for Islam an insurance of incalculable value, ensuring further protection and subsequent growth. It also held out prospects of further entrenchment with the political authorities, and the possibility of affecting the desired changes in society.

In this evolutionary approach the choice of the sphere of action was no less significant. Political power and influence seemed to have been both a magnet and a lodestar for Islam. Even at the earliest stages the Muslim community always had some members who were near the seats of political (as well as military) power and influence. As the Muslim community expanded, it depended for its growth and security on the political influence of the powers that be, whether Muslims or not. It was this inherent tendency of Yoruba Islam or, indeed, of Islam in general to obtain political power ultimately that explains much of this Yoruba Muslim attitude towards political authorities in Yorubaland. The underlying idea seems to have been the eventual attainment of political influence and power – by converting the ruling hierarchies and thereby attaining for Islam more political influence and power.

It is rather difficult to see what non-political relationship the Muslim community maintained with the society in peace time. Officially the community as a group stood aloof from all such communal activities as the local festivals, which were un-Islamic in content or by connection. But, in practice, it was more usual for this type of relationship to be decided upon on the individual level. The mallams, Muslim officials and the pious ones would use their influence to ensure strict Muslim orthodoxy, but essentially it was the individual who decided whether or not he would participate in any local festival; and if so, the extent of such participation.

This did not mean that every Muslim had to participate in 'pagan' activities, communal or otherwise; the leaders and scholars did not, but the more lax Muslims were, and can still be, close to traditional society. It is the more observable action of this group that brought out the erroneous and opprobrious expression among the Yoruba that 'bo ti wu ni la nse 'male eni' ('We do what we like with our Islam').[43]

The crucial question here is the reaction of the community to such lax Muslims. Their individual action was necessarily disapproved of by the entire community, which had the duty of preserving its good Muslim name and furthering the cause of Islam. The Muslim community was often particularly concerned whenever it found *any* of its own titled men engaged in an activity, that savoured of paganism. In such a case, word went round about the erring official, and after a while, if such an officer did not return to the straight path, he was often brought up for discussion at the central mosque after the *Jum'a* prayers. A demand could be made for his removal from office. It is noteworthy that even such a highly-placed officer as an Imam in a certain big town was in this way disciplined when found harbouring certain 'pagan' materials[44] used in idol worshipping.

The Muslim community as a group tried to share such interests of the society as were not incompatible with their religion. Throughout the period under study Muslims took part in the war efforts of their states. Even when, especially for those at Ibadan, this involved fighting against Ilọrin, a Muslim town, the Muslims still co-operated under the leadership of Arẹ Latosisa. This was largely because the Muslim opponents of Ilọrin saw the central issue as one of politics, trade and security rather than as a straightforward question of religion. Indeed, it would be hard to describe the Yoruba wars of this period as being directly motivated by religion.

It is therefore essentially in the context of the friendly relations between Muslims and non-Muslims that Islam was in a position to make some impact on Yoruba society, and much of the Islamic impact in Yorubaland was cultural.

First, the Yoruba language was enriched.[45] This was consequent in a great measure on the contact of the Yoruba with Islamic culture largely through the Hausa and Nupe. Some Yoruba words which are peculiar to the Muslims, such as *mọṣalaṣi*, 'mosque', *takada*, 'paper', can be traced easily to the languages of these neighbouring Muslims.[46] But strictly speaking, most of the loan words are derived from their Arabic parallels.[47] In a social context where most Arabic speakers were Muslims, and where Islam and Arabic are closely interrelated, it is difficult not to see Islam at work in the transference of these words into the Yoruba language.

The largest single contribution to the Yoruba language was in the sphere of religion. Present in the Yoruba language and accepted as Yoruba were certain words borrowed from Arabic through Islam. For example, there were *adura* (*al-du'ā*: prayer); *alufa* (*laffa*: turban);[48] *Keferi* (*Kafir*: non-Muslim); *Waasu* or *waasi* (*Wa'z*: a religious sermon, admonition); and *wolii* (*Waliyy*: holy man, saint).

There were some loan words which have a religious significance in the donor language but which became secularised by usage in Yoruba. For example, *anfani* (*naffa*: useful),[49] *suna* (*sunna*: to be proper); *aniyan* (*niyya*: intention, care); *aṣiri* (*sirr*: secret); *Tuba* (*Tawba*: repentance); and *gafara* (*ghafara*: to beg one's pardon). Ever since these words were recorded by Bowen and Crowther, they had become current. A few words of this category such as *alubarika* (*baraka*: blessing) were not mentioned by these nineteenth-century writers.

There were also loan words which are ethical in meaning and usage. These included *Kadara* (*qadar*: fate; lot); *Munafiki* (*munafiq*: hypocrite, double-leader); *Musiba* (*Muṣiba*: misfortune); *Sina* (*Zina*: adultery).

Next in importance to the group of religious words were loan words with a basic trade connotation. These relate to articles of trade such as *alubọsa* (*al-basala*: onion), and *alumagaji* (*al-miqas*: a pair of scissors). They also included words describing trade relations and attitudes such as *alukawani* (*al-muqawala*: agreement, promise); *haramu* (*haram*: unlawful, cheating); *lada* (*ladda*: enjoyment, pleasure gain); and *riba* (*ribh*: interest, profit[50]).

There were also a few loan-words about time: *saa* (*sā'a*: time period); *Samani* (*Zamān*: period, age); and *wakati* (*waqt*: hour, time).

So also there were some words of a political nature. There were titles such as *Ajẹlẹ* (resident), *Shehu* (*shaikh*: an old man). Other words such as *ṣeria* (*shari'a*: law); *fitina* (*fitna*: trouble, unrest); *Sakani* (*Sakān*: dwelling, place, area of jurisdiction); and *labari* (*khabār*: report, news) can be used in a political context.

There were a few general words about natural phenomena such as *Ara* (*ra'd*: thunder); and *Sanmo* (*Samā'*: sky, clouds).

And, of course, there were also a few loan words dealing with the art and range of writing. These included *Kalamu* (*qalam*: pen); *Satara* (*satar*: line, row); and *hantu* (*Khatt*: script, writing).

The range of loan words from Arabic to Yoruba reveals the areas of Yoruba life on which this religious language had made some impact – on the time-measurement, religious, economic, political and literary aspects of the Yoruba language.

The degree of assimilation of these loan words into Yoruba (whereby their pronunciation reflects that of native words and is hardly recognisable from it) indicates that the period of their introduction into Yoruba must be three generations, at least. Indeed, their general distribution and acceptability in all Yoruba areas, Muslim or otherwise, would indicate that these words must have entered the Yoruba language perhaps before the religion became widespread in the nineteenth century.[51]

One other aspect of the cultural effect of Islam was manifest in the dress of the Yoruba. For the *Jum'a* service, the various Muslim festivals, and for the five daily prayers, proper decent attire including the turban[52] is counselled. The Yoruba dress of *Agbada* may or may not have been introduced into Yoruba society by Muslims; but contemporary observers often testified to the generally proper and decent outfit of the Muslims in contrast to their pagan contemporaries. The case was well put in 1861 by Burton, who noted that in Abẹokuta 'the best looking were decidedly the Moslems [*sic*]. . . . They were conspicuous for their decent dress.'[53] This was particularly true for the women. After a tour into the interior, it was clear to Burton also that 'bodily exposure of the woman's form first disappeared permanently among the Moslem converts from heathenry'.[54]

A noteworthy aspect of the impact of Islam on Yoruba society was the enlarged scope, the new dimensions, it introduced. It brought the *Hajj*, which enriched the experience and widened the scope of the pilgrim. The convert joined a community that provided him ready acceptance in the neighbouring non-Yoruba Muslim areas. It taught and obliged converts to cherish and practise cleanliness of body as well as of the mind, symbolised in ablution. As Muslims, the Yoruba could trade much more easily among the Muslims in the neighbouring areas. It was not a co-incidence that many of the Ibadan, Ogbomọṣọ and Ijẹbu long-distance traders were Muslims. It is probably not much of a wild conjecture to state the hypothesis that Islam has been a factor promoting the external overland trade of the Yoruba.

The enrichment of Yoruba language, the improvement of dress and the widening of their cultural horizon were no doubt important by themselves; but they formed only a part of the general new civilisation which Islam provided for the Yoruba society.[55] By far the greatest symbol of this enriching civilisation was literacy in Arabic. Through Muslim education, the Yoruba were exposed not only to Islamic literature but also to new ideas and the entire Arabic literary world. And a particularly remarkable feature of this exposure to a different civilisation was the fact that the Yoruba Muslims blended the old and the new cultures, which gave them considerable confidence and self-respect and enabled them to develop roots in their society. This also meant that Islam offered an alternative access to civilisation other than through Christianity and submission to European cultural domination.

This general civilising impact of Islam still continues, perhaps in greater strength. Today Yoruba Muslim contacts with the Arab countries widen and get stronger, particularly since the time of Nigerian independence. Their womenfolk are educated and are participating with the men; above all, they are more than ever before conscious of their position in the society. They feel the Christian challenge, and that they are being discriminated against. They want to redress their former neglect of the practice of Islam, and also desire to make a greater impact on their society. Consequently there is a growing *esprit de corps*; and as a group, they are today, more than ever before, organised into various religious and 'modernist' societies prosecuting the cause of Islam in very many ways.

Notes

1 NAI, C50 1/1, Denton to Chamberlain, 19 December 1898.
2 T. Ola Avoseh, *A Short History of Epe*, pp. 26–7.
3 *Iwe Itan Isedale Esin Imale ni Iwo*, ms. 'awọn ogbogan abọriṣa nkirun'. This manuscript was compiled by two Muslims under the leadership of Imam Akinlade. I am grateful to the community for allowing me to use this.

4 At the interview with the Muslim community, Fiditi, in April 1965. The heathen background of these converts is often regarded as embarrassing and information about it is whispered only in confidence. In this particular regard, he is a certain Gbadamọsi, during the tenure of office of the second Imam, Imam Sanni.

5 Interview with the younger Afa Kokewukobere, Ilọrin. As a young man, the informant often accompanied his uncle, the older Kokewuko- bere, on his preaching tours of Yorubaland and Dahomey. His information here has been borne out by evidence collected from the Muslim communities in the towns concerned. See Bibliography: Oral Evidence.

6 *Ibid.*

7 See Chapters 1 and 5.

8 This was virtually ritual baptism. The new convert was thoroughly bathed, taught the *shahādat* (the Muslim profession of faith) and the five pillars of the religion. See T. W. Arnold, *The Preaching of Islam*; and Gaudefroy-Demombynes, *Les Institutions Musulmanes*. He was often given new or fresh clothes to wear, and henceforth he was often guided by a mallam.

9 One of the most popular songs is
   Ajẹbiwe, ko jẹ bẹ mọ
   Asuregbasuna lo ma jẹ
   This means that the new convert formerly known as the Efficacious Herb will no longer be so called, but will henceforth be known as one- who quickly-runs-to-accept-the-faith.

10 'Nwọn npọfọ, nwọn si nṣepe'; ('they chanted incantation and uttered curses').

11 Interview with the Muslim community, Abẹokuta in June 1963. See *Tukuru Papers*.

12 *Abọriṣa* means pagan worshipper. *Iwe Itan Isedale Esin Imale ni Iwo*.

13 Interview with the Chief Imam and others at Ado-Ekiti, June 1965.

14 *Iwe Itan Isedale Esin Imale ni Iwo.*

15 Interview with the Chief Imam and others at Ado-Ekiti, June 1965.

16 Curfews were sometimes imposed especially after dusk to enable the votaries of traditional religion to perform certain rites and sacrifices on behalf of a town or community.

17 There are many of these short songs composed by various preachers.

18 *Olundu*, that is, a god dummy.

19 Interview with the Muslim Community, Badagry, in August 1963. Present were informed Muslim historians including Rufai Tukuru, the Balogun; Abdul Gafar Tijani, the Chief Imam; Muhammad Adelakun, and Mustafa Lawal Ajape, the Onitafusiru.

20 That the leaves and tree of this plant have a sacred place in Yoruba life, see R. C. Abraham, *Dictionary of Modern Yoruba*. Compare the similar use of the tender offshoots of the Palm Tree (Yoruba: *Mariwo*).

21 Interview with the Muslim communities in these places. See Bib- liography: Oral Evidence.

22 This is his pet-name (lit. 'till tomorrow') derived from his religious ditty that the hypocrite will be exposed on the 'O da laira ka to mọ alabosi'. *Al-Akhira* means the hereafter; and the expression 'O da laira' has become 'O dọla' ('till tomorrow').

23 This is also another pet-name derived from the habit of the Muslim exclaiming in Arabic: 'Qul lahum' ('Say to them').

24 Compare the position elsewhere, for example in Ashanti where 'all levels of society' were affected by Muslim charm; see Ivor Wilks, 'The Position of Muslims in Metropolitan Ashanti in the early nineteenth century', in I. M. Lewis (ed.), *Islam in Tropical Africa*, pp. 318–39.

25 See Chapters 3 and 4.

26 Interview with the Chief Imam, Ilaro, and with al-hajj Adewumi, the son of the Adewumi, at Ilaro, June–July 1963.

27 *Ibid.*

28 It is observed that in centralised states in Tropical Africa, '*Īd al-Kabir* provides the opportunity for public payment of homage to kings and chiefs. See I. M. Lewis (ed.), *op. cit.*, pp. 70 *et passim*; S. F. Nadel, *A Black Byzantium: the Kingdom of Nupe*, p. 217. P. C. Lloyd, 'Salah at Ilorin', *Nigeria Magazine*.

29 This is called *Tira Ọdun* (lit. 'the book of the Year'). *Kitāb al-Sana* is an anonymous work, found with many mallams in Yorubaland.

30 This can be the Chief Imam, or the Onitasfusiru.

31 Divination is forbidden in Islam; see Qur'ān 72, 8; 34, 14 and so on. See also *EI*, article on 'Kahin'. It has survived, however, in Yoruba Islam; and it exists in Yoruba culture.

32 It can symbolise rebellion and opposition. *cf.* I. M. Lewis (ed.). *op. cit.*, p. 217.

33 *Awujalẹ Papers*: Bello Naibi to Awujalẹ (n.d.) See also Chief Ilamuren (Joseph Asekunle) to Awujalẹ, *ibid.*

34 NAI, CSO 26, Ijẹbu Prof. J. 569.

35 NAI, CSO 26, Ijẹbu Diary 1903.

36 Particularly in Lagos, the Eleko's involvement in the recognition of certain Muslim appointments such as the Onitafusiru brought on a storm that rocked not only the Muslim community but also the politics of Lagos and indeed of Nigeria till the late 1920s. See particularly Suit No. 111 of 1915, Bashorun and others *v.* Ẹkẹmọde.

37 This did not rule out attempts at arbitration by other Muslim communities interested in the case. But with the failure of their own officers to effect a settlement, the next step was arbitration by the Ọba and, perhaps, his council.

38 It was strange because the Muslims otherwise denounced these bodies as secret societies. Although the bodies were, strictly speaking, arms of the Government, yet it was true that they operated *in camera* and performed certain rites and customs, e.g. initiation, trial by ordeal, oath taking, which were objectionable to Muslim belief. See A. F. Abell, *Intelligence Report: Ijẹbu Remo* (1935); Captain J. A. Mac-Kenzie, *Intelligence Report, Ijẹbu-Igbo* (1940); and J. H. Blair, *Intelligence Report, Abeokuta* (1933).

Similarly, the Christians dismissed the bodies as pagan; see J. F. Ade Ajayi, *Christian Missions in Nigeria*, p. 110: '. . . all agree that it [Ogboni] is inconsistent with the principles of the Christian religion . . .'

39 This is without prejudice to their ultimate desire to establish Islamic law and state. See Chapter 6.

40 See action of the Alafin in Chapter 1.

41 See Chapter 4.

42 *Ibid.* To cite just one example: Parrinder notes that 'when the Alafin of Ọyọ became a Muslim and made the pilgrimage to Mecca, many of his people became Muslim because their father had done so'; E. G. Parrinder, 'Divine Kingship in West Africa', *Numen*.

43 Both Crowther and Burton noted this Yoruba saying in the nineteenth century; see R. F. Burton: *Negro Wit and Wisdom*, p. 283, and S. Crowther, *A Grammar and Vocabulary of the Yoruba Language*, p. 283. There is also a figurative use of this expression to mean individual liberty of action.

Compare also the Yoruba derogatory saying, 'Bo kirun, bi o kirun, nṣọ ni mọṣalaṣi' (lit. 'Whether you perform the *salat* or not, just proceed to the mosque'). Note also 'ebi ko pa Imale, o ni oun ko jẹ aya, ebi pa Sule o jẹ ọbọ' (lit. 'When the Muslim is not hungry, he says he does not eat monkey-flesh. When Sule is hungry he eats it'); see R. F. Burton, *op. cit.*, p. 183. Islam, of course, has to be followed as laid down in the Qur'ān and in the religious books, and is not subject to individual caprice.

44 People interviewed were reluctant in disclosing his name, out of respect for the dead, as well as for his family.

45 See Appendix II for a list of Arabic loan words in Yoruba.

46 In Hausa the mosque is *masallaci*; paper, *takarda*; see R. C. Abraham, *A Dictionary of the Hausa Language*.

47 Arabic is the language of the Qur'ān and it is the *lingua franca* of the Muslims.

Compare also the impact of Arabic words on Hausa; see J. Greenberg, 'Arabic Loan Words in Hausa', *Word*; and 'Kanuri Influence on Hausa', *Journal of African History*.

48 This word might also have been derived from *Allafa* to write, compose. This is possible because the Muslim mallam was the first class of person to be seen writing in Yorubaland. T. J. Bowen in his *Grammar and Dictionary of the Yoruba Language* translates this word, *Alufa*, as 'a learned man, religious'.

49 This word might have been derived from *naf*: 'use, benefit', which is also from the same root *n-f-'*.

50 This word has in Yoruba the connotation of an unmerited profit.

51 This section on the age of the loan words owes a lot to Biodun Adetugbo, who has kindly read it and made some useful comments. He feels that the words must be 'over 100 years old in Yoruba'.

52 Qur'ān 62, 9–11.

53 R. F. Burton, *Wanderings in West Africa*, vol. 1, pp. 103–4.

54 *Ibid.*

55 Compare the position particularly in Hausaland, where this is much
   so. See D. P. L. Dry, *The Place of Islam in Hausa Society*, p. 138 *et*
   passim. He shows that Islam provides the ideals in social, religious,
   political and economic spheres.

Conclusion

Islam has a long history in Yorubaland, even though its very beginnings are enveloped in a fog of secrecy and ignorance. As the materials relevant to this early phase of Islam in Yorubaland have so far been scanty, it has not been possible to provide here more than a bare outline of the history and features of Islam in the period before the Jihād. In the later period, however, the sources available both in written and oral form are more diverse and considerable though largely incidental and indirect. Within the limits provided by the sources, a bolder attempt can be made to construct the history of the growth of Islam among the Yoruba in the second half of the nineteenth century.

The Jihād and its aftermath obviously constituted a watershed. Rather than improving the position of Yoruba Muslims, however, initially it had rather tragic effects, scattering the Muslims and threatening their position. They mostly came under a cloud, and for a long time could worship only in secret and as individuals. Though shaken, however, Islam was not broken. As the Yoruba society settled down, the Muslims reconstituted themselves, surviving to a great extent, the tragedy, prejudices and opposition of the previous decades.

The survival and growth of Islam henceforth were a major feature of the history of Yorubaland in the second half of the nineteenth century. True enough, certain features of the past, such as facial marking and the leadership of the Parakoyi, gave way; but other traditions persisted. New developments were evident, for example in the evolution of the Imamate. It is clear that the Yoruba Muslim community was adopting some social traditions while at the same time making its own social and political impact.

In the resurgence of Yoruba Islam, a noticeable role was played by external forces. From outside came the sustaining support provided by the overseas Muslims; and the various mallams and teachers from Ilọrin and beyond helped to raise the level of knowledge and worship, and earned for the Muslims considerable respect. But more significant was the support found within the society itself. The abatement of the Ilọrin threat, the Yoruba attitude of toleration and the conversion of the Yoruba social and political elite combined to work in the Muslims' favour. And the Muslims themselves exhibited a considerable degree of earnestness, adaptability and tact in their efforts to establish their community.

The Muslim community developed separately in each Yoruba town, although those in the important large towns tended to wield some influence over those in the subordinate nearby ones. In all of them, however, certain common features could be observed regarding their organisation, development, beliefs and ideas.

The growth of the Muslim community received great challenges from the new forces of Christianity and colonial rule. These had some stimulating influence and in spite of Christian endeavour, Islam waxed stronger; and Muslims tried to serve on the new administrative bodies introduced by the British. Above all, they came to accept some Western ideas and values, notably the Western system of education.

It was the combination of these new developments in Yoruba Islam, together with the rapid growth of Islam both in size and status, that marked the turn of the nineteenth century as the era when Islam in Yorubaland reached a high watermark in its social and political development.

In the course of its growth Islam had been exerting considerable influence on the rest of Yoruba life and history. It had widened the scope of its connections, and enriched the content of its culture. Altogether, it had provided an elevating civilisation. As an alternative to the 'colonial' Western civilisation ushered in at this period, this Muslim civilisation was particularly salutary since it better preserved African values and dignity; moreover, open to Western ideas, they offered to the society a cultural synthesis richer than anything hitherto available.

But from the beginning of the twentieth century onwards, the Muslims were to feel the adverse effects wrought by the changing circumstances of the age. The establishment of native law and custom, not to mention English law, effectively checkmated the eventual introduction of Islamic law which the political development of Islam had presaged. Also, the monopoly of Western education which Christianity had initially enjoyed put the Muslims at some disadvantage in the rise of the new elite.

The Muslims have been trying to salvage the situation by forming various Muslim societies. The most notable of these are the Ijẹbu Muslim Friendly Society, the Ansar ud-Deen, the Ahmadiyya, the Muslim Literary Society and the Nawair ud-Deen which arose in the early decades of the twentieth century. These societies constitute a dynamic force actively prosecuting both the reform of Yoruba Islam and the cause of Muslims in Nigeria as a whole. Indeed, they have opened a new era of Muslim history in Nigeria; and their overall influence today should not be underestimated.

Appendix I

List of Chief Imams in some Yoruba Towns

Abẹokuta[1]
1 Umoru son of Salu Bale Itoku in Oke Aleji
2 Sunmonu Oyegebi Sofo of Igbore
3 Lawani Tegbese of Erunwa
4 Abdullahi Ibunnuoba
5 Uthman Akewugberu
6 Badiru of Oke Aleji

Apomu
1 Abdullahi of Alapomu's compound
2 Saidu [from Bida]
3 Oseni, father of Raji [from Iseyin]
4 Lawani, son of Apedeoru [nickname]
5 Lawani Aiyegbayin of Oke Jago compound
6 Bello Agbagirimokewu
7 Abiola of Arẹ compound

Badagry
1 Abudu Salami Alalukurani
2 Sanni
3 Al-hajj Tijani
4 Uthman Asiru
5 Awesu Akewusola
6 Abudu Gafar

[1] Another list is father of Badaru of Oke Aleji; [2] Akewugberu of Igbore, [3] Badaru, son of first Imam; [4] Imam Baba of Oke Ijeun; [5] Imam Baba of Ijeja; [6] Imam Qudus; [7] Imam Ibrahim of Eruwon; and [8] Imam Jafaru of Itoku.

Ẹdẹ
1 Nurudeen of Ogbagba Quarter
2 Muhammad of Talafia Quarter
3 Kadiri
4 Alimi
5 Muhammad Sulu

Ejirin
1 Sanusi Afigong
2 Sadiku
3 Bello from Ikire
4 Buari from Ilorin
5 Adamu, 'from the North'
6 Oseni Obadimeji, from Epe
7 Sanni Adigun Abdullahi

Ẹpẹ
1 Awudu
2 Alamu
3 Awesu
4 Alantakun
5 Uthman Audu
6 Musa
7 Ismaila Alaru
8 Tukuru Uthman
9 Abudu Lasisi Awesu
10 Abudu Alayaki
11 Salia Tukuru

Ibadan
1 Abudulai Gunnugun
2 Ismail Basunmu
3 Jibril Qifu
4 Tijani
5 Suleiman Garuba Alagufon
6 Suleiman Gambari
7 Abudulai Basunmu
8 Yesufu Inakoju
9 Lawal Jibril Qifu
10 Haruna of Oke Gege
11 Ajagbe Afasegbejo
12 Muili Ayinde Basunmu

Ifẹ

1 Afa Daniyan
2 Kasumu Adeosun
3 Raji of Agbedegbede [from Ẹdẹ]
4 Hussein Imam
5 Al-hajj Bello Hassan

Igboho[2]

1 Asani, of Mọlaba Quarter
2 [Years of inter-regnum] Aminu of Ilọrin
3 [Years of inter-regnum] Abubakare
4 Aliyu
5 Mustafa
6 Present Chief Imam

Ijẹbu-Ẹpẹ

1 Kadiri Mota
2 Bello
3 Disu Akeju
4 Kadiri Oluwo

Ijẹbu-Ode

1 Sanni Oborumboro
2 Alli Akanyinode I of Igbogunja
3 Sanni Sangosanya of Ita Ntebo
4 Bakare Akanyinode II of Igbogunja
5 Sanni Okona of Isase [Imamate dispute]
6 Al-hajj Shittu Olufowomu of Imopa

Ikire

[Apomu, Ikire used to come to Ikire to have the Jumat – Friday Service – together; later they had their own central mosques, with their chief Imams].
1 Ahmad [from Ọyọ]
2 Gbadamọsi of Alagba compound
3 Raji Omolaiye of Ọlota compound
4 Damalu, son of the first Imam
5 Al-hajj Gbadamọsi
6 Al-hajj Kareem Agbongon

[2] I was informed by the Muslim Community that up to 1962 there had been eighty-four Imams in Igboho, but recollection of their names proved an uphill task.

Ikirun
1 Mallam Bako
2 Abdullai Jibril Oyeteju
3 Musa
4 Abudurahman
5 Salau Ajani Abiodun

Iṣẹyin
1 Momodu of Idi-Ose
2 Idrisu Momodu
3 Apara of Adabo
4 Olokun family
5 Daiyero Family in Ijẹmba
6 Oye in Ijẹmba
7 Sule of Oke-Ola
8 Leasu of Ijamba
9 Momodu Egbrongbe of Olukuta family
10 Lawani Alaikimba
11 Layiwola of Adabo
12 Busari of Ijẹmba
13 Mustafa of Adabo
14 Samino of Oke-Ola
15 Raji Ajirin of Idi-Ose
16 [Disputed]

Iwo
1 Muhammad Akinlade
2 Hisimonu of Oke-Adan
3 Sakariyau of Omorodo
4 Gbadamọsi of Ile Akinlade
5 Busari of Ile Ikoyi
6 Suberu Momini
7 Asafa of Oke-Adan
8 Abudu Karimu of Petugbele
9 Asafa of Ikoyi
10 Al-hajj Jabari Akinlade

Lagos
1 Salu
2 [Sule Gana]

3 Nafiu
4 Norla
5 Ibrahim
6 Ligali

Modakẹkẹ
1 Sabiu from Ipetumodu [from Sare, Ilorin]
2 Buari from Ipetumodu
3 Lawani, father of Amida
4 Ashiru, son of the first Imam
5 Sanusi, son of Agbede of Oke-Eso compound
6 Oseni Alabeloje
7 Al-hajj Salami Osoaro

Ogbomọṣọ
1 Nafiu
2 Muse of Oke Masifa Quarter
3 Gbadamọsi of Adurin Quarter
4 Abudu Rahmon of Isale Ora Quarter
5 Muhammad Nafiu
6 Sanusi of Oke Masifa Quarter
7 Mahmud of Oke Agbede Quarter
8 Salau Gbadamọsi
9 Buari Abudu Rahmon
10 Marufu Abegunde Muhammad

Oke-Iho
1 Ibraimo Bibilari
2 Arunya Iyanda
3 Aibu Adisa
4 Sanni
5 Arikewusola Abudu Ramoni Ajani
6 Yusau Akanbi
7 Al-hajj Imam Muhammad Niala
8 Al-hajj Abdul Karim Akano

Oṣogbo
1 Buraimọ
2 Abdukadiri of Igbagi
3 Abudurahman [Imam Anisere?]
4 Abudukadiri

5 Sunmonu of Batedo
6 Lawani Oseni of Olokuta
6 Busari of Atanka
8 Abibu ibn Abdukadiri
9 Awesu of Ile Aka
10 Abudu Salami Alabaja-iro
11 Hafsir of Idi Ako

Ọyọ
1 Aliyu Ajokidero
2 Abubakare of Ile Imam Akewugberu
3 Badaru
4 Silikifuli
5 Asimi
6 Aliyu Odunlami
7 Tunkuru
8 Al-hajj Oyibi

Shaki
1 Abiba
2 Saliu Asunnara [from Parakou]
3 Amadu of Agbede
4 Sadiku of Oke-Oro
5 Musa of Isale-Onikoko
6 Gafata Aliyu [a Hausa]
7 Gbadamọṣi [alias Aberesola] of Igbola
8 Caruba of Isale-Onikeke
9 Lawani of Idi-Agbede

Appendix II

List of some Arabic loan words in Yoruba

A. RELIGIOUS

(i) *Non-secularised*

Adura:	Prayer (Arabic: *al-duʻā*)
Alaji:	Pilgrim (Ar.: *al-ḥajj*)
Alufa:	Mallam, a devout Muslim (Ar.: *Laffa*: turban)
Alujanna:	Heaven, Paradise (Ar.: *al-janna*)
Aluwala:	Ablution (Ar.: *al-wuḍūʻ*)
Keferi:	Non-Muslim (Ar.: *Kāfir*)
Lemọmu:	Imam (Ar.: *Imām*)
Maleika:	Angel (Ar.: *Malaika*)
Nasia:	Advice, admonition (Ar.: *Nasīha*)
Sare:	Ramadan early meal (Ar.: *Sahūr*)
Saree:	Gravel, burial ground (Ar.: *Darīh*)
Setani:	The Devil (Ar.: *Al-Shaitān*)
Seria:	Muslim Law (Ar.: *Al-Shariʻa*)
Waasi:	Sermon (Ar.: *Waʻiz*)
Walaa:	A wooden board used for learning (Ar.: *al-lawh*)
Wolii:	Prophet (Ar.: *Waliyy*)
Yidi:	Muslim festival-ground outside the town (Ar.: *ʻId*)

(ii) *Secularised*

Aasiki:	Fame, prosperity, talent (Ar.: *rizq*)
Alubarika:	Blessing (Ar.: *al-baraka*)
Anfani:	Use, benefit (Ar.: *al-nafʻ*, *naffa*)
Aniyan:	Intention (Ar.: *al-niyya*)

Asiri:	Secret (Ar.: *al-sirr*)
Gafara:	Pardon, permission (Ar.: *ghafara*: to pardon)
Jonmon:	Group of persons (Ar.: *Jama'a*: a group, community (Muston))
Suna:	Orthodox, (Ar.: *Sunna*)
Sunno:	Naming Ceremony (Ar.: *Sunna*)
Tuba:	Repent (Ar.: *Tawba*)

(iii) *Ethical*

Kadara	Fate (Ar.: *Qadr*)
Kamu:	Lot, fate (?Ar.: *Kamm Qāma*)
Manafiki:	Michief, hypocrite (Ar.: *Munafiq*)
Musiba:	Misfortune (Ar.: *Muṣiba*)
Sina:	Adultery (ar.: *Zina*)

B.   SECULAR

(i) *Trade*

Adeun:	Agreement, promise (Ar.: *Al-'ahd*)
Alubosa:	Onion (Ar.: *al-basal*)
Alukembu:	Stirrups (Ar.: *al-rikāb*)
Alumagaji:	Pair of scissors (Ar.: *al-miqass*)
Haramu:	Thief, cheat (Ar.: *ḥarām*)
Riba:	Bribe (Ar.: *Ribā*)

(ii) *Political*

Fitina:	Trouble, unrest (Ar.: *Fitna*)
Labari:	Report, information (Ar.: *al-Khabār*)
Sakani:	Place, province (Ar.: *Sakan*)
Ṣeria:	Judgement, Law (Ar.: *Sharī'a*)
Shehu:	A title (Ar.: *Shaikh*)

(iii) *Time*

Saa:	Period, age (Ar.: *Sā'a*)
Samani:	Times (Ar.: *Zamān*)
Wakati:	Hour, time (Ar.: *Waqt*)

(iv) *Writing*

Alufaa:	A learned Muslim (Ar.: *Allafa*: to write, compose)
Hantu	Writing (Ar.: *Khaṭṭ*)

Kalamu:	Pen (Ar.: *Qalam*)
Satara:	Line (Ar.: *Satr*)

(v) *General*

Alafia:	Peace (Ar.: *al-'āfiya*)
Ara:	Thunder (Ar.: *al-ra'd*)
Halaka:	Trouble (Ar.: *Halaka*: to destroy)
Sababi:	Cause (Ar.: *Sabab*)
Sanmo:	Sky (Ar.: *Samā'*)

Appendix III

No. 1 Report of the Muslim School[1]

Bankole Street School,
Lagos,
31st August, 1896.

This School opened on the 15th day of June last with 41 boys and 46 young men, the boys have now increased to 45.

The boys are divided into 5 classes. 12 boys in the first class and their lessons are Reading Standard one to three and sometimes with translation into Yoruba orally. Arithmetic Simple Subtraction to Simple Division, only one of them can do Compound Addition to Division.

There are 5 boys in the 2nd Class their lessons are Reading 3rd Primer, Arithmetic Numeration and Simple Addition.

All of the above boys had been attending English Schools before, but, they are making fine progress since they began to attend here.

The rest of the children are divided into three classes where lessons are reading First Primer and numeration.

Some of them had been attending School before but those of them who commenced their education at the time the School was opened have been attending the School regularly and have nearly finished spelling and reading, in the first Primer, a book of 32 pages. In Arithmetic some of them have commenced to do Addition and others are learning Numeration Table and notation.

Arabic is taught with the meaning and translation into Yoruba orally. It will take sometime before these boys will be able to translate Arabic into English and English into Arabic, because their previous teaching was limited to simple reading and writing of the Quran without translation.

[1] *Correspondence Relative to Appointment of Blyden as Agent of Native Affairs, UIL.*

The young-men I am sorry to say have decreased to 8 in number. This is owing to the fact that they are employees and traders, but those who have been attending to the School regularly and punctually have finished the reading of the Sunday School Primer a book of 36 pages and are doing subtraction in Arithmetic.

The School is taught five days in each week from Saturday to Wednesday from 9.00 a.m. to 1.30 and the youngmen from 11.00 a.m. to 12.30 p.m.

The teachers are earnest and faithful.

(I. A. Animasaun)
Principal

Appendix IV

Translation of the letter of the Muslims of Lagos to His Excellency the Acting Governor[1]

In the name of God. . . .

This letter is from His Honour Yusufu Shitta Bey, Ibrahima, the Almany and His Deputy, Ahmad Tijani and all Muslim Sheikhs Viziers and c in Lagos.

We all send to humbly salute Your Excellency and sincerely congratulate you on your return amongst us in safety and good health we thank God for that and sincerely hope you will enjoy long life and happiness.

We approach now with reference to the understanding which we had with his Excellency Governor Carter. When we asked his permission to allow us to endeavour to make peace between our Muslim brethren at Ilọrin and the government here he kindly gave us permission to write to Ilọrin for that purpose and assured us that our messenger would go and return here safely. We then sent our messenger to Ilọrin and he was kindly received by the Emir and the people.

The Emir of Ilọrin was pleased with the message we sent and he would like to send his own messengers to the Government here; but he was afraid that they might be stopped on the road and punished. But if our messenger brought him back assurance that his messengers would not be molested he the Emir would if God please send his message by one, two three or four good and trustworthy men. These are the words of the Emir of Ilọrin.

[1] *Correspondence Relative to Appointment of Blyden as Agent of Native Affairs, UIL.* The Arabic original of this letter cannot be found.

When he Governor Carter was about to leave the other day we asked him what was to be done when our messenger returned from Ilọrin, he said that the Governor who would come to take his place is a good and faithful man and a peacemaker and he would adjust all matters in a right way. This was the understanding we had with Governor Carter on the eve of his departure.

We approach he the Acting Governor because we want to send back to the King and people of Ilọrin and would beg the assistance of His Excellency to give us permission in writing and the assurance that the messengers from the Emir of Ilọrin will be allowed to come to the Governor here with his message and return safely to Ilọrin. This is our desire and our determination. May God assist His Excellency greatly and give to him and to His Excellency Governor Carter length of days and prosperity.

God Save the Queen.

Dated at Lagos this 7th day of the Muslim month of Safar in the year of Hijra 1314 corresponding to the 19th day of July, 1896.

Appendix V

The Growth of Mohammedanism[1]

Resolved on the motion of the Rev. A. W. Smith, seconded by the Rev. S. M. Abiodun, 'that the rapid growth of Mohammedanism in the Yoruba country calls for serious consideration and prompt action on the part of the Church'. The Rev. A. W. Smith, who spoke in English, said that it was an awful *fact* that Mohammedanism was rapidly gaining ground in the Yoruba country. The Church, he went on, must face this fact as a country faces an enemy, and determine upon a definite plan of campaign. The Church *must* act *immediately*, and not sit down allowing the deadly enemy of Christianity to advance practically unchecked. Judging by the inaction of the Church she was turning blind eyes to this terrible fact. Mr. Smith spoke of the danger of trusting to statistics. He had sent out into various districts in the country 8 questions for the clergy to answer:

1. *When was Mohammedanism first introduced into the country?*

From replies it would appear that with the exception of Ogbomọșọ, it was of quite recent date. There it dated from 140 years ago, whilst in Ijẹbu country, it was introduced as 1893. The opening up of the country has meant the advice of first, and within the memory of many it has grown from a small stream into a mighty river, and that river practically unchecked.

2. *The estimated number of Mohammedans in your district and the population of Mohammedans to Christians and Heathen?*

Lagos: Three-fifths of the population.
Ijẹbu-Ode: One half of the population.

---

[1] *Proceedings of the Third Session of the First Synod of the Diocese of Western Equatorial Africa, May 7, 1908* (Exeter 1908), pp. 36–7.

230

Ibadan: One tenth of the population.
Ondo: 26% of the population.
Ogbomọṣọ: About 1,000 Mohammedans.

3. *Number of Mosques?*

Ibadan, 70;
Ijẹbu-Ode, 12;
Ijẹbu-Igbo, 20;
Ogbomọṣọ, 37;
Lagos, three times as many mosques as Churches of all denominations.

4. *To what causes do you attribute the growth of Islam in your district?*

Sanction of polygamy, sensuality and vice, encouragement of works of merit, love of dress, the sanction of making and selling charms, the attraction offered by the grand and showy demonstrations at the annual festivals, the outward show of self-denial in the way of fasting, ablutions, attendance at the fixed times of prayer.

5. *What is the social status of Mohammedans in your district?*

The social status of Mohammedans would appear to depend rather upon their private position than upon the fact of their religion.

6. *The social evils associated with the spread of Mohammedanism?*

All that minsters to the flesh, gross immorality, fraud, deception and extortion, obscene language in the streets, deliberate wickedness, murder, indifference to the care of their girls etc. etc.

7. *What efforts are being made to check the progress of Mohammedanism?*

No special effort other than the ordinary open-air preaching, and in Ondo is added to that, the visiting of the Mosques.

8. *What methods do you suggest for dealing with Mohammedan question*[6]

The same as that adopted in India and Persia. The appointment of men competent in the Arabic language and literature, Quran, commentaries and ritual, who will deal with the Mohammedans in the spirit of gentleness, humility and love.

Prayer and teaching the rising generation Arabic in our schools. Reading the Quran in the original with the educated Mohammedans and pointing out the excellency of the Bible. Reading the Quran in Yoruba with those who cannot read it in the original.

Seeking to lead them into a state of conviction of sin so that they may know their need of a Saviour. In seconding the motion, the Rev. S. M. Abiodun, who spoke in Yoruba, emphasized the points already referred to by the Rev. A. W. Smith.

The motion was supported by Mr. J. Adelagun and Mr. C. W. Wakeman; the latter referred to the Koran in Yoruba which is selling very slowly, and suggested that a missionary to the Mohammedans be sent by the Synod.

Appendix VI

Muslims' Petition for Islamic Law Courts[1]

May it please Your Excellency,

The humble petition of the undersigned on behalf of themselves and the other Muslim residents in Lagos sheweth:—

1. That the Muslim population of Lagos is in number about one half of the entire population of the town proper, and is ever increasing.

2. That pursuant to the law and customs of our faith most of the Muslims who have attained mature age, have contracted marriage and begotten children.

3. That under the English Common and Statute Law as applied to this colony by which the proceedings in our local courts of judicature are administered it is open to persons to contend.

(a) That our marriages are not legal.

(b) That our children are not legitimate and

(c) To seek to alter the manner and mode in which the property and estates of deceased Muslims would naturally devolve under the ordinary Muslim law and practice.

4. In the Empire of India where there is a large and increasing Muslim population, who constitute however but about one sixth of the population of that great empire under British rule (whereas, as previously pointed out in clause 1 of this memorial, in this colony the proportion of Muslims to the followers of other faiths is much greater), this anomaly and apparent injustice has been perceived and recognised and the Crown, with that tender solicitude for the welfare of its subjects so characteristic of the great and noble British race, has decreed that all Muslim subjects in India shall be

---

1 Text of Petition from the Muslims to His Excellency The Governor, Published in Nigerian Newspapers for which see *The Lagos Weekly Record*, 28 July 1894.

judged, in regard to their civil rights and grievances according to the law and usages of their own faith. And this wise provision of an enlightened government has been provocative of great good and has worked well for the interest of the Muslim population of the Indian Empire, and has greatly strengthened their loyalty and attachment to the British Crown.

We your memorialsts therefore humbly pray that your Excellency will be pleased to favourably consider this matter which we feel to be of serious importance to our community and provide in your wisdom some means whereby the Muslims of this colony may be placed upon a similar footing and have and enjoy the same legal rights and privileges as their co-religionists and fellow subjects in India have the felicity of duly enjoying.

And your petitioners will as in duty bound ever pray to the Almighty Ruler of all things to long preserve the life of your Excellency and also that of your Excellency's Royal and August Mistress, our most noble and Gracious Sovereign Queen Victoria.

Signed by us all at Lagos on the 6th day of the month of Moharram in the year of the Hegira of our Blessed Prophet (upon whom be everlasting peace) 1312, answering to and corresponding with the date which Christians describe as the tenth day of July 1894.

(Signed Mohammed Shitta Bey, Yusufu Shitta, Allmam Ibrahim, Ahmad Tijani, Othman Animashwun, and others.)

Bibliography

I PRIMARY SOURCES

Written information directly relevant to this topic is scanty; and much of the available historical material is only marginally useful. Any research worker in this field will, therefore, be well advised to cast his net very wide in his search for relevant material.

A. MUSLIM RECORDS

Available Muslim records and writings which are in Arabic are dealt with separately below. Muslim records in Yoruba and English can be found in private hands and in the offices of record-conscious Muslim societies such as the Ansar-ud-Deen Society and the Nawair-ud-Deen Society. Most of the records in this group relate to recent times, and can occasionally provide useful hindsight into the more remote past. As a class, however, they form an obvious invaluable source material.

B. CHRISTIAN MISSIONARY RECORDS

Some missionaries often took interest in the spread of Islam in their areas of work, and the records, journals and letters of such missionaries I have found extremely useful. Caution is essential, however, in the use of some of these materials as they may be biased one way or the other.

The records which I found particularly valuable are the CMS Papers which are classified into two groups:
(i) CA2: Yoruba Mission, 1842–80.
(ii) G3 A2: Yoruba Mission, 1880–1914.

These are available in microfilm in the Library of the University of Ibadan.

There are also some missionary papers in the National Archives, Ibadan.
(i) CMS (Y) 1/5–4/1.
These contain a few letters, minutes and reports of some committees.
(ii) Wesleyan Missionary Records.
A few of these records are available in NAI, where they are classified as W.M.M.S.

Occasionally useful are some Baptist Papers, notably *Correspondence of the Missionaries of the Southern Baptist Convention: Yoruba Mission, 1850–1890*. This is available in microfilm in the Library of the University of Ibadan.

More accessible, however, are the printed missionary records, which often drew upon the written records. I used the following:
(i)   *The Church Missionary Gleaner*, 1845–1914.
(ii) *The Church Missionary Intelligencer*, 1890–9.
(iii) *The Proceedings of the Church Missionary Society for Africa and the East*, 1908–14.
(iv) *The Niger and Yoruba Notes*, 1895–1904.
(v)   *The Proceedings of the Synod of the Diocese of Western Equatorial Africa*, 1902–14.
(vi) *The Annual Report of the Lagos Church Missions*, 1894–1917.

C. GOVERNMENT RECORDS

(i) NATIONAL

Those I consulted are available mostly in the National Archives at Ibadan and Kaduna, where they are catalogued in the C.S.O. series.

CSO 1/1 series are very useful: they contain the despatches between London and Lagos.

CCSO 1/8 contain the Instructions to Government.

CSO 26 series are mainly the Government files.

(ii) DIVISIONAL

The records of Divisional offices which are serialised under Ijẹbu Prof, Ọyọ Prof and the like are occasionally useful.

In the local Divisional offices some files have proved quite helpful in giving details of local issues, disputes and the background to such.

(iii) COURT RECORDS

Those used are in the Supreme Court, Lagos. Published cases can be found in the Library of the Supreme Court under West African Court of Appeal (W.A.C.A.), and Nigerian Law Reports (N.L.R.).

(iv) REPORTS

Abell, A. F., *Intelligence Report on the Ijebus*, 1933.
Blair, J. H., *Intelligence Report, Abeokuta*, 1938.
Bovill-Jones, T. B., *Intelligence Report on Ijebu Ode Town and Villages*, 1941.
Childs, H., and Gibbons, E. J., *Epe Reorganisation Report*, 1934.
Childs, H., and Gibbons, E. J., *A Report on the Administrative Reorganisation of the Epe District Native Treasury Area*, 1939.
Lethem, G. J. and Tomlinson, J., *The History of Political Propaganda in Nigeria*, Confidential Report, London 1927.
Mackenzie, Captain J. A., *Intelligence Report on Ijebu-Igbo*, 1940.
Weir, N. A. C., *Intelligence Report on the Ado District*, 1933.

(v) REPORTS (PRINTED)

Colonial Reports – Annual, Lagos, 1888–1902.
Colonial Reports – Annual, Southern Nigeria, 1899–1909.
Lagos Blue Books, 1897–1908.
Lagos Official Handbook, 1897–8.
Lagos Government Gazette, 1903.

(vi) PARLIAMENTARY PAPERS (BRITISH)

1862, Papers relating to the Occupation of Lagos C. 2982.
1865, V, Report from the Select Committee on State of British Settlements on the West Coast of Africa.
1887, Correspondence Respecting the War between Native Tribes in the Interior and the Negotiations for Peace conducted by the Government of Lagos. 1887. C. 4957.

1887, Further Correspondence Respecting the War between Native Tribes in the Interior and the Negotiations for Peace conducted by the Government of Lagos. C. 5144 in continuation of C. 4957.

1893, Despatch from Sir Gilbert T. Carter furnishing a general Report on the Lagos Interior Expedition. C. 7227.

D. PRIVATE PAPERS

(i) *Abass Papers* in the possession of two sons of Seriki Abass who are at Badagry and Aiyetoro. These papers yield much material on the activities of Seriki Abass in Egbado, his family affairs and relations with the Government.

(ii) *Adẹyẹmi Cole Papers* in possession of the owner (now deceased). He was for many years the Treasurer of the Ansar ud-Deen Society Lagos, and was himself related to the Muslim repatriates from Sierra Leone. His papers, fortunately, do throw some light on these two issues though more on the former than the other.

(iii) *Awujalẹ Papers* in the Palace of Awujalẹ. These papers contain valuable petitions and reports mostly from the whole of Ijẹbu.

(iv) *Daramola Papers* in the possession of the owner; B. A. Daramola of Ijẹbu-Ode. An elderly (over 65) Muslim gentleman, he has been closely connected with the more elderly Muslims in Ijẹbu-Ode and he is much respected for his contribution to the educational progress of Muslims.

(v) *Macaulay Papers* in the Library of the University of Ibadan. These throw more light on some notable families in Lagos, and the contact between the government and outstanding personalities in Lagos.

(vi) *Tukuru Papers* in the possession of the owner. These bear on the development of the Muslim community in Abẹokuta.

II ARABIC SOURCES

Note: Various Arabic manuscripts are being found among mallams in Yorubaland. I have not read all of them, and only a selection is given here – those which were popular, and are of historical interest. Their location is indicated by certain symbols.

B: Brockelmann.
CAD: Centre of Arabic Documentation, University of Ibadan.
P: Private Collections in the possession of various mallams
          in Yorubaland.
UIL: University of Ibadan Library.

Abū Bakr b. Abī Bakr, *'ilm al-Tawḥīd*	P
Aḥmad b. Abī Bakr Kokoro, *Ta'lif Akhbār al-qurūn*	
min umarā bilād ilūrin	P; CAD
Risāla ilā Wazīr Bida	CAD
Aḥmad b. Maḥmud, *Qasīda fī al-Madḥ*	P; CAD
Aḥmad al-Rufā'i, *Tārīkh al-Islām fī Ibadan*	UIL
Ashmawi	B; UIL
'Abd al-Rahmān b. 'Awf, *Kitāb al-Wa'z*	P
'Abdallāh b. Fūdī, *Maṭīyat al-Zād*	UIL
'Abdallāh Muḥammad b. al-Sinhājī *Kitāb al-Naḥw*	B; UIL
'Alī Ahmad b. 'Isa, *Qasīda fī al-Madḥ*	P
'Ali b. Hussain, *Durr al-durar fī madh Khair al-bashār*	UIL
Badamāṣī, *Qaṣīda*	UIL
Ibn Bābā al 'Alawī al-Maghribī, *Muniyat al-Murīd*	UIL
Khalīl b. Ishāq, *Mukhtaṣar*	B; UIL
Muḥammad Bello, *Qawā' id al-Ṣalāt*	UIL
Muḥammad b. Salīm al-Awjalī, *Shahādat al-Islām*	B; UIL
Muḥammad 'Abdallāh al-Qairawānī	B; UIL
Muḥammad b. Jibrīl b. al-Kuqināwī, *Tafakkur*	UIL
Muḥammad b. Mu'tī b. 'Alī al-Sūdānī, *Tafhīm al-*	
Mubtadī n	UIL
Muḥammad b. al-Wardī, *Fī ladā al-durr*	P
Tuḥfat al-Wardī	UIL
Shihāb al-Dīn, *Kitāb fī al-Ṣalāt*	UIL
'Umār b. Aḥmad b. al-Bukhārī, *Tuḥfat al-Sibyān*	P

Anonymous authors

Māqama ladā sidrat at muntahā	P
Hal mā Shī ta fī darain tas'ad	P
Kitāb al-Anwār	P
Raghba ladā Allah	P
Kitāb al-Tawḥīd	P
Qawā' id al-Ṣalāt	P

Qaṣīda fī   P
Al-ḥamdu l-Allah Huwa
   al-wāhid   P

III SECONDARY SOURCES

A NEWSPAPERS

The Lagos Weekly Record, 1891–1920
The Lagos Times, 1880–93
Times of Nigeria, 1914–20
African Messenger, 1924
The Lagos Weekly Times, 1890–1
The Truth, 1961–7

B LOCAL HISTORY

Abiola, J. D. E., *Iwe Itan Ileṣa* (History of Ileṣa), 1st edn. Ileṣa, 1932
Adeleke, Wale, *Iwe Itan Ilu Iseyin* (History of Iseyin). Iseyin, 1964
Aguda, Chief, *A Brief History of the Central Mosque, Lagos.* Lagos, n.d.
Agunwa, D., *Iwe Itan bi Ẹsin Imale ti ṣe de Ilu Ọtta* (History of the coming of Islam to Otta). Yaba, 1947
Ajisafe, A. K. (formerly Moore, E. O.), *History of Abeokuta*, 2nd edn. Bungay, Suffolk, 1924
Akinyele, I. B., *Iwe Itan Ibadan* (History of Ibadan). Ibadan, 1911
Outlines of Ibadan History. Lagos, 1946
Animasaun, A. I., *The History of the Muslim Community of Lagos.* Lagos, n.d.
Apena, M. B. O., *Iwe Ikekuru ti Itan Ijebu* (A Short History of Ijebu), 2nd edn. Ibadan, 1937
Avoseh, T. Ola, *A Short History of Epe.* Epe, 1960
The History of Badagry. MSS, 2nd edn. 1960
Epega, Rev. D. O., *Iwe Itan Ijebu ati awon ilu Miran* (A History of Ijebu and other towns), 2nd edn. Lagos, 1934
Johnson, S., *The History of the Yorubas.* CMS, Lagos, 1957
Laotan, A. B., *The Torch Bearers or old Brazilian Colony in Lagos.* 1943
Losi, J. B. O., *The History of Lagos.* Lagos, 1914

Oguntuyi, A., *A Short History of Ade-Ekiti*, Part II. Ibadan, 1967
Ojo, S. O., *Iwe Itan Ondo* (History of Ondo). Ondo, 1940
A Short History of Ilorin. Oyo, 1957
Oyerinde, N. D., *Iwe Itan Ogbomosho* (History of Ogbomosho). Jos, 1934

C BOOKS

Abraham, R. C., *A Dictionary of Modern Yoruba*. London, 1958
A Dictionary of the Hausa Language. London, 1949
Adams, Captain John, *Remarks on the Country extending from Cape Palmas to the River Congo*. London, 1823
Ajayi, J. F. Ade, *Population Census of Nigeria, May 1962*. Ibadan, 1962
Christian Missions in Nigeria 1841–1891. Longman, 1965
Akindele, A., and Aguessy, C., *Dahomey*. Editions Maritimes et Coloniales, Paris. 1955
Contribution à l'étude de l'histoire de l'ancien royaume de Porto-Novo. Dakar, 1958
Arberry, A. J., *An Introduction to History of Sufism*. London, 1942
Arnett, E. J., *The Rise of the Sokoto Fulani*. Kano, 1922
Arnold, T. W., *The Preaching of Islam*. London, 1913
Ayandele, E. A., *The Missionary Impact on Modern Nigeria*. Longman, 1966
Holy Johnson: Pioneer of African Nationalism 1836–1917. Frank Cass, 1970.
Baeta, C. G., *Christianity in Tropical Africa*. Oxford University Press, 1968
Bascom, W. R., *Ifa Divination; communication between gods and men in West Africa*. Indiana University Press, 1969
Bello, M., *Infāq al-Maisūr*
Biobaku, S. O., *The Egba and their Neighbours, 1842–1872*. Oxford, 1957
Sources on Yoruba History. Oxford, 1973
Blyden, E. W., *Christianity, Islam and the Negro Race*, 2nd edn. London, 1889
Bovill, E. W., *The Golden Trade of the Moors*. Oxford, 1961
Bowen, Rev. T. J., *Grammar and Dictionary of the Yoruba Language with an Introductory Description of the Country and People of Yoruba*. Washington, Smithsonian Institute, 1858
Adventures and Missionary Labours in the Interior of Africa, 1849–1856. Charlestown, 1857

Brockelmann, C., *Geschichte der Arabischen Litteratur*. Leiden, 1937–49.

Burns, Sir Alan, *History of Nigeria*. London, 1964

Burton, R. F., *Abeokuta and the Cameroons Mountains*, vol. I. London, 1863
Wanderings in West Africa from Liverpool to Fernando Po, 2 vols. London, 1863
Negro Wit and Wisdom. London, 1865

Campbell, Robert, *A Pilgrimage to my Motherland: An Account of a Journey among the Egbas and Yorubas of Central Africa in 1859–1860*. London, 1861

Clapperton, Captain Hugh, *Journal of a Second Expedition into the Interior of Africa from the Bight of Benin to Seccatoo*. London, 1829

Coleman, James S., *Nigeria: Background to Nationalism*. California, 1958

Coulson, N. J., *A History of Islamic Law*. Edinburgh, 1964

Cregg, K., *Counsels in Contemporary Islam*. Edinburgh, 1965

Crowder, M. and Ikime, O., (eds.) *West African Chiefs* African Publishing Corporation. Ife, 1970

Crowther, Rt Rev. Samuel Ajayi, *A Grammar and Vocabulary of the Yoruba Language*. London, 1852
Experiences with Heathens and Mohammedans in West Africa. London, 1892

Curtin, P. (ed.), *Africa Remembered*. Ibadan, 1967

Delano, I. O., *The Soul of Nigeria*. London, 1937

Elgee, C. H., *The Evolution of Ibadan*. Lagos, 1914

Ellis, A. B., *The Yoruba-Speaking Peoples of the Slave Coast of West Africa*. Chapman and Hall, 1894
Encyclopaedia of Islam. Leiden, 1913 and 1960

Farrow, S. S., *Faith, Fancies and Fetish*. London, S.P.C.K., 1926

Fisher, H. J. L., *Ahmadiyya*. Oxford, 1963

Flint, J. E., *Sir George Goldie and the Making of Nigeria*. London, 1960

Freeman-Grenville, G. S. P., *The Muslim and Christian Calendars*. Oxford, 1963

Fyfe, C. H., *A History of Sierra Leone*. Oxford, 1962

Fyzee, A. A., *Outlines of Muhammadan Law*. Oxford, 1955

Gaudefroy-Demombynes, *Les Institutions Musulmanes*. Paris, 1953

George, J. O., *Historical Notes on the Yoruba Country and its Tribes*. Lagos, 1895

Gibb, H. A. R., *Modern Trends in Islam.* Chicago, 1947

Grimely, J. B., and Robinson, G. E., *Church Growth in Central and Southern Nigeria.* Michigan, 1966

Groves, C. P., *The Planting of Christianity in Africa,* 4 vols. London, 1948–55

Hinderer, Anna, *Seventeen Years in the Yoruba Country: Memorials of Anna Hinderer, wife of the Rev. David Hinderer, C.M.S. Missionary in Western Africa. Gathered from Her Journals and Letters with an Introduction by Richard B. Hone M.A., Archdeacon of Worcester.* London, 1872

Hitti, P., *History of the Arabs,* 8th edn. Macmillan, 1963

Hodgkin, T., *Nigerian perspectives: An Historical Anthology.* London, 1960

Hogben, S. J., *An Introduction to the History of Islamic States of Nigeria.* Oxford, 1967

Hogben, S. J. and Kirk-Greene, A. H. M., *The Mohammedan Emirates of Northern Nigeria.* Oxford, 1965

Idowu, E. B., *Olodumare: God in Yoruba Belief.* London, 1962
African Traditional Religion: A definition. London, S.C.M., 1973

al-Iluri, A. A., *Tārikh al-Islām fī Nijīriya wa 'Uthmān b. Fūdī.* Cairo, n.d.
Qāla al-Shaikh. Cairo, n.d.
al-fawāk al-sāqita. Cairo, n.d.

Jeffrey, A. (ed.), *A Reader on Islam.* Mouton, 1962

Johnston, Sir H. H., *The Negro in the New World.* London, 1910

Johnston, H. A. S., *The Fulani Empire of Sokoto.* Oxford, 1967

Kensdale, W. E. N., *A Catalogue of Arabic Manuscripts preserved in the University Library, Ibadan.* Ibadan, 1955–8

Kiev, A. (ed.), *Magic, Faith and Healing: Studies in Primitive Psychiatry Today.* New York, 1964

Koelle, S. W., *Polyglotta Africana or a Comparative Vocabulary of nearly 300 words and phrases in more than 100 distinct African Languages.* CMS 1856

Lander, Richard, *Records of Captain Clapperton's Last Expedition to Africa,* vols i–ii. London, 1830

Lander, Richard and John, *Journal of an Expedition to explore the Course and Termination of the Niger: with a narrative of a voyage down that River,* 2 vols. 2nd edn. London, 1838

Levtzion, N., *Muslims and Chiefs in West Africa: A study of Islam in the Middle Volta Basin in the Pre-Colonial Period.* Oxford, 1968

Levy, R., *The Social Structure of Islam.* Cambridge, 1957

Lewis, B., *The Emergence of Modern Turkey*. Oxford, 1961
Lewis, G. L., *Turkey*. London, 1954
Lewis, I. M. (ed.), *Islam in Tropical Africa*. Oxford, 1966
Lloyd, P. C., *Yoruba Land Law*. Ibadan, 1962
Lloyd, P. C., Mabogunje, A. L., and Awe, B. (eds.), *The City of Ibadan*. Cambridge, 1967
Lucas, J. O., *The Religion of the Yorubas*. Lagos, 1922
Lynch, H. R., *Black Spokesman: Select Published Writings of E. W. Blyden*. Frank Cass 1971.
Mabogunje, A. L., *Yoruba Towns*. Ibadan, 1962
Marty, P., *Études sur l'Islam au Dahomey*. Paris, 1926
Maudūdī, Abul A'la, *Islamic Law and Constitution*. Lahore, 1960
Mendelsohn, Jack, *God, Allah and Juju*. New York, 1962
Millot, L., *Introduction à l'étude du droit Musulman*. Paris, 1953
Monteil, V., *L'Islam Noir*. Paris, 1964
Morgan, K. W. (ed.), *Islam, The Straight Path*. New York, 1956
Nadel, S. F., *A Black Byzantium: the Kingdom of Nupe*. Oxford, 1942
Nasr, Abun, *The Tijaniyya: A Sufi Order in the Modern World*. Oxford, 1965
Nasr, S. H., *Ideals and Realities of Islam*. London, 1966
Newbury, C. W., *The Western Slave Coast and its Rulers*. Oxford, 1961
British Policy Towards West Africa: Select Documents, 1786–1874, vol. i. Oxford, 1965.
Nicholson, R. A., *Studies in Islamic Mysticism*. Cambridge, 1921
    A Literary History of Arabs. Cambridge, 1956
    The Mystics of Islam. London, 1963
Okediji, F. D. and Okediji, O. O., (eds.) *N. A. Fadipe: The Sociology of the Yoruba*. Ibadan, 1970.
Palmer, H. R. (trans.), *Bornu, Sahara and the Sudan*. London, 1936
    Sudanese Memoirs, vol. iii. Lagos, 1928
Panikkar, K. N., *The Serpent and the Crescent, A History of the Negro Empires of West Africa*. Asia Publishing House, 1963
Parrinder, E. G., *Religion in an African City*. Oxford, 1953
    The Story of Ketu: An Ancient Yoruba Kingdom. Ibadan, 1956
    African Traditional Religion. London, S.P.C.K., 1962
    What World Religions Teach. London, Harrap, 1963
    Religion in Africa. London, 1969
Payne, John Augustus Otonba, *Table of Principal Events in Yoruba History with Certain other Matters of General Interest Compiled*

Principally for use in the Courts within the British Colony of Lagos, West Africa. Lagos, 1893

al-Qur'ān

Rahman, F., *Islam*. London, 1966

Rodrigues, Jose Honoric, *Brazil and Africa*. University of California Press, Berkeley, 1965

Rondot, F., *L'Islam et les Musulman d'aujourdhui*. Paris, 1958

Schacht, J., *An Introduction to Islamic Law*. Oxford, 1964

Sharif, M. M., *A History of Muslim Philosophy*. Wiesbaden, 1963

Skinner, E. P., *The Mossi of the Upper Volta, the political development of a Sudanese People*. Stanford, 1964

Smith, M., *Baba of Karo*. London, 1954

Smith, W. C., *Islam in Modern History*. Princeton, 1955

Stock, E., *History of the Church Missionary Society*, vols 2, 3 and 4. London, 1899

Talbot, P. A., *The Peoples of Southern Nigeria*. Oxford, 1926
Life in Southern Nigeria. London, 1936

Tomlinson, G. J. F., and Lethem, G. J., *History of Islamic Political Propaganda in Nigeria*. London, 1927

Trimingham, J. Spencer, *The Christian Church and Islam in West Africa*. London, S.C.M., 1955
A History of Islam in West Africa. Oxford, 1962
The Influence of Islam upon Africa. London, Longmans, 1968
Islam in West Africa. London, 1959

Tucker, Miss, *Abeokuta or Sunrise within the Tropics. An Outline of the Origin and Progress of the Yoruba Mission*. London, 1853

Turner, H. W., *African Independent Church* vol. 1. Oxford, 1967

Vansina, J., Mauny, R., and Thomas, L. V. (eds), *The Historian in Tropical Africa*. Oxford, 1964

Walker, F. D., *A Hundred Years in Nigeria: The Story of Methodist Mission in the Western Nigeria, 1841–1942*. London, 1942

Watt, W. M., *Islamic Philosophy and Theology*. Edinburgh, 1962

Webster, J. B., *The African Churches Among the Yoruba 1888–1922*. Oxford, 1964

Whitford, J. L., *Trading Life in Western and Central Africa*. Liverpool, 1877

D ARTICLES

Abuja, J. B., 'Koranic and Moslem Law Teaching in Hausaland' *Nigeria*, 37, 1951

Ajayi, J. F. Ade, 'How Yoruba was reduced to writing', *Odu*, 8, October 1960
  'Henry Venn and the Policy of Development', *JHSN*, i, 4, December 1959
  'Political Organisation in West African Towns in the Nineteenth Century: the Lagos Example', in *Urbanisation in African Social Change*. Paper presented at the inaugural Seminar at the Centre of Africa Studies, Edinburgh, 1963
Akinjogbin, I. A., 'The Prelude to the Yoruba Civil Wars', *Odu*, i, 2, January 1965
  'A Chronology of Yoruba History', *Odu*, ii, 2, January 1966
Allison, P., 'Koranic Schools in Northern Nigeria', *West African Journal of Education*, vii, 3, 1963
Ayandele, E. A., 'The Mode of British Expansion in Yorubaland in the second half of the nineteenth century: the Ọyọ Episode.' *Odu*, iii, 2, January 1967
  'An Assessment of James Johnson and his Place in Nigerian History (1874–1917)', Parts I and II. 2, 4, December 1963; and 3, 1, December 1964
Bascom, W. R., 'The Sanctions of Ifa Divination', *Journal of the Royal Anthropological Institute*, 71, Part II, 1941
  'Ifa Divination: Comments on Clarke's Paper', *Man*, 42, 1942
  'Social Status among the Yoruba', *American Anthropologist*, liii, 4, October–December 1951
  'Urbanisation among the Yoruba', *American Journal of Sociology*, lx, 5, March 1955
  'Urbanism as a Traditional African Pattern', *Sociological Review*, vii, 1, July 1959
Bascom, W., and McClelland, E. M., 'Two Studies of Ifa Divination', *Africa*, xxxvi, 4, October 1966, pp. 406–31
Bassir, O., 'Marriage Rites among the Aku in Freetown', *Africa*, xxiv, 3, July 1954
Beals, R. L., 'Urbanism, Urbanisation and Acculturation', *American Anthropologist*, liii, 1, 1951
Biobaku, S. O., 'Ogboni, the Ẹgba Senate', *Proceedings of the C.I.A.O.* Ibadan, 1949
  'An historical sketch of Ẹgba traditional authorities', *Africa*, xxii, 1952
  'The origin of the Yorubas', in *Lugard Lectures*, Lagos, 1955
Bivar, A. D. H., 'Arabic Documents of Northern Nigeria', *BSOAS*, 22, 1959

Blyden, E. W., 'The Koran in Africa', *JAS*, viii, July 1903
'Mohammedanism in West Africa', *Methodist Quarterly Review*, January 1871
'Mohammedanism and the Negro Race', *Fraser's Magazine*, New Series, xii, Nov. 1875
Clarke, J. D., 'Ifa Divination', *Journal of Royal Anthropological Institute*, 69, Part II, 1939
Cragg, K., 'West African Catechism', *The Muslim World*, xlviii, 3, July 1958
Debrunner, H. D., and Fisher, H., 'Early Fante Islam', *The Ghana Bulletin of Theology*, i, 7, December 1959; i, 8, Trinity Term 1960
Doi, A. R. I., 'The Yoruba Mahdi', *Journal of Religion in Africa*, iv, 2, 1971 pp. 119–38
Gbadamosi, G. O., 'The Establishment of Western Education among Muslims in Nigeria', *JHSN*, iv, 1, December 1967
'The Imamate Question among Yoruba Muslims', *JHSN*, vi, 2, December 1972
Goddard, S., 'Town and Farm Relationships in Yorubaland: A Case Study from Ọyọ', *Africa*, xxxv, 1, Jan. 1965
Greenberg, J., 'Some aspects of Negro–Mohammedan Culture among the Hausa', *American Anthropologist*, xliii, 51–61, 1941
The Influence of Islam on a Sudanese Religion', *New York American Ethnological Social Memoir*, 15, 1946
'Arabic Loan Words in Hausa', *Word*, 3, 1947
'Kanuri Influence on Hausa', *Journal of African History*, 1960
Halligey, J. T. F.,'Yoruba Country, Abeokuta and Lagos', *Journal of the Manchester Geographical Society*, 9, 1893
Hiskett, M., 'Material relating to the state of learning among the Fulani before the Jihad', *BSOAS*, 19, 1957
'Problems of Religious Education in Muslim Communities in Africa', *Overseas Education*, xxxiii, 3, October 1960
Hodder, B. W., 'Badagry: One hundred years of change', *The Nigerian Geographical Journal*, vi, 1, June 1963
Law, R. C. C., 'The Chronology of the Yoruba Wars of the Early Nineteenth Century: a Reconsideration,' *JHSN*, v, 2, June 1970
Lloyd, P. C., 'The traditional political system of the Yoruba', *South Western Journal of Anthropology*, x, 4, Winter 1954
'Salah at Ilorin', *Nigeria Magazine*, lxx, 19
'The Yoruba Lineage', *Africa*, xxv, 3, July 1955

'The Yoruba Town Today', *Sociological Review*, 9, 1959

MacGregor, Sir William, 'Lagos, Abeokuta and the Alake', *JAS*, iii, 12, July 1904

Mason, M., 'The Jihad in the South: an outline of the nineteenth century Nupe Hegemony in North-eastern Yorubaland and Afenmai', *JHSN*, ,v 2, June 1970

Moloney, Sir Alfred, 'Notes on Yoruba and the Colony and Protectorate of Lagos, West Africa', *Journal of the Royal Geographical Society*, v, 12, 1890

Monteil, V., 'L'Islam Noir', *Rev. Tunisienne Sor.*, ii, 4, Dec. 1965

Morton-Williams, P., 'The Atinga Cult among the South-Western Yoruba: A Sociological Analysis of a witch-finding movement', *West African Institute of Social and Economic Research*, 1952

'The Egungun Society in South-Western Yoruba Kingdoms', *Proceedings of the Third Annual Conference of the West African Institute of Social and Economic Research*. Ibadan, 1956

'The Yoruba Ogbẹni Cult in Oyo', *Africa*, xxx, 1960

'An outline of the Cosmology and Cult Organisation of the Oyo Yoruba', *Africa*, xxxiv, 3, July 1964, pp. 243–61

Oke, R. O., 'Islam in Ibadan', in *Ibadan*, a publication presented to the Third International West African Conference, 1949

Parrinder, E. G., 'Divine Kingship in West Africa', *Numen*, iii, 2, 1956

Peel, J. B. Y., 'Religious change in Yorubaland', *Africa*, July 1969, pp. 292–306

Proudfoot, L., 'Mosque Building and Tribal Separation in Freetown', *Africa*, xxix, 4, 1959

Schacht, J., 'Islam in Northern Nigeria', *Studia Islamica*, viii, 1957

Schwab, W. B., 'The Growth and Conflicts of religion in a modern Yoruba community', *Zaire*, vi, 8, October 1952

Skinner, E. P., 'Christianity and Islam among the Mossi', *American Anthropologist*, lx, 6, Pt 1, Dec. 1955, pp. 1102–19

'Mossi Society', *Africa*, xxx, 4, October 1960

'The Diffusion of Islam in an African Society', *Annals, New York Academy of Sciences*, xcvi, January 20, 1961

'Strangers in West African Societies', *Africa*, xxxiii, 4, October 1963

Smith, H. F. C., 'Arabic Manuscript Material Relating to the History of the Western Sudan', *Supplement to Bulletin of News*, Historical Society of Nigeria, iv, 2, 1959

'The Islamic Revolutions of the Nineteenth Century', *JHSN,* ii, 1, 1961

Turner, H. W., The Place of Independent Religious Movements in the Modernisation of Africa', *Jo. Relig. Pub. in Africa,* ii, 1, 1969, pp. 43–63

'Pagan Features in West African Independent Churches', *Practical Anthropology,* xii, 4, July–Aug. 1965, pp. 145–51

Verger, P., 'Notes sur le culte des Orisa et Vodun à Bahia'. *Mémoires,* IFAN, 51, 1957

'Influence du Brésil au Golfe du Bénin', in *Les Afro-Americaines. Mémoires,* IFAN 27, 1952

'The Yoruba High God', *Odu*

Watt, W. M., 'Some Problems before West African Islam', *The Islamic Review Quarterly,* iv, 1, April 1957, pp. 43–51

Webster, J. S., 'The African Churches', *Nigeria Magazine,* 70

Wirth, 'Urbanism as a way of Life', *American Journal of Sociology,* xliv, 8, 1938,

E THESES

Adeleye, R. A., *The Overthrow of the Sokoto Caliphate, 1879–1903.* Ph.D., Ibadan, 1967

Aderibigbe, A. A. B., *Expansion of the Lagos Protectorate, 1861–1900.* Ph.D., London 1959

Adetugbo, B., *The Yoruba language in Western Nigeria: its major Dialect areas.* Ph.D., Columbia University, 1967

Agiri, B. A., *Development of Local Government in Ogbomosho, 1850–1950.* M.A., Ibadan, 1966

Akintoye, S. A., *The Ekitiparapo and the Kiriji War.* Ph.D., Ibadan, 1966

Atanda, J. A., *The New Oyo Empire: A Study of British Indirect Rule in Oyo Province, 1894–1934.* Ph.D., Ibadan, 1967

Awe, B. O., *The Rise of Ibadan as a Yoruba power in the nineteenth century.* D.Phil., Oxford, 1964

Ayandele, E. A., *The Political and Social Implications of Missionary Enterprise in the Evolution of Modern Nigeria, 1875–1914.* Ph.D., London 1964

Ayantuga, O., *The Ijẹbu and Its Neighbours.* Ph.D., London, 1965

Bascom, W. R., *Secret Societies, Religious Cult groups and Kinship units among West African Yoruba: A Study in Social Organisation.* Ph.D., Department of Anthropology, 1939

Biobaku, S. O., *The Egba State and Its Neighbours, 1842–1872*. Ph.D., London, 1951

Cordwell, J. W., *Some Aesthetic Aspects of Yoruba and Benin Cultures*, Ph.D., Northwestern, 1952

Dry, D. P. L., *The Place of Islam in Hausa Society*. D.Phil., Oxford, 1956

Fadipẹ, N. A., *The Sociology of the Yoruba*. Ph.D., London, 1940

Fọlayan, K., *Ẹgbado and Yoruba–Aja Power Politics, 1832–1894*. M.A., Ibadan, 1967

Hodder, B. W., *Markets in Yorubaland*. Ph.D., London, 1963

Hopewell, J. F., *Muslim Penetration into French Guinea, Sierra Leone and Liberia before 1850*. Ph.D., Columbia, 1958

Hopkins, A. G., *An Economic History of Lagos, 1880–1914*. Ph.D., London, 1964

Jenkins, G. D., *Politics in Ibadan*. Ph.D., Northwestern, 1965

Knight, C. W., *History of the Expansion of Evangelical Christianity in Nigeria, 1842–1942*. Ph.D., Southern Baptist, 1951

Last, D. M., *Sokoto in the Nineteenth Century with Special Reference to the Vizierate*. Ph.D., Ibadan, 1964

Lynch, H. R., *Edward Wilmot Blyden, 1832–1912, and Negro Nationalism*. Ph.D., London, 1964

Olowukure, J. O. K., *Christianity in Ijesaland, 1858–1960*. M.A., Ibadan, 1970

Peterson, J. E., *Freetown: a study in the Dynamics of Liberated African Society, 1807–1870*. Ph.D., Northwestern, 1963

Schwab, W. B., *The Political and Social Organisation of an Urban African Community*. Ph.D., Pennsylvania, 1952

Tamuno, S. M., *The Rise and Development of British Administrative Control of Southern Nigeria, 1900–1912: A study in the Administration of Sir Ralph Moor, Sir William MacGregor and Sir Walter Egerton*. Ph.D., London, 1962

Walsh, M. W., *The Catholic Contribution to Education in Western Nigeria, 1861–1926*. M.A., London, 1951

Welldon, R. M. C., *The Human Geography of a Yoruba Township in Western Nigeria*. B.Litt., Oxford, 1957

IV ORAL EVIDENCE

The use of oral evidence for historical purposes has become accepted by now.[1] Indeed, it is really inevitable in a work of this nature where written evidence is, by and large, small as compared with any work on the Christian missionaries.

I discovered, however, that the Yoruba Muslims do possess a remarkably high sense of history. In each Yoruba community that I visited, the people cherish a knowledge of their beginnings and development. This has greatly facilitated the collection of historical data. This sense of history explains why there was not only a number of published local works on the history of Islam, but also a considerable number of manuscripts on this subject. These manuscripts were sometimes prepared in readiness for my interview.

I visited a large number of Muslim communities in Yorubaland, sometimes more than once, in order to collect and check evidence relating to this work. In a letter to them, I always informed them beforehand about the purpose and date of my visit. On my arrival, there was often need for a fuller explanation of my purpose, myself, and sponsors; sometimes my previous experience was subtly asked for. Soon enough, I found the people enthusiastic and co-operative, especially as they came to know about my academic leanings, my interest in the community, and my knowledge of Arabic (I was often called *muallim* or *ustadh*). A formal interview took place with the leaders and elders; and within a short time, people became relaxed. I listened to the story told me, with very few interruptions. When there was some considerable pause, I asked a few questions to clarify what had already been said. Otherwise, I managed to lead them on to fresh topics. Open meetings with elders could be twice or thrice.

This was often followed by 'unofficial' interviews with individual Muslims and non-Muslims in their private homes. A lot of interesting detail sometimes emerged here, particularly from the womenfolk who remembered praise names and other interesting data fairly well.

My interviews were sometimes with local historians, relatives of Muslims, and others who by their age or connections might have some relevant information to give. The chiefs and elders – above fifty – were the most helpful.

While I generally gave free scope to the people interviewed, there were topics on which I often had to ask for their evidence.

[1] See particularly Vansina (ed.), *The Historian in Tropical Africa*.

These included the various itinerant mallams, their songs (which I recorded on tape), the Arabic manuscripts locally read or written, relations with non-Muslims, pilgrimage and the like.

I stayed with Muslims for most of the time during my tours of Yorubaland. Often I was a guest with the Chief Imam, or with any other Muslim as fixed for me by the Muslim elders. Sometimes I had to stay in the Government Rest Houses. Based in one town, I visited other neighbouring towns and villages, conducting my interviews. Quite apart from official work, it was a very useful and interesting experience to move so closely with all the Yoruba communities, and with people so dedicated to and fervent in the cause of their living faith.

During interviews there were sometimes some difficulties. Two can be cited. First, there was some difficulty in fixing dates. This problem I tried to solve by reference to fairly fixed chronologies: in Ijẹbu, age-grades; and elsewhere, king lists, and Imam lists. In using historical events as a time framework, I found Ajayi's *Population Census* useful; but I often had to supplement or even correct these by using the records in the files of the local administrative offices. Even by these methods, however, only approximate dates could sometimes be given.

Secondly, it was not always easy to get information about the 'pagan' background and 'pagan' connections of some Muslims, particularly the prominent ones. There is an open reserve about this. And although gossip and private discussions could be revealing here, yet these had severe limitations for historical purposes. However, disputes among Muslims often throw up a lot of material on this aspect; and reports of these, which are available in various government and private records, can be useful. But, even here, there is some obvious need for circumspection in handling such materials.

Generally, however, a valid story can be pieced together by a careful use of both oral and written evidence.

Below is a *select* list of places I visited and the people interviewed.

Abẹokuta, June 1963

1 Al-hajj Bamgbola
2 Al-hajj Yaya
3 Mr Kaseem
4 Al-hajj Zubair Badmos Imam

5 Al-hajj A. K. Uthman
6 Afa A. A. Olusunmade of Idiape, Owu, Abẹokuta
7 Chief Ayọ Ṣofolukẹ.
  Chief Ṣofolukẹ is an Ẹgba historian: he has written *Awọn Akọni Mejila*, and has made many broadcasts on Ẹgba history and customs.

Ado-Ekiti, June 1965
1 Afa Jimọ, the Chief Imam of Ado
2 Balogun Sanni, aged about 60
3 Jinadu Alowoyọ Idemọ (about 60)
4 Chief Ẹkẹrin Buraimọ Irọna
5 Al-hajj Saliu Ajijọla, Chairman of the Central Mosque Committee
6 S. S. Balogun, Secretary of the Nawwar-al-Dīn.
  The chief Imam was the son of the first Imam of Ado-Ekiti.

Badagry, August 1963
1 Abdul Gafar Tijani, the Chief Imam, Warako Quarter, Badagry
2 Rufai Tukuru, the Balogun
3 Muhammad Adelakun, the Ọnaṣokun
4 Al-hajj Muhammad
5 Mustafa Lawal Ajapẹ, the Onitafusiru
6 Afa Mujitaba Awesu.
  The Chief Imam is the son of Tijani, the third Chief Imam of Badagry.

Ẹdẹ, May–June 1965
1 Ọba Lagunju, the Timi of Ẹdẹ
2 Alimi B. Sadiku, the Chief Imam of Ẹdẹ
3 Agbo-Ile Imale, Ẹdẹ.

Ejirin, June 1963
1 Chief S. M. A. Balogun, the Elejirin of Ejirin
2 Sanni Adigun, the Imam of Ejirin
3 Chief S. Ade. Ologuda, a chief of the town
4 Kadiri Olokun of Obalende Ward III
5 Shaikh Mallam Tijani of Seriki Ward I
6 Abdul Karim, the head of Tafsir, of Ago-Ijẹsa Ward.
  Chief Sanusi Ologudu was an early Ejirin convert.

Ẹpẹ, June 1963

1 Chief D. A. Ajayi, the Ọlọja of Ẹpẹ
2 Mallam Salia Tukuru (about, 55), the Chief Imam of Ẹpẹ
3 T. Ọla Avoseh, a local historian of Ẹpẹ (and Badagry)
4 The Ijẹbu Balẹ of Ẹpẹ.

Ibadan, February–March 1965

1 Al-hajj Abdulsalami
2 Al-hajj Mudasir (Muritala?)
3 The Chief Imam.

Igboho, April 1965

1 Chief Imam
2 Salami Jaiyeọla
3 Onibode Igboho.

Ijẹbu-Igbo, August 1963

1 The Chief Imam
2 Al-hajj Rufai Arikewuyọ.

Ikẹrẹ, May–June 1965

1 Afa Isa, the Chief Imam
2 Al-hajj Jimọ Ajijọlanabi, the Imam of Ahmadiyya
3 Al-hajj Ibrahim Suberu, Onitafusiru
4 Mallam Sule Bakare
5 Mallam Shehu Ajagunna
6 Mallam B. O. Ọlagoke, the local manager of the AUD, Ikarẹ.
Others were Bakare Ọtum of Ile Bariba, Balogun Salami of Odo-Ọja and Yesufu Adegbite.
Al-hajj Ibrahim Suberu and Al-hajj Jimọ Ajijọlanabi showed a remarkable amount of knowledge about the history of Islam in Akoko. The former had been the Onitafusiru in Ikarẹ for over thirty years; and had travelled widely in Akoko area.

Ikirun, June–July 1965

1 The Chief Imam
2 Nọibi
3 Afa Yaqub's family.

Ilaro, June–July 1963

1 Al-hajj Lawani Adewumi (about 80)

2 Al-hajj Abudu Salami Adewumi, the head of the Zumrat al-Hujjāj, Ilaro
3 Muhammad Mustafa Adewumi, the Chief Imam
4 Al-hajj Wahabi Adewumi
5 Asani Bada, the Seriki of Ilaro
6 Al-hajj Lawal Musa.

Ileṣa, June 1965
1 The Chief Imam
2 A. K. Arowojọbẹ
3 Al-hajj S. A. Famuyide
4 Chief Bello Risa Iro
5 Al-hajj Musa Sarumi.

Iliṣan, July 1963
1 Alli Yesufu, the Imam's deputy
2 Abdullai Jinadu, Afa Agba
3 Hassan Soso
4 Sanni Oduṣina, the head of the Ansar ud-Deen Society
5 Lawani Okubọtẹ.

Ilọrin, April–May 1965
1 Salu Gambari, Emir of Ilọrin
2 Aliru b. Muhammad Ani
3 Imam Gambari
4 Imam Fulani
5 Imam Oke Male
6 Imam Yorūba
7 Balogun Gambari
8 Afa Girgisu
9 Afa Nda, the Muqadam of Tijaniya, Ilọrin
10 Al-hajj K. S. Apaokagi
11 Afa Salawu b. Ismaila Tajidni
12 Afa Muhammad Salisu Kokewukobere
13 Afa Agbagi
14 Al-hajj Ibrahim
15 Afa Mubarak Ali
16 Afa Gali
17 Al-hajj Eleha
18 Afa Asukuti.

Iṣẹyin, April 1965

1 Al-hajj Kasimu, the Senior Mugaddam of the Tijaniyya
2 Al-hajj Yaya in Ijẹmba Quarter
3 Afa Muhammad Sanni of Ọmọlewu, Idi-Ose Quarter
4 Al-hajj Abudu Wahabi of Agbaji Quarter – the Onitafusiru of Iṣẹyin
5 Afa Kasimu Ratibi Agbaji Quarter.

Al-hajj Kasimu showed a remarkable grasp of the development of Sufism in Iṣẹyin.

Iwo, June 1965

1 Jabari Akinlade, the Chief Imam of Iwo
2 Al-hajj Baki, the head of the Islah of Al-Dīn, Iwo
3 The Ọmọ-Ọba, Iwo.

Al-hajj Baki, an intelligent Arabic scholar, was particularly helpful in describing the development of Islamic studies in Iwo and its environs.

Kishi, May 1965

1 Imam Karimu
2 Afa Busari Ogunbade
3 Afa Ile Tefa
4 Imam Mustafa
5 Al-hajj Yusuf
6 Al-hajj A. Tijani.

Odo Adegbajo, June 1965

1 Ismaila Badaru, the Chief Imam
2 Kasumu Ogunselu
3 Ashiru Disu, a well-informed local historian.

Ogbomọṣọ, May 1965

1 Afa Maruf b. Mahmud Abegunde, the Chief Imam of Ogbomọṣọ
2 Al-hajj Oseni
3 Afa Aliru, the Parakoyi
4 Al-hajj Badawiyu, the head of the Alhajj's (Yoruba: Olori Alalaji)
5 Iliasu, the Balogun Imale.

Al-hajj Oseni was from the royal family; and he was helpful on information relating to that side.

Okeho, April–May 1965

1 Al-hajj Abudu Karimu Akano, the Chief Imam of Okeho
2 Baba Onisu
3 Afa Atiku, the head of the mu'allims
4 Afa Busari, the Parakoyi
5 Baba Tijani Akano
6 Tiamiyu A. Salami of Ansār-al-Dīn School.

Baba Onisu was a local historian who furnished much relevant information about family relationship, and developments in Okeho generally. Afa Atiku, the oldest mu'allim around, was useful on developments within the local Muslim community.

Ondo, June 1965

1 S. O. Oyeneyin
2 Junaid, Secretary of the Central Mosque Committee.

These are very active members of the Muslim community and educated as they are, they occupy a respectable place in the community.

Oṣogbo, mid May–June 1965

1 Afa Hafsir, the Chief Imam of Oṣogbo
2 his deputy
3 Afa Bello Arikalamu
4 Afa Muhammad Rabiu, the Oṇitafusiru
5 Al-hajj Salmanu
6 Al-hajj S. B. Lawal.

The Chief Imam is a descendant of the first Chief Imam, and he is related to Afa Haruna of Oke Gẹgẹ. He exhibts a considerable fund of historical knowledge.

Ọtta, August 1965

1 Afa Ọtta, Al-hajj Baṣọrun
2 Al-hajj Ṣango, the Oṇitafusiru.

Ọyọ, March 1965

1 Al-hajj Imam Oyibi, the Chief Imam of Ọyọ
2 Al-hajj Shehu, the Parakoyi
3 Al-hajj Salmon
4 Al-hajj Adediran
5 Mr Animaṣaun
6 Afa Isiaka Ogunbado.

Ṣagamu, July–August 1963

1 Abdul Kadiri Buraimọ, the Chief Imam
2 Al-hajj the Balogun (over 90)
3 Ibrahim Tairu, the Imam's deputy
4 Afa Buraimọ, Parakoyi
5 Sadiku Giwa of Killa Society
6 Kasumu Ibrahim.

The Chief Imam and the aged, though virile, Balogun were particularly well informed.

Shaki, April 1965

1 The Chief Imam
2 Al-hajj Nafiu
3 Al-hajj Shitu (Pupa) Akewulabi
4 Afa Yakubu, Ọtun Imale
5 Afa Momodu, Ọnitafusiru
6 Afa Shehu Tijani Olohun Ẹrọ
7 Afa Balogun Sadiku.

Index

Index

Bornu, 4, 6
Bowen, T. J., 34, 125, 207
Bower, Captain, 182, 183
Braimah Edu, 171
Braithwaite, Rev. I. A., 129, 132, 133, 134–5
Brazilian Group of Muslims, 28, 30
British rule, 26, 84, 107, 108, 109, 124, 134, 159
  and attitude to Islam, 163, 187, 215
  (*and see* Colonial Office)
Buhler, Rev. G. F., 125
Buraimo Aina, 29
Burke, Edward, 132
Burton, *Sir* Richard:
  visit to Lagos, 31, 34, 35, 36, 39, 62, 161
  visit to Abẹokuta, 39, 208
  visit to Kosọkọ, 160

Carr, Mr H., 171
Carter, *Sir* Gilbert T. (Governor), 52, 66, 136, 165–8, 170–1
  Expedition (1892–3), 178ff
  negotiations with Ilọrin, 180
  (*and see* Appendix IV)
Chamberlain, Joseph, 173
'charms' (in religious use), 132, 142, 200
Christ, Muslim view of, 134
Christianity, 2, 26, 53, 85
  missionaries, 98 (*and see* CMS)
  lower social status of, 125
  use of Arabic in, 128–30
  and dialogues with Muslims, 131–3
  propaganda for, 135, 142
  few converts to, 139–40
  admiration of Islam, 143–4
  challenged by Islam, 215–16
Clapperton, H., 8, 11, 12
cloth (*see* Ijebu)
CMS, 125, 126, 127, 136, 142, 143
Coker, Rev. R. A., 141
Cole, Rev. (later Canon) M. S., 129, 130
Colonial Office, 173, 181, 183
Crowther, Ajayi, 26, 28, 145, 207

Dendi Muslims, 5
Denton, Captain G. C. (Acting Governor), 105, 171, 174, 185, 187
divination, annual, 203
  (*and see* Ifa)
drumming (Lagos), 186–7

education: Western, 32, 135, 145, 163, 177, 215, 216
  elementary (*Ile-kewu*), 36
  Muslim, 99–100, 102–4, 167
  Christian-sponsored, 135–7, 139
  Ordinance (1887), 138, 168
  Board of, 164, 167
  British policy in Nigeria on, 165
  Code of 1887, 167
  Inspectors of Schools, 170, 171, 175
  and Muslim teachers, 177
  (*and see* Appendix III; Arabic; English; Islam)
Egungun, 3, 198
Ekiti, the, 33, 87, 142
  kola, 32
Ekiti Parapọ War, 53
Elegungun, 199
English, 32, 146
  teaching of, 136, 165
Erinmope attack, 185
Euler-Ajayi, Rev. M. T., 129
Ewi Aladesanni Ajimudaoro, 88
Eyin Ogan mosque, 89
Ẹdẹ, 24, 68, 71, 72
Ẹgbado, 23
Ẹgbẹ (societies), 53
Ẹiyẹ War, 202
Ẹpẹ, 26, 69, 72, 73, 108, 135, 161
  Eko Ẹpẹ, 69
  Ijebu-Ẹpẹ, 69
  Mosque, 70
  missionary failures in, 134
  Christian schools in, 136
  Muslim theological dispute in, 161–3
  Government Muslim school, 171–2, 175
  (*and see* Kosọkọ)